"Rabbi Shmuel Goldin demonstrates in his two volumes of *Unlocking the Torah Text* a remarkable knack for identifying [compelling] topics. He surveys the classic approaches to the issues addressed and then adds a new and often surprising layer of interpretation that addresses contemporary concerns and sensibilities. Many of Rabbi Goldin's novel insights serve as a springboard to vigorous classroom discussion and debate. The combination of the old and the new provides for an enriching and vigorous learning experience for a wide range of audiences.... [A] major contribution to serious study of Chumash in our day."

– **Rabbi Chaim (Howard) Jachter**
Rebbe, Torah Academy of Bergen County;
Co-rabbi, Shaarei Orah, the Sephardic Congregation of Teaneck;
Dayan, Beth Din of Elizabeth; author, three volumes of *Gray Matter*

"Rare is a study of the weekly parsha which speaks to all the generations. Rabbi Goldin's *Unlocking The Torah Text* breaks new ground not only in its clear, fascinating insights into the Torah text but in its compelling appeal to young and old alike. Many of our school's parents use Rabbi Goldin's books as the basis of their Shabbat dinner Torah discussions and have shared with me how much their children look forward each week to the challenging and dramatically presented questions which Rabbi Goldin explores. For any parent and Jewish educator seeking to inspire their children with the love of Torah, *Unlocking The Torah Text* is essential."

– **Dr. Elliot Prager**
Principal, The Moriah School, Englewood, NJ

UNLOCKING
THE TORAH TEXT

AN IN-DEPTH JOURNEY
INTO THE WEEKLY PARSHA

VAYIKRA

SHMUEL GOLDIN

gefen
publishing house בית הוצאה לאור
JERUSALEM ◆ NEW YORK Est. 1981

Layout Design: KPS
Typesetting and Cover Design: S. Kim Glassman

ISBN 978-965-229-450-0

Edition   3   5   7   9   8   6   4   2

Gefen Publishing House Ltd.   Gefen Books
6 Hatzvi Street, Jerusalem 94386, Israel   600 Broadway, Lynbrook, NY 11563, USA
972-2-538-0247 • orders@gefenpublishing.com   1-800-477-5257 • orders@gefenpublishing.com

www.gefenpublishing.com

Printed in Israel   *Send for our free catalogue*

Dedicated, with love and unending respect, to my parents

My father, Isaac Goldin, of blessed memory, set an example of honesty, loyalty and personal integrity that continues to inform my life each day.

Although he passed away over twelve years ago, I still find myself gauging my own actions by his standards.

Without fanfare, his word was his bond, his commitments resolute and his love for and devotion to family unwavering.

I can only hope to teach my children and grandchildren as he, through action, taught us.

My mother, Pnina (Pearl) Goldin, may she live and be well, continues to amaze us all.

Her life journey, from Seattle to Brooklyn to the Adirondack Mountains to West Hempstead, Long Island, and, finally, to Israel has been defined by her generous heart and her warm love.

Her remarkable aliya to Israel after a decades-long teaching career in the United States has led to new friends and experiences, even more learning, deeper religious devotion and an ever-growing commitment to Torah ideals.

She is an unassuming family matriarch who, without realizing it, sets a benchmark for us all.

And, once again, to Barbara

Every page of this volume has your name on it.

Without your devotion, sacrifice, advice and constant encouragement, these thoughts and words never would have seen the light of day.

When I was certain that it could not be done, you made me see that it could. When I was ready to quit, you simply would not let me.

I love you and will always be grateful.

Contents

Acknowledgments

I am ever-impressed by the talent and professionalism of the staff and management at Gefen Publishing House and by their dedication to their craft.

Ilan Greenfield, the publisher at Gefen, made this project his own from the moment we began. We both knew, however, that Vayikra would be the real challenge. His unfailing support, sage advice and constant encouragement continue to make all the difference.

What a wonderful surprise when Michael Fischberger, a friend from the past, became a new partner at Gefen and a most welcome addition to an already excellent team. His exciting new ideas, fresh perspective, and enthusiasm energized this endeavor.

Smadar Belilty, Gefen's project coordinator, kept our feet on the ground and our noses to the grindstone. With real expertise and an eye constantly focused on the finish line, she carefully shepherded the multiple production elements of this volume from beginning to end.

The best thing I can say about my editor, Kezia Raffel Pride, is that I miss working with her between volumes. Her keen eye, sharp insight, breadth of knowledge, editorial expertise and refreshing sense of humor make the editing experience a pleasure. Her grace under pressure, as the deadline neared, ensured our timely completion.

* * *

The publishing of this volume saw a new and welcome partnership with the Union of Orthodox Jewish Congregations. I am deeply grateful to Rabbis Menachem Genack, Simon Posner and Gil Student for their confidence in me and in this project. The imprimatur of the OU press adds great stature to our venture.

* * *

Raphael and Linda Benaroya, Daniel and Thalia Federbush, Kenneth and Susan Greif, Jonathan and Mindy Kolatch, Lee and Cheryl Lasher, Solomon and Sharon Merkin, Drew and Careena Parker, and Dina Perry and her family provided generous material assistance and warm personal support through their sponsorship of this volume. I cannot thank them enough. Their cherished friendship means the world to me.

Once again, my administrative assistant, Eileen Gorlyn, somehow manages to keep my hectic professional life in order, against great odds. With a steady hand, consummate skill and a calm manner she enables me to accomplish much more than I ever could without her.

My talented associate rabbi, Chaim Poupko, has become a valued partner in my rabbinate. His full participation in every sphere of our communal endeavor has enhanced our congregation and aided me immeasurably.

* * *

A quarter of a century is a long time. I have passed that mark in my tenure as rabbi of Congregation Ahavath Torah. What is amazing, however, is the sense of "newness" that still pervades my relationship with my synagogue. Each day is a fresh adventure. Mine is an extraordinary congregation, filled with immeasurable human resource, sincere intellectual search, genuine warmth, acts of inestimable kindness, deep commitment to the Jewish community throughout the world and a real love for all aspects of our Jewish heritage. I can think of no setting that could have provided me with a richer professional experience than my synagogue. I look forward to the journey ahead.

Many of the lessons found within this volume stem from my shared learning with my community. Reflected as well are countless hours of study, discussion and debate with my students at Yeshiva University, the Eve Flechner Institute, the Isaac Perry Beit Medrash and various other venues. I am grateful for our shared exploration.

* * *

My children – Avi and Rena, Yossi and Shifra, Yehuda and Noa and my twins, Donny and Rivka – fill me with pride each day. As I watch each of my children define his or her own life path and unique place within the fabric of our people, I realize how blessed I am. It is, after all, wonderful to watch your kids become adults and to truly like the adults that they have become.

As for my grandchildren – Isaac, Benjamin, Temima and Jacob – what can I say? They are *nachat* personified. They fill my days with joy.

Children and Grandchildren, as I have said before, you are "what it is all about."

Special thanks to Yossi and to my mother for, once again, serving as "in-house editors" of this text.

* * *

Finally, this volume is dedicated with unending love to my parents and, once again, to my wife, Barbara.

Whatever I have accomplished find its roots in the home that my parents created for me and my sisters, a home in which we learned to connect to our tradition through heart and mind. Whatever I continue to accomplish belongs to Barbara. I know what no one else really knows. Without her, nothing would be possible.

Introduction

Just wait until you get to Vayikra…

I have lost count of the number of times this comment has been gleefully offered to me by observers upon their discovery that I am writing a series of volumes on the Torah.

Bereishit and Shmot are easy. Just wait until you get to Vayikra…

The point is well taken. Consider, after all, the unique nature of this third book of the Torah. In place of the gripping drama and captivating narrative of the preceding volumes, Vayikra offers chapter upon chapter of detailed sacrificial law, Temple rites, ritual observances, holiday regulations, seemingly obscure themes such as biblical leprosy, etc.

Granted, Vayikra also contains some of the most powerful, far-reaching interpersonal edicts in the Torah, including the commandment considered by Rabbi Akiva and Hillel to be the central decree of Torah law: "You shall love your fellow as yourself." Nonetheless, by the time the reader arrives at these towering edicts he has waded through page after page of difficult text, with little apparent relevance to his world.

The challenge as I approached this book was, therefore, clear. Deeply gratified by the response to the first two volumes of this series, could I now produce a similar volume on Vayikra that would speak compellingly to the reader? Would the many of you who have shared in the excitement of our joint Torah study find Vayikra as captivating as I know it can be? Would we, together, discover meaningful messages in the passages of a book which, at first glance, speaks largely of rituals and concepts exceedingly distant from our lives?

Just wait until you get to Vayikra…

Here, then, is our volume on Vayikra. And, while I admit that it has not been easy, I hope that you will agree that the challenge has been successfully met.

Once again, when we least expect it, the Torah surprises us with the timeliness of its ideas, values and lessons. Even further, the experience of discovering these lessons specifically within texts that initially elude us only serves to heighten our respect for the Torah as God's eternal blueprint for our lives. We are reminded that, as we have often noted before, every portion of the Torah has something to say to each of us, regardless of our prior level of knowledge, educational background or religious affiliation. Even the most seemingly obscure passages of this divine, timeless tome yield countless lessons of continued relevance, each with the potential to inspire ongoing study, discussion and debate in every generation.

With great pleasure and excitement, therefore, I again invite those of you who have been traveling with us to continue – and those who are beginning now to join – our shared journey through the text. An extraordinary adventure awaits us as we open the book of Vayikra and join the newly formed Jewish nation standing at the foot of Mount Sinai, receiving God's law. We will remain, with that nation, rooted at the mountain's base for the entire book of Vayikra. Nonetheless, we will travel widely – through difficult concepts, esoteric ideas and lofty edicts – as together we probe the text for lessons that can shape our lives.

To set the stage for this journey, I repeat a brief review of the parameters of our search. (This review is reprinted, with minor changes, from the introduction to the Shmot volume. A fuller discussion of these principles can be found in the introduction to Bereishit.)

1. While traditional Torah study is based on a fundamental belief in the divine authorship of the text, questioning and challenging the text itself is not only allowed but encouraged. Unless we struggle with the narrative, God's word and God's intent remain distant and unclear and the Torah remains a closed book.

2. The treasures of the Torah can only be uncovered when the narrative itself is seen as the truth, comprised of real events that happened to real people. The heroes of the Bible were human beings, not gods, and the stories of their lives are not fables.

3. No part of the text or its contents will be off-limits to our search. We will explore the motives and actions of the personalities who populate its pages. We will probe God's desires for us reflected in His unfolding law and we will attempt to discern what the Torah reveals about His divine will. We will seek to understand why events took place as they did and how the

narrative might inform our lives. And we will explore the deep philosophical currents coursing through the laws and events described to us.

4. Two distinct approaches to the Torah text are reflected in rabbinic literature: *pshat* and *drash*.

Pshat refers to the straightforward explanation of the text. When we operate within the realm of *pshat*, we search for the literal, concrete sense of the narrative before us. *Proper understanding of pshat reveals deep, unexpected meaning within the text itself.*

Drash refers to rabbinic commentary serving as a vehicle for the transmission of lessons and ideas beyond the literal narrative. Many authorities maintain that Midrashic commentary is not meant to be taken literally, nor is it meant to be seen as an attempt to explain the factual meaning of a specific Torah passage. The key question in the realm of *drash* is: *What are the rabbis trying to teach us?*

When, as unfortunately often happens, we confuse these two approaches to text – when we ignore the *pshat* and instead offer *drash* as the literal interpretation of the text – we end up understanding neither of these interpretive realms. In our studies, therefore, we will make every attempt to distinguish between *pshat* and *drash* and to present each approach appropriately.

5. Each of our studies on the parshiot of Vayikra will raise a series of questions designed to strike to the core of a particular passage of the text.

Our search for answers to the questions raised will take us on a journey through traditional commentary and original thought. In each study, a sampling of rabbinic opinion on the issues will be reviewed and original approaches will be offered as we humbly continue our own struggle with the text.

Finally, most studies will include a "Points to Ponder" section in which connections are made between the Torah passage and relevant concerns that touch our lives. This section is specifically designed to encourage ongoing thought and debate.

As I have in the past, I close with the hope that our continuing journey will be, for each of us, a passionate one, inspiring continuing exploration and thought, sparking conversation, dialogue and debate each week in homes, synagogues, schools and beyond, as together we unlock the treasures of the Torah text.

Vayikra

CHAPTER 1:1–5:26

ויקרא

פרק א:א-ה:כו

Parsha Summary

From the Sanctuary: a call to ritual...

The curtain rises on Parshat Vayikra with the newly formed Jewish nation still encamped at the foot of Mount Sinai. There they will remain throughout the book of Vayikra.

God launches a new chapter of Jewish experience by calling to Moshe from the Sanctuary and commanding him concerning Judaism's sacrificial rite.

Included in the list of korbanot (sacrifices) detailed in Parshat Vayikra are voluntary offerings, burnt offerings, meal offerings, sin offerings and peace offerings.

1 Confronting *Korbanot*

Context

With the opening of the book of Vayikra, we enter the world of *korbanot*.[1]

In chapter upon chapter of text, God commands the newly formed Jewish nation, encamped at the foot of Mount Sinai, concerning the rituals that will define the sacrificial rite in the Sanctuary.

Questions

The very existence of *korbanot* creates a powerful quandary.

On the one hand, no area of Torah law seems more alien to modern sensibilities than that of *korbanot*. As we confront the Torah's sacrificial rite, we find ourselves at a total loss, unable to relate to these seemingly primitive rituals, wondering why an all-powerful, incorporeal God would demand the offering of animals and grain in His worship.

On the other hand, we cannot deny that the sacrificial rite is an integral part of Jewish law. Not only are substantial portions of Torah text dedicated to detailed descriptions of *korbanot*, but these rituals apparently remain, to this day, a critical component of our national aspirations and dreams. Jewish liturgy is replete with prayers seeking the rebuilding of the Temple and the reinstatement of the sacrifices.

An honest approach towards the Torah text demands that we not ignore the existence of *korbanot*. The questions raised by these puzzling rituals must be dealt with head-on.

Why does God demand offerings of animals and grain as part of His

---

1. The term *korban* is usually translated as "sacrifice" or "offering." As will become clear in this study, however, these translations do not do the concept justice. The root of the term *korban* literally means "to draw near." *Korbanot* are, therefore, rituals through which the supplicant attempts to "draw near" to an unfathomable God. For want of a better alternative, however, we will initially use the popular translations in our text.

worship? An all-powerful, transcendent God certainly has no need for physical gifts from man.

Does the Torah-mandated sacrificial rite speak to us, on any level, today? Can any relevant lessons be learned from these seemingly archaic rituals?

Do we really desire a return to the practice of *korbanot*?

Approaches

I. Historical Development

Our analysis begins, as it should, at the beginning, with a brief review of the historical development of *korbanot* as described in the Torah. This review reveals a number of surprising and significant points.

—— **A** ——————————————————————————

The first textually recorded physical offering to God is brought during the second generation of man's existence by Kayin, the eldest son of Adam and Chava. Kayin is promptly followed in this act by his brother, Hevel.[2]

As we have noted previously (see *Bereishit*: Bereishit 3, *Approaches* D), the Torah's testimony concerning God's selective acceptance of these offerings is particularly telling: "And God turned to Hevel and to his offering, but to Kayin and to his offering He did not turn."[3]

The language seems superfluous. The Torah could have made its point by simply stating, "And God turned to Hevel's offering while to Kayin's offering He did not turn." Why specify that God turns to "Hevel and to his offering" but not to "Kayin and to his offering"?

Apparently, with the very advent of man's physical offerings to the Divine, God wants to establish that He will not consider these rituals in a vacuum. God does not "accept" or "reject" *korbanot* or, for that matter, any ritual observance, arbitrarily. He bases His judgments upon the motivations and actions of the supplicant. While the Torah is not clear why, something in Hevel's behavior moves God to accept him and his offering. Conversely, Kayin's conduct apparently merits divine rejection.

---

2. Bereishit 4:3–4. While the Talmud does maintain that Adam offered *korbanot* (Talmud Bavli Avoda Zara 8a) we will limit our discussion to the evidence of textual *pshat* (straightforward explanation of the Torah text).

3. Bereishit 4:4–5.

Kayin is unable or unwilling to appreciate the ramifications of this rejection. Paralyzed in the face of the divine demand for personal introspection and behavioral change, he instead lashes out against his brother, with tragic consequences.

With the first appearance of ritual worship in the Torah, God immediately places such worship in its proper context. Through a seemingly simple turn of phrase, He communicates that He does not seek meaningless, arbitrary acts from man, but, instead, thought-filled, meaningful religious devotion (see *Bereishit*: Bereishit 3).

— **B** —————————————————————————————

Another telling, continuing pattern is initiated in the Torah with the offerings of Kayin and Hevel. From this point on, until the birth of the Jewish nation with the Exodus from Egypt, *all* korbanot *emerge in the Torah as man-initiated events*. Driven by a desire to communicate with an unfathomable God, early man, of his own accord, develops a sacrificial rite.

Noach, Avraham, Yitzchak and Yaakov each voluntarily bring offerings to God. At no point does God demand any of these sacrifices.

The only two possible exceptions to this rule prove, upon analysis, not to be exceptions at all.

1. During the *Brit bein Habetarim*, the Covenant between the Pieces, God commands Avraham to slaughter a series of animals and divide each animal into two. "Passing through" the pieces, God then reveals to Avraham a prophetic vision of the Israelites' eventual descent into bondage and their ultimate redemption.[4]

On a level of *pshat*, however, the scholars maintain that the animals used in this ritual are not offerings in the classical sense. Rashi, for example, explains that, as God enacts a covenant with Avraham, He employs symbolism common to the society of the time. "It was the custom of those involved in a covenant to divide animals and to pass through them."[5]

2. During Avraham's most dramatic test, *Akeidat Yitzchak* (the aborted sacrifice of Yitzchak), God commands the patriarch to "raise" his son as an

---

4. Ibid., 15:9–16.
5. Rashi, Bereishit 15:10.

offering on the summit of Mount Moriah. This "offering," however, never takes place. Avraham is stopped at the last moment by a heavenly angel.[6]

While the true purpose of the *Akeida* remains an ongoing subject of discussion (see *Bereishit*: Vayeira 4), one aspect of the event remains unchallenged. The only offering actually brought on the summit of Mount Moriah occurs after Yitzchak is spared. At that point Avraham, of his own initiative, offers a ram "in place of his son."[7]

Once again, the *korban* actually offered is not commanded by God.

— C —

Everything changes, however, centuries later, on the eve of the Exodus from Egypt. As the Egyptians brace for the final, devastating plague, the Israelites retreat, upon God's command, to their homes. There, in separate family meals, they participate in the first God-commanded sacrifice recorded in the Torah: the *Korban Pesach*.[8] Simultaneous with the birth of the Jewish nation, a divinely ordained sacrificial rite is "born." Beginning with that event, *korbanot* became an integral part of Jewish tradition.

Why do things change so dramatically with the birth of the Jewish nation? Why, at this point, are *korbanot* transformed from man-initiated to God-commanded rituals? Why does God now desire *korbanot*? Answers to these questions are suggested in the deliberations of the rabbis.

II. Philosophical Approaches

— A —

Two separate approaches proposed by the Rambam are central to the rabbinic discussion of *korbanot*.

1. In his halachic magnum opus, the *Mishneh Torah*, the Rambam categorizes *korbanot* as *chukim*, mitzvot for which no reason is given in the Torah. While one is encouraged to seek meaning in such mitzvot, says the Rambam, God's true reasoning may well remain elusive. Shrouded in mystery, *chukim* such as *korbanot* emerge as a true test of our loyalty to God's will.[9]

---

6. Bereishit 22:1–12.
7. Ibid., 22:13.
8. Shmot 12:3–28.
9. Rambam, *Mishneh Torah*, Hilchot Meila 8:8; Hilchot Temura 4:13.

2. In his *Guide to the Perplexed*, however, the Rambam offers a vastly different, rational approach to the inclusion of *korbanot* in Jewish law.

Many phenomena in the Torah, he maintains, are based upon the principle that abrupt major change in human behavior is impossible. *Man simply cannot journey immediately "from one extreme to the other"* (see *Shmot: Ki Tissa* 2, *Approaches* A).

God cannot expect the Israelites, reared in idolatrous surroundings replete with sacrificial rite, to totally reject rituals that they have come to see as necessary for communion with the Divine. He therefore commands his chosen people to sanctify the profane by adapting aspects of the prevailing sacrificial rite to His worship within the Sanctuary. *From this perspective, korbanot emerge as a divine concession to man's need.* The Israelites' difficult transition to their newfound faith is eased through the incorporation of a familiar ritual path.[10]

While the Rambam's rational explanation for *korbanot* in the *Guide to the Perplexed* sets off a firestorm of controversy among his contemporaries and later scholars (see below), his observations may not be as revolutionary as they seem. The Rambam's theories, according to some authorities,[11] are actually foreshadowed in an earlier Midrashic source recorded in Vayikra Rabba:

> Rabbi Pinchas said in the name of Rabbi Levi: The matter [of sacrifices] can be compared to the story of a prince whose haughtiness leads him to the consumption of despicable substances. The king determines: "Let my son attend my table regularly and he will abstain [from his evil doing] of his own accord."
>
> Similarly, because the Israelites were drawn to idolatrous practices in Egypt and regularly sacrificed to pagan deities, the Holy One Blessed Be He declared: "Let them offer their sacrifices before Me at all times in the Sanctuary and they will separate themselves from idolatry."[12]

---

10. Rambam, *Moreh Nevuchim* 30:32.

11. Abravanel, introduction to Vayikra, chapter 4. Note: Other authorities maintain that this Midrash does not support the Rambam's views but only suggests that involvement with Torah ritual will inevitably result in abstinence from idolatrous practices (see Rabbi David Zvi Hoffman, *Sefer Vayikra* [Jerusalem: Mossad Harav Kook, 1972], pp. 60–61).

12. Midrash Rabba Vayikra 22:7–8.

Even the Torah text itself seems to lend credence to the Rambam's approach with the following commandment concerning the centrality of the Temple service: "And they shall bring [their offerings] to the entrance of the Tent of Meeting to the Kohen…and they shall no longer slaughter their offerings to the demons after whom they stray.…"[13]

Finally, the Rambam's suggestions also find support in the earlier described historical development of *korbanot* in the Torah. Sacrifices emerge as man, of his own initiative, determines a mode of communication with the Divine (see above). With the birth of the Jewish nation, God recognizes the Israelites' continuing need for such symbolic communication and allows for the retention of the sacrificial rite in his newly given law.

—— **B** ————————————————————————————————

Many authorities defend the Rambam's rational explanation for the existence of *korbanot* in Jewish law.[14] Numerous other scholars, however, remain severely critical of the Rambam's approach, unwilling to categorize the Torah's extensive, detailed sacrificial rite as a concession to human frailties.

After dismissing the Rambam's proposals as "empty words which address a deep concern in superficial fashion,"[15] the Ramban quotes an alternative approach for those seeking a rational foundation for *korbanot* (the Ramban himself prefers a mystical approach). Sacrifices are offered, he notes, in large measure as a response to man's failure and sin. God, therefore, designs the steps of the sacrificial rite to correspond to the three components of human activity through which sin occurs: *thought, words* and *deeds*.

Sins committed through deed are addressed through the ritual of *smicha*, whereby the individual bringing the *korban* "lays his hands" upon the animal prior to its slaughter. Sins committed through speech are reflected in the *vidui*, the verbal confession offered by each supplicant. Finally, the sinful thoughts and desires that have coursed through the supplicant's heart and soul are referenced through the animal's consumption in the fire of the altar and through the sprinkling of its blood.

---

13. Vayikra 17:5–7.
14. Ritva, *Sefer Hazikaron*, Parshat Vayikra; Abravanel, introduction to Vayikra, chapter 4.
15. Ramban, Vayikra 1:9.

As an individual witnesses and participates in these graphic rituals, he is forced to recognize the extent of his own sinfulness and culpability. Were it not for God's merciful acceptance of this *korban* "in his stead," the petitioner himself would have merited a place upon the altar.[16]

———C———

Numerous additional approaches to the concept of *korbanot* are offered within traditional Jewish literature. Following are several of them.

Rav Saadia Gaon maintains that the sacrificial rite enables the Israelites to demonstrate the depth of their dedication to God by offering of the "best of their possessions."[17]

The Ba'al Hachinuch remains true to his general postulate that a person's thoughts and sentiments are shaped, in great measure, by his concrete actions. The performance of symbolic mitzvot is thus critical to the process of attitude formation. A sinner cannot purify his heart simply through a passive confession "between himself and the wall." Such confession requires no real effort and, therefore, has minimal effect. If, however, the individual is forced to act – if he becomes obligated in a demanding series of atoning rituals; if he must select from his flock, bring his offerings to the Sanctuary and participate in the detailed sacrificial rite – he will then become acutely aware of the extent of his sin and he will avoid such failure in the future.

The Ba'al Hachinuch also suggests that the very act of offering a *korban* reminds man of the tenuous nature of his own superiority over the beasts of the field. Man's distinctiveness lies in his ability to reason. When an individual's reasoning fails and he consequently sins, that individual loses his status as a man and becomes no different from the animal. The Torah, therefore, commands the sinner to offer a *korban* in the Sanctuary. The slaughter of the animal and the consumption of its remains upon the altar graphically demonstrate that a "reasonless" being is valueless and ultimately destined to destruction. The depth of the supplicant's failure and the toll of that failure upon his soul are thus underscored.[18]

For his part, the Maharal of Prague perceives the sacrificial rite, with its intimations of mortality, as a fundamental reflection of the

---

16. Ibid.
17. *Emunot V'deiot* 3:10.
18. Sefer Hachinuch, mitzva 95.

inconsequentiality of all creatures in the face of God's greatness. Nothing exists in the world except as a result of God's kindness and munificence.[19]

Finally, numerous commentaries move beyond general explanations for the phenomenon of *korbanot* and painstakingly analyze the symbolic significance of each detail of the Temple ritual. We will encounter some of their observations in our continued analysis of the book of Vayikra.

—— **D** ——————————————————————

Perhaps the most telling aspect of the Torah's sacrificial rite, however, is the most obvious: *the vast majority of* korbanot *are simply not "sacrifices" in the commonly accepted sense.*

With singular exceptions (such as the Olah, the burnt offering, which is consumed in its entirety upon the altar), portions of every *korban* are *designated as food* for the Kohanim, their dependents and/or the individuals bringing the offering to the Temple.

Even more, the very first obligatory *korban* recorded in the Torah, the *Korban Pesach* of the Exodus, was, in its entirety, *a family meal* (see above, I, *Approaches* C). No altar was present, no Temple service involved. The Israelites were, instead, commanded, on the eve of the Exodus, to physically consume the Paschal Lamb within the sanctity of their homes and to burn the remainder in the morning.

What then, defines the Paschal Lamb as a *korban*? How does this puzzling, seminal ritual set the stage for the entire sacrificial rite to follow? Why were portions of so many of the later *korbanot* designated as food? Shouldn't each *korban* have been a true offering to God, consumed entirely in flames upon the altar?

We are forced, it would seem, to reexamine our understanding of *korbanot*.

In contrast to classical "sacrifices," consumed entirely on the altar, *korbanot* were, in large measure, *shared meals with God*. Faced with the naturally developing distance between man and his Creator, forced to address the separation from God that results from sin, the Torah proposes a path, astoundingly profound in its simplicity: *invite God to your table.*

A *korban*, deriving from the root word *karov*, "to draw near" (see Vayikra 1, note 1), is the mechanism through which an individual can begin to

---

19. *Sefer Gevurot Hashem* 5:69.

repair and reestablish his relationship with a personal God. Just as, in the human realm, a shared meal is a powerful relational tool, so too, a meal consumed with God's symbolic participation can begin to address His estrangement from our lives.

Consumed with pomp and circumstance in the very shadow of the Holy Temple – with some portions placed upon the altar and others shared with the priests and, often, with the supplicants themselves – each *korban* became a potentially powerful rehabilitative tool. God's presence as an invited, honored guest was palpable and concrete. To the participants these observances were far from meaningless rituals. *They were, instead, shared meals with God, the first steps back to a fuller awareness of the Divine in their lives.*

—— **E** ————————————————————————

What, however, of the future? Do we truly anticipate a return to sacrifices, as maintained in our prayers? Or, is the sacrificial rite rooted in a past from which our nation has moved on?

The vast majority of classical Jewish thinkers insist that our final redemption will feature not only the rebuilding of the Temple but a full return to the sacrificial rite. Particularly noteworthy is the position of the Rambam. In spite of this scholar's willingness to postulate the origin of *korbanot* as a concession to man's limitations (see above, II, *Approaches* A), he gives no indication that this earthly origin limits the future applicability of these rituals. After dedicating major portions of his *Mishneh Torah*, his practical compendium of laws, to the strictures surrounding *korbanot*, the Rambam clearly states towards the end of that work:

> The Messianic king is destined to rise in the future and reestablish the Kingdom of David, to build the Temple and to gather the dispersed of Israel. In his day, all the laws will return to their original state. *Korbanot will be offered* [my italics], the *Shmita* and *Yovel* years will be observed.... Anyone who does not believe this, or does not await his

[the Mashiach's] arrival, not only denies the words of the prophets but denies the Torah and Moshe, our teacher.[20]

A solitary alternative position is raised by the first chief rabbi of the State of Israel, Rabbi Avraham Yitzchak Hacohen Kook.

After first maintaining that "with regard to sacrifices it is correct to believe that all aspects will be restored to their place," Rav Kook builds on kabbalistic literature and envisions a "distant time" when all aspects of the world will be elevated. At that time, he states, humans will no longer need to take the lives of animals for their physical, moral or spiritual needs. The prophet Malachi perhaps references this future period when he states, "Then the *grain offering* of Judah and Jerusalem will be pleasing to God as in the days of old and as in former years."[21] Strikingly absent from Malachi's vision is the reinstatement of animal offerings. The Midrash seems to go even further with the startling prediction "With the exception of the thanksgiving offering, all sacrifices will be nullified in the future."[22]

To further strengthen his position, Kook identifies a series of clues within the Torah itself which he claims reflect the secondary status of animal sacrifices. These offerings remain appropriate as long as man makes use of animals for other needs, such as food and clothing. The time will come, however, when man, reaching his highest state of refinement, will no longer feel the need to take animal life for any purpose. At that point, only grain sacrifices will be offered in the Temple.[23]

Points to Ponder

A number of years ago I fielded a strange phone call in my synagogue office. "I represent," the caller said, "a group of Korean Christian ministers who, in the interest of studying comparative religions, would very much like to visit your synagogue during a Sabbath morning service."

I was immediately struck by two concerns.

Firstly, I wondered how my congregation would react when a group of Korean Christian ministers walked in, en masse, without warning one

20. Rambam, *Mishneh Torah*, Hilchot Melachim 11:1.
21. Malachi 3:4.
22. Midrash Rabba Vayikra 9:7.
23. Rabbi Avraham Yitzchak Hacohen Kook, *Otzrot Hare'aya*, vol. 2, pp. 101–103; *Olat Re'aya*, vol. 1, p. 292.

Shabbat morning. Secondly, and more importantly, I wondered what the ministers themselves, absent prior preparation, would make of our service. They would not understand the language; the rituals would be alien and difficult to follow; and, to top matters off, the apparent lack of decorum would be startling (this was before our synagogue's successful efforts at decorum improvement). How would these ministers respond, for example, to children running up and down the aisles, to groups of adults talking at various points and on various topics during the service? The entire prospect carried, it seemed to me, potential for disaster.

I therefore made a stipulation. The group would be welcome, I said, as long as they were willing to come to the synagogue beforehand for a private briefing with me. At that time, I would explain the various symbols within the sanctuary, the nature of our service and our approach to prayer. We would then schedule and announce their Shabbat visit to the community, thus preparing my congregation for their appearance.

The caller readily agreed and the date was set for my preliminary meeting with the group at the synagogue.

Having spoken before to groups of other faiths about Judaism, I knew that I had to be prepared for the unexpected during the question period that would inevitably follow my presentation. It is always difficult, and at the same time refreshing, to view our traditions through the eyes of total outsiders. On one such previous occasion, for example, the first question raised by a group of Catholic schoolchildren was, "What is the significance of the different colored skullcaps that you wear? Do they represent a hierarchy within your tradition?"

Armed by this time with years of experience, however, I felt prepared for whatever might come my way.

Early on a Thursday morning, therefore, I found myself in conversation with a group of roughly twenty Korean Christian ministers in the main sanctuary of my synagogue. After reviewing some of the philosophical and practical particulars of our Shabbat service and after showing them various ritual items such as the Torah scroll, the *aron kodesh* and the *ner tamid*, I opened the floor for questions.

There was a moment of silence…

Suddenly a hand shot up: "Rabbi, where do you do the animal sacrifices?"

"What?" I stammered, caught completely off guard.

"Where do you do the animal sacrifices?"

Regaining my composure, I began to explain that animal sacrifices were indeed a part of our tradition but that they had been suspended since the destruction of the Temple.

My visitors, however, would not let go. For forty-five minutes they continued to pepper me with educated questions concerning animal sacrifices, convinced that somewhere, somehow, I was hiding a goat or cow in the basement of the synagogue.

Halfway through the session, I began to realize what was really happening. The assumptions of my guests actually said more about the foundations of their own faith tradition than about mine.

Fundamentalist Christians, these ministers were driven by a simple developmental equation. Man, tainted with sin, cannot relate to God directly. To address this basic problem, the "Old Testament," therefore, prescribes a Temple rite in which offerings of animals and grain enable man to gain atonement and approach an unfathomable God. These sacrifices serve as "substitutes" upon the altar, taking the place of the sinners themselves and redeeming them from sin. Upon entering the world stage, however, Christianity moves past the "primitive" Temple rite by substituting the death of Jesus for the sacrifices. When Jesus "dies for the sins of man," he replaces the animals on the altar and becomes the essential intermediary between limited man and a limitless God.

The possibility that Judaism could be practiced without sacrifices was, therefore, to the minds of my guests, simply unthinkable. Given our lack of belief in Jesus, how else could we relate to an unreachable God? Only a Judaism incorporating sacrifices as intermediaries between man and the Divine could serve as a precursor to their own faith system.

No amount of persuasion on my part could, therefore, convince my guests of Judaism's fundamental belief in a direct relationship with God without intermediary. No explanation of the sacrificial rite as symbolic or educational in purpose could sway them from their firm assumptions.

While my guests and I parted ways agreeing to disagree, and while their Shabbat visit to my congregation a few weeks later went without a hitch, their powerfully mistaken assumptions concerning *korbanot* have haunted me for years. Not because they need to know the truth, but because we do.

I find myself wondering… How many of my students or congregants would have been able to respond to the questions raised by the ministers who visited my synagogue those many years ago? How many Jews today give even a second thought to the purpose and significance of the sacrificial rite within our tradition?

We understandably avoid confrontation with elements of our tradition which, like *korbanot*, are difficult to comprehend and uncomfortable to encounter. Such evasion, however, cedes the intellectual high ground to those who would challenge our beliefs and question our traditions.

As our brief study of *korbanot* has demonstrated, every element of the Torah is filled with relevant meaning and message. We avoid the discovery and study of those messages to our own detriment and at our own risk.

2 The Anatomy of a Sentence

This study might seem, at first glance, highly technical in scope. Focusing on only one sentence, we will examine a series of linguistic variations in the text.

Our analysis will show, however, that, in the Torah, even the slightest textual deviation can be extremely significant.

Context

God opens the book of Vayikra with a general directive to Moshe concerning voluntary *korbanot*: "Speak to the children of Israel and say to them: *Adam ki yakriv mikem korban la'Hashem, min habeheima min habakar u'min hatzon takrivu et korbanchem*, 'If a man should bring from among you an offering to the Lord, from the domestic animal, from the cattle or from the flock shall you bring your offering.'"[1]

Questions

On the surface, God's commandment to Moshe is clear and straightforward. A closer look, however, reveals a series of striking technical difficulties.

Why does the Torah use the word *adam* in this sentence? The term consistently used in the Torah to indicate an individual is *ish*.

The word *mikem*, "from among you," seems superfluous. Any Israelite offering a *korban* would by definition be "from among" the people.

Even if a case can be made for the inclusion of the word *mikem*, its placement in the sentence is clearly problematic. The text should have read

---

1. Vayikra 1:2.

16

"if a man *from among you* should bring" rather than "if a man should bring *from among you*." The current construction seems to indicate that the *korban* itself is coming "from among" the nation, a clear impossibility in a tradition that adamantly rejects the very idea of human sacrifice.

Finally, the sentence opens in the singular (*Adam ki yakriv*, "If a man should bring"), but closes in the plural (*takrivu* [plural] *et korbanchem*, "shall you bring your offering"). Why the switch?

Approaches

Through careful analysis of each element of this introductory sentence, the commentaries glean a myriad of foundational lessons, ranging from the halachic parameters of the sacrificial rite to philosophical truths that reverberate well beyond the theme of *korbanot*.

I. *Adam ki yakriv...korban,* "If a man should bring...an offering"

—A—

Numerous authorities within the Talmud and Midrash view the term *adam* in this sentence as halachically inclusive in nature, deliberately broadening the population base from which *korbanot* will be received. Not only are all loyal Jews (men, women,[2] born Jews and converts[3]) delineated as eligible participants in the Sanctuary's sacrificial rite, but some authorities even derive the eligibility of non-Jews from this term as well.[4]

Whatever the actual textual source, the halachic acceptance of specific *korbanot* from Gentiles is a well-established phenomenon. The Talmud notes that non-Jews may bring burnt offerings to the Temple where the priests will attend to their *korbanot* as they would to those of Jews.[5] In addition, in contrast to Jews whose offerings must be brought to the Temple, "Gentiles are permitted to offer burnt offerings to God anywhere in the world and it is permissible to instruct them and teach them how to sacrifice to God's name, Blessed be He."[6]

---

2. Midrash Hachaifetz Vayikra 1:2.
3. Talmud Yerushalmi Shekalim 1:4.
4. Chizkuni, Vayikra 1:2. The Talmud Bavli (Nazir 62b), however, derives the inclusion of Gentiles from a different textual source (Vayikra 22:18).
5. Talmud Bavli Menachot 73b; Chulin 13b.
6. Rambam, *Mishneh Torah*, Hilchot Ma'aseh Korbanot 19:16.

The inclusion of Gentiles as eligible participants in the Torah's sacrificial rite carries no hidden agenda. Non-Jewish worship is accepted as independently valid in its own right, even when such worship takes place within a Jewish setting or context.

The Torah thus repeats, at the very outset of its detailed description of *korbanot*, a message sounded often and clearly within the text. *God's selection of the Jews as a "chosen people" does not connote exclusivity. Even after the birth of the Jewish nation, God continues to relate to all of mankind* (see *Bereishit*: Noach 4, *Approaches* A).

—— **B** ——————————————————————————————

Choosing a different, Midrashic path, Rashi explains the Torah's use of the word *adam* by quoting one of a number of sources that connect this sentence to Adam, the first man, ancestor of all mankind: "Why is the term *adam* used? Just as the first man, Adam, by definition did not offer stolen material to God, [as he alone existed in the world and] all in the world was his; so too, [God commands the Israelites] 'Your *korbanot* should not consist of stolen goods.'"[7]

At first glance, this Midrashic admonition seems gratuitous. Why should the Torah find it necessary to prohibit the sacrifice of stolen material as an offering to God? Certainly, a just God would not accept *korbanot* that originate in sin!

And yet, the sobering litany of horrifying deeds performed across the ages "in God's name" demonstrates the clear need for the Torah's warning. How often have zealous "believers" found license for all sorts of aberrant behavior in the fulfillment of their perception of "God's will"? From the ancient proponents of human sacrifice to the "fundamentalists" of our day, zealots have redrawn the laws of morality to justify actions purportedly perpetrated in the pursuit of specific "religious" goals.

In stark contrast, Jewish law shapes the interface between ritual observance and ethical behavior through the application of the legal maxim "A mitzva that results from the commission of a sin is simply unacceptable."[8] No amount of spiritual devotion exempts a religious practitioner from the basic laws of morality that apply to all of mankind.

---

7. Rashi, Vayikra 1:2; Midrash Rabba Vayikra 2:7.
8. Talmud Bavli Succa 29b–30a.

As the sacrificial laws begin to unfold in the book of Vayikra, therefore, the Midrash sees God reminding the Israelites: *Your religious worship must always be observed within a moral framework. Under no conditions will actions in My name relieve you from universal ethical responsibilities towards your fellow man.*

—— **C** ——

Returning to the realm of *pshat*, another explanation for the phrase in question can, perhaps, be offered.

The term *adam* derives from the word *adama*, "earth," and references man's creation by God from the "dust of the earth." The root of the word *korban*, on the other hand, literally means to "draw near" (see Vayikra 1, note 1), emphasizing the role of the sacrificial rite as a vehicle through which a supplicant attempts to reach heavenward and approach an unfathomable God.

The phrase *adam ki yakriv*, therefore, in addition to its contextual meaning, "if a man should bring [an offering]," also literally translates as "if an earthly individual would draw near…"

How does one draw near to God? How does limited man begin to approach a limitless Deity?

As we have noted before, many faith traditions maintain that the quest for holiness requires the relinquishing of the "earthly" dimensions of man's existence. Only by escaping the defiling constraints of the physical world, these traditions claim, can we begin to approach the heavens.

Judaism, however, demurs.

From a Jewish perspective, man's singularity derives from the fact that he, alone within creation, is fashioned *min ha'elyonim u'min hatachtonim*, from the upper and lower spheres of creation.[9] Only man is, at once, a member of the animal kingdom and at the same time a philosopher, poet, artist and sage. Man is a creature in conflict, continually striving to reconcile heaven and earth, the two realms that define his existence. Sanctity, for the Jew, is to be found in that reconciliation, in the investiture of the physical world with holiness through concrete actions that sanctify God's name (see *Bereishit*: Bereishit 1, *Approaches* D; *Shmot*: Shmot 3, *Approaches* E; *Shmot*: Yitro 2, *Approaches* C).

---

9. Midrash Rabba Bereishit 12:8.

The message that God conveys to the Israelites, as He introduces the sacrificial rite, now becomes clear: *If you wish to approach to the heavens you must remain earthbound. Recognize that your greatness lies in the fact that you are adam ki yakriv, an earthly creature who can draw near. You will find Me, not in a distant mystical domain, but at the intersection of the physical and the spiritual in your lives.*

Always remember, the rituals that you are about to receive are ultimately designed to help you find yourselves; to aid you in discovering the heavenly potential with which you, as my partners, can invest your physical world.

II. ...*ki yakriv mikem korban*, "...should bring from among you an offering"

——A——

If the word *adam* halachically expands the population pool from whom *korbanot* are accepted (see above), many authorities maintain that the word *mikem*, "from among you," creates a countering limitation. At issue is a fundamental concern which will ultimately stretch well beyond the Sanctuary's walls. How will Jewish tradition balance the desire for inclusiveness with the need for realistic boundaries? Not all behaviors can be accepted within a religious community. And yet, can we completely close the door on any individual? As the Torah launches its sacrificial rite, a question looms that will reverberate in changing forms and in a myriad of settings across the ages: *with regard to affiliation with the Jewish community, who is in and who is out?*

The discussion begins in the Talmud as follows: "*Mikem v'lo kulchem*, 'from among you, but not from all of you'; from this phrase we learn that *korbanot* are not accepted from apostates."

Refining the equation further, the rabbis maintain that no such distinction is made in the case of Gentiles, all of whom, regardless of their beliefs, are eligible to offer sacrifices to God. Counterintuitively, the bar is set higher for Jews than it is for non-Jews.

Finally, the rabbis declare, only those apostates whose rebellion strikes to the basic core of Jewish belief are excluded. The acceptance of these individuals would, apparently, connote validation of their convictions and thus present too great a threat to the community. The door, however, remains open to others, whose rebellion is less pervasive, in the hope that they will return to normative Jewish practice.[10]

At the dawn of our nation's history, the struggle to define acceptable communal boundaries is joined – a struggle that rages to this very day.

— **B** —

Moving from the legal to the philosophical realm, a different approach to the inclusion of the word *mikem* and to its placement in the text is offered by a number of authorities, including the Sforno.

God specifically commands "from *among you* an offering," because the most important part of a *korban* is the piece that the supplicant offers "from himself."[11]

As we have noted before (see Vayikra 1, *Approaches* A) and as the remonstrations of prophets across the ages underscore,[12] *korbanot* are only meaningful if they occur within a proper attitudinal and behavioral context. God responds not to the ritual alone but to the petitioner himself. "The Lord does not desire," says the Sforno, "fools who bring offerings without the prerequisite personal humility."[13]

Each *korban* must come "from us." Ritual that is devoid of personal investment is unacceptable to God.

III. ...*takrivu et korbanchem*, "shall you bring your offering."

— **A** —

Finally, the textual journey from the singular *Adam ki yakriv* to the plural *takrivu et korbanchem* informs the reader that, in contradistinction to many other *korbanot* which can only be offered by one individual alone,

---

10. Talmud Bavli Eruvin 69b.
11. Sforno, Vayikra 1:2.
12. Shmuel I 15:22; Yeshayahu 1:11–17; Yirmiyahu 6:20; Amos 5:22.
13. Sforno, Vayikra 1:2.

a voluntary animal Olah (burnt offering) may be brought by a group in partnership or even by an entire community.[14]

The Torah thus creates a balance between individual religious search and shared spiritual experience.

Too often, in the realm of spirituality, we journey at the extremes. We either engage in an isolating personal search that distances us from those around us or we fail to engage in personal struggle at all, choosing to hide behind rote communal observance. By insisting that some sacrifices can only be brought by individuals while others can be offered in partnership, the Torah encourages us to find a balanced path.

Religion is meaningless if it does not engage each of us on a deep individual, personal level. At the same time, religion is empty if the journey is not shared.

Points to Ponder

One of my favorite stories tells of a prison guard who is assigned to a minimum-security prison camp before the fall of the Soviet Union. Inmates of this camp report for work early in the morning and retire nightly to lodgings outside the gates. Our guard is charged with the task of ensuring that, as the workers leave for the night, no one walks away with property belonging to the camp.

On the very first day, one particular inmate catches the guard's attention by wheeling out, through the camp gates, *a wheelbarrow full of straw.*

The guard stops the prison inmate, empties the straw from the wheelbarrow, searches the straw, searches the wheelbarrow, finds absolutely nothing and allows the prisoner to proceed.

On the very next day, the same thing occurs. The prisoner exits the camp with a wheelbarrow full of straw, the guard empties the wheelbarrow, searches the straw, searches the wheelbarrow, finds absolutely nothing and allows the prisoner to proceed.

Day in and day out, week in and week out, month in and month out, year in and year out…for thirty-five years, this scene replays over and over again. Every day the prisoner wheels out a wheelbarrow full of straw. Every day the guard searches and finds nothing.

---

14. Rashi, Vayikra 1:2; Torat Kohanim 2.

Finally, after thirty-five years, the guard turns to the prisoner as he exits the prison gates and says, "Listen! I am about to retire. I promise you that your secret is safe with me. But, if you don't tell me the truth, it's going to bother me for the rest of my life. Can you please tell me why, each day for the past thirty-five years, you've been stealing straw?"

The prisoner turns towards the guard with a glint in his eye and says, "You still don't get it, do you? For the past thirty-five years I have not been stealing straw. *I have been stealing wheelbarrows.*"

The Torah text is viewed, by many of us, through a prism of familiarity: stories we have heard before, passages we have read and reread, texts we have encountered year after year. Some of these texts, we feel, have already revealed their secrets, while other passages (such as those dealing with *korbanot*) have nothing to say to us in the first place. In either case, we perceive nothing new; we've seen it all before.

The problem, however, is that, concerning the Torah, familiarity works against us. We see in the text what we've "learned to see" rather than what's really there.

It takes a second look to perceive the "wheelbarrows" instead of the "straw."

In the above study, when we stopped to read carefully and to ask the right questions, a sentence easily dismissed as irrelevant to our lives was transformed. A technical passage, dealing with ancient ritual, suddenly spoke to us concerning the Jewish attitude towards non-Jewish worship, the search for sanctity in a physical world, the interface between religion and ethics, the philosophical boundaries of the Jewish community and more.

Who knows what other treasures lie within familiar texts, waiting to be revealed, if only we take a second look?

3 Only a Mistake?

Context

As Parshat Vayikra unfolds, God mandates a series of sin offerings to be brought as part of the atonement process for crimes committed *b'shogeig*, unintentionally.

The text outlines specific *korbanot* to be offered by priests, communities, rulers or individuals in the aftermath of these unintentional sins.[1]

Questions

What are the parameters of the category of *shogeig*, unintentional acts for which *korbanot* are brought? Are all unintentional acts "equal" in the eyes of Jewish law? Does negligence affect the way an unintentional sin is perceived? How is the issue of intentionality generally dealt with in Jewish ritual and criminal law?

In the realm of *korbanot*, why are sin offerings specifically linked to unintentional acts? In what way, if any, do these sacrifices serve as appropriate correctives specifically for acts committed *b'shogeig*?

Approaches

—A—

A review of Jewish law reveals a spectrum of potential responsibility for acts performed, based upon the degree of intentionality in an individual's actions. Three distinct signposts are found along this continuum.

At the top of the range are acts that carry the greatest degree of guilt: acts committed *b'meizid*, with full intent. Jewish law will punish these acts to the fullest extent of the law.

---

1. Vayikra 4:1–35.

At the bottom of the spectrum lie acts that fall into the category of *oness*, coercion or force of circumstance (accident). Legally, acts committed through *oness* are considered totally unintentional and carry no guilt.

Somewhere in the middle of the range lies the category of *shogeig*, unintentional acts for which the perpetrator, nonetheless, bears a certain degree of responsibility. Although unintended, acts committed *b'shogeig* could have been avoided through greater care and attention. The very existence of this category indicates that, in the eyes of Jewish law, not all unintentional acts are "equal."

While the legal category of *shogeig*, however, is repeatedly referenced in the Torah, the exact parameters of the category are left for determination in the Oral Law. What, the rabbis ask, is the level of intentionality that classifies an act as *shogeig*? What, if any, is the degree of negligence involved?

—— **B** ———————————————————————————

In the area of capital crimes, debate concerning the criteria for *shogeig* centers on the interpretation of a foundational passage in the book of Devarim. There, the text considers the guilt of a woodcutter who, in the act of cutting a tree, mortally wounds a bystander *b'shogeig*. The case is outlined in the text as follows.

Two individuals are in a public forest where one of them is cutting trees. Suddenly, *v'nashal habarzel min ha'etz*, "the iron slips from the wood," striking the bystander and killing him. Once convicted of the crime, the woodcutter is exiled to a city of refuge, one of a number of such designated cities to which all individuals convicted of killing *b'shogeig* are exiled.[2]

The rabbis, however, are puzzled. What are the details of this crime? At issue is the meaning of the enigmatic phrase *v'nashal habarzel min ha'etz*, "the iron slips from the wood." The text is open to interpretation. What exactly causes the death of the bystander?

Two distinct opinions are presented in the Mishna.

Rebbe (Rabbi Yehuda Hanasi) maintains that the Torah refers to a case where a *chip of wood* flies from the tree as the ax strikes, finding and killing the bystander.[3] Rebbe's rabbinic colleagues, however, insist that the Torah

---

2. Devarim 19:5.
3. Talmud Bavli Makkot 7b; Rashi, ibid. Note: the Rambam (*Mishneh Torah*, Hilchot Rotzeiach U'shmirat Hanefesh 6:15) differs from Rashi and explains Rebbe as referring to a case where the ax head separates from the handle as a result of striking the tree

refers to a case where the *ax head* separates from its handle, becoming a lethal projectile which strikes and kills the victim.[4]

Rebbe's benchmarks for guilt are clearly much more onerous than those of his colleagues. The woodcutter is guilty, *b'shogeig*, even for lethal damage caused by a flying splinter, a phenomenon which reflects minimal negligence on the part of the woodcutter. Had the ax head killed the victim, Rebbe feels, exile would not have been adequate punishment. The woodcutter's degree of guilt for failing to keep his equipment in good working order would have placed him too high on the spectrum of intent, somewhere between *shogeig* and *meizid* (intentional acts).[5]

Rebbe's colleagues, on the other hand, adopt a more lenient view. The category of *shogeig* reflects the case where the ax head causes the damage. Had the wood chip killed the victim, the woodcutter would have been almost blameless, not responsible for indirect events beyond his control.[6]

The practical applications of the debate between Rebbe and his colleagues are potentially manifold, even in our day. What, for example, is the level of guilt of the driver of a car that tragically strikes and kills a pedestrian? What would the legal verdict be, according to each of the halachic protagonists, if the accident were the result of brake failure of a recently inspected car? What if the car was neither recently inspected nor properly maintained? What if the driver was talking on a cell phone, otherwise preoccupied, or even inebriated at the time of the accident? Which of these cases would be classified as *shogeig* and which would fall elsewhere on the spectrum of intention?

While the Rambam and other halachists codify the practical law in favor of the lenient position of Rebbe's colleagues,[7] more important for our purposes is the debate itself. This rabbinic discourse demonstrates the great care exerted within the halachic process to determine the exact level of intentionality involved in any crime, in order to ensure proper treatment of the perpetrator under the rule of law.

---

and his colleagues as referring to a case where the ax head separates from the handle before striking the tree. Rabbeinu Chananel (Makkot 7b) cites both the position of Rashi and the position of the Rambam in his commentary.

4. Talmud Bavli Makkot 7b; Rabbeinu Chananel, ibid.
5. Rabbeinu Chananel, ibid.
6. Talmud Bavli Makkot 8a; Rambam, *Mishneh Torah*, Hilchot Rotzeach U'shmirat Hanefesh 6:15.
7. Rambam, ibid.

— **C** ———————————————————————

For the vast majority of us, the relationship between intent and responsibility in the area of capital crimes will remain, God willing, only a theoretical concern. Of more practical relevance is the issue of intent in the arena of ritual law.

What role, for example, does intent play in the area of Shabbat observance? Are all unintentional Shabbat transgressions equal, or are some more severe than others?

Here the halacha suggests a fundamental distinction between two categories: the category of *shogeig* – unintentional acts which, as we have seen, carry a measure of guilt – and acts falling into the grouping of *mit'asseik*, totally inadvertent acts for which the perpetrator bears little or no responsibility.

The rabbis distinguish between these two categories of intentionality as follows.

Shogeig with regard to Shabbat laws includes acts performed by someone who is aware of his actions but is either ignorant of the law or of the fact that the day is Shabbat. If an individual, for example, turns on an electric light on Shabbat because he is unaware that the use of electricity is prohibited, he is considered a *shogeig*. Similarly, if an individual who is knowledgeable of the Shabbat laws turns on an electric light on Shabbat because he is convinced that it is Sunday, he is also a *shogeig*.[8] While unintentional, his act in each of these cases carries a measure of guilt. The individual should have been more aware, respectively, either of the law or of the weekly calendar.

Mit'asseik, on the other hand, refers to someone who, while aware of the law and of the day of the week, is oblivious to the act that he performs. An individual who, moving alongside the wall of a crowded room, accidentally brushes against a light switch on Shabbat and turns on the light falls into the category of *mit'asseik*. In this case, his action was totally unconscious and carries little or no guilt.[9]

---

8. Talmud Bavli Shabbat 70b; Rashi, Shabbat 72b; Rambam, *Mishneh Torah*, Hilchot Shgagot 7:2–4.
9. Talmud Bavli Kritot 19a–b; Rashi, ibid. Note: because of specific complexities unique to the laws of Shabbat, the parameters of *mit'asseik* with regard to Shabbat observance are different from the parameters of this category with regard to other areas of halacha (*She'eilot U'tshuvot Rebbe Akiva Eiger* 18; Shimshon Raphael Hirsch, Vayikra 4:2).

While the distinction between these two categories of intentionality seems clear, there is still great room for debate as the details of the cases change. What would the verdict of halacha be, for example, concerning someone who walks into a room and, without thinking, turns on a light switch? Would we consider such a case to be *mit'asseik* because of the reflexive and unthinking nature of the act? Or, would this case fall higher on the spectrum of responsibility because, after all, the individual turns on the light of his own accord? What would the verdict be in a case where an individual could have avoided transgressing the Shabbat law had he been a bit more careful? Does his carelessness take him out of the category of *mit'asseik* or can we still point to the inadvertent nature of the act itself? For example, how would halacha judge an individual who sets an alarm clock before Shabbat to wake him on Shabbat morning, knowing full well that he tends to reflexively shut off the alarm, without thinking, when suddenly awakened?

While it might seem that we are splitting "halachic hairs," such deliberation actually shows the great care with which Jewish law treats the issue of intent. An individual cannot rely with impunity on the excuse "it was only a mistake" in all cases of inadvertent behavior.

The effort we put into determining these and other issues of Jewish law also reflects our willingness to accept the halachic system as central to our lives and to devote real time and energy towards its proper implementation. As we have noted previously, such acceptance and devotion is the primary demand of the system itself (see *Shmot*: Yitro 5, *Points to Ponder*).

— **D** —————————————————————

Finally, we return to the realm of *korbanot*. As indicated above, Jewish law stipulates that only certain acts committed *b'shogeig* create the obligation for an atoning sacrifice.

Why should this be so? What is the relationship between unintentional transgressions and *korbanot*? Why do sacrifices serve as appropriate correctives only for acts committed *b'shogeig* and not for other sins?

The answer to these questions may well lie in the root failure that gives rise to the category of *shogeig*.

Rabbi Shimshon Raphael Hirsch observes:

> The [human] soul must submit to the "fire" of God and allow itself *uninterruptedly* to be ruled by its light and warmth.… In the moment

of *shegaga* the perpetrator is not conscious of, does not worry about, the legality or otherwise of his act…. It is just *this lack of attention, this carelessness* as to whether his actions are in accordance with the demands of law, wherein lies the sinfulness of his mistake.[10]

A sin committed *b'shogeig* represents a temporary suspension of what is meant to be a continuous, uninterrupted relationship with God. When this lapse results in an unintentional transgression, *the lapse itself, and not the act, demands atonement*. Somehow, the transgressor must be made aware of the depth of his unique failure, which, unlike the failure of the intentional sinner, is rooted not in outright rebellion but in an absence of caring. Somehow, he must return to the point where God's presence is again felt in his life, guiding every moment of each day.

The Torah therefore mandates a *korban* as part of the *shogeig*'s corrective journey. By "inviting God to his table" (see Vayikra 1, *Approaches* II D) the *shogeig* addresses his lapse and begins his journey back to a fuller, more constant awareness of God in his life.

Points to Ponder

Which is worse, active rebellion or the absence of caring?

My years in the rabbinate have taught me a surprising truth: as long as there is engagement there is hope…

Like all rabbis, I have witnessed the tragedy of deep relationships disintegrating into rancor. I have seen how the loss of love can engender hate. And yet, as heartbreaking as those bitter situations may be, equally if not more frightening are the cases where personal caring descends into the emptiness of apathy. Nothing is more disquieting than the scene of those who were once close and who now simply no longer care. Any emotional connection, even a bitter one, is better than no connection at all, and carries the possibility, however remote, for repair.

Perhaps that is why the Torah treats the category of *shogeig* so seriously, granting those who transgress *b'shogeig* an atonement path all their own. Even a momentary lapse in our relationship with God and his law must be addressed, lest with the passage of time, that break grow into continued carelessness, or, God forbid, an absence of caring.

---

10. Rabbi Shimshon Raphael Hirsch, Vayikra 4:2.

4 The Leadership Quandary

Context

As mentioned in the previous study, the Torah outlines a series of cases where acts committed *b'shogeig* give rise to obligatory sin offerings. Covered in the text are unintentional sins committed by priests, communities, rulers and individuals.

In each of the above situations the Torah raises the *possibility* of sin, with one glaring exception...

When the Torah describes the potential sin of a *nasi* (leader), the text reads: *Asher nasi yecheta*, "When a leader sins..."[1]

Questions

Why does the Torah state "*when* a leader sins" rather than "*if* a leader sins"?

Approaches

—— **A** ——

A number of commentaries are unwilling to take this phrase at face value. The Torah, they feel, could not be predicting inevitable sin on the part of the leader.

The Ibn Ezra and the Chizkuni, for example, avoid the problem entirely. Using technical grammatical formulae they simply rework the text in order to arrive at the more comfortable definition "if a *nasi* sins."[2]

Rashi, on the other hand, chooses a Midrashic route. Referencing a Talmudic passage that connects the word *asher* (when) to the word *ashrei* (fortunate), he suggests the following interpretation: "Fortunate is the

---

1. Vayikra 4:22.
2. Ibn Ezra, ibid; Chizkuni, ibid.

generation whose leader [honestly admits his failings] and offers a *korban* for his unintentional sin."[3]

————— **B** —————

There are scholars, however, who are willing to embrace the *pshat* of this phrase and the troubling philosophical message it conveys. This straightforward approach is mirrored in the comments of the Sforno: "[The Torah states] 'When a leader sins' ...for, after all, *it is expected that he will sin*."[4]

At the dawn of history, the Torah establishes a truth most famously verbalized centuries later by the nineteenth-century moralist Lord John Emerich Edward Dalberg Acton: "Power tends to corrupt, and absolute power corrupts absolutely."[5]

Through a simple twist of text, God warns of the dangers of leadership. From the Torah's perspective the issue is not "*if* a leader will sin" but "*when* a leader will sin." Whether because of the corrupting influence of power or simply because of the risks a leader must take, the assumption of a leadership position carries with it the inevitability of sin.

What, however, is the lesson the Torah wishes to convey? If sin and leadership are synonymous, does the Torah's moral system discourage the assumption of leadership roles?

————— **C** —————

A strange Talmudic passage may well shed light upon the rabbinic attitude towards the interface between leadership and sin.

> The rabbis taught: Four individuals died "at the urging of the serpent" [i.e., sinless: their deaths did not result from their own sins but from the mortality introduced into man's existence, at the instigation of the serpent, in the Garden of Eden]. They were: Binyamin, the son of Yaakov; Amram, the father of Moshe; Yishai, the father of David; Kil'av, the son of David.[6]

---

3. Rashi, ibid.
4. Sforno, ibid.
5. Expressed in a letter to Bishop Mandell Creighton in 1887.
6. Talmud Bavli Bava Batra 17a.

The contemporary scholar Rabbi Zevulun Charlop notes that the Talmudic identification of each of these individuals is strange. Why, he asks, doesn't the Talmud simply list their names? Why identify each historical figure by his relationship to another: Binyamin, *the son of Yaakov*; Amram, the *father of Moshe*; Yishai, *the father of David*; Kil'av, *the son of David*?[7]

Clearly, the Talmud wants us compare each of these four individuals to a more well-known relative. When we do so, a striking truth emerges. Each of the four figures identified in the Talmud as having died "without sin" pales in comparison to a close relative who cannot make that claim. While some Midrashic traditions maintain otherwise,[8] the straightforward reading of events indicates that Yaakov, Moshe and David certainly sin, and that their sins are recorded for posterity in the Tanach and rabbinic literature. Nonetheless, their place in Jewish history is unsurpassed. In spite of faults and human failings, Yaakov remains the greatest of our patriarchs,[9] Moshe the greatest of our prophets,[10] David the greatest of our kings.[11]

Is it preferable to be Binyamin or Yaakov, Amram or Moshe, Yishai or David, Kil'av or David? While all of these personalities were righteous men deserving of emulation, the Talmud's answer is clear: *Better to risk sin and rise to leadership than to remain unblemished in the shadows.*

Points to Ponder

A cursory glance at trends within Jewish day school and yeshiva education today reveals that we are not training the best of our children towards Jewish communal leadership.

So much emphasis is placed in the "yeshiva world" on the goals of personal piety and Torah study that many of our brightest are loathe to venture outside the walls of the *beit midrash* (house of study). Success within the system is defined by a willingness to engage in full-time Torah study. As

---

7. Rabbi Zevulun Charlop, Shabbat *drasha*.

8. As we have noted before (see *Bereishit*: Lech Lecha 2, *Questions*; Toldot 4, *Approaches* A), a spectrum of opinion exists within rabbinic thought concerning the potential fallibility of biblical heroes. At one end of the spectrum are those who refuse to see any possible failing on the part of the heroes of the Torah and Tanach. A clear example of this approach is the Talmudic statement "Anyone who says that David sinned is mistaken" (Talmud Bavli Shabbat 56a).

9. Midrash Sechel Tov Bereishit 33.

10. Devarim 34:10.

11. Midrash Tehillim Mizmor 1.

a result, many young men and women whose contributions to the Jewish nation are potentially invaluable remain cloistered, unwilling to take the risks associated with involvement with the community at large.

At the same time, for years, the choice of a career in Jewish leadership has rarely been promoted by parents in the Modern Orthodox and non-Orthodox communities. Within those sectors, the rabbinate is generally perceived as "no job for a good Jewish boy" and teaching is often discouraged as a vocational choice. The hours in both the communal and educational spheres are seen as long, the burdens overwhelming, the responsibilities great, the social position lonely, the material rewards (in many cases) limited.

The rabbis, already in Talmudic times, acknowledged the moral risks inherent in positions of power. They determined, however, that the benefits of communal involvement far outweigh the cost. Today, we are challenged to recapture for ourselves and to communicate to our own children that sense of commitment and mission.

Thankfully, strides have been made to increase the professional stature and financial remuneration of those who choose careers in Jewish leadership. We still have a ways to go, however, before those careers become as attractive and as respected as other opportunities available to the young men and women of our community.

The incentives for a change in attitude towards professional communal contribution are manifold. At a time when many young people are searching for greater meaning, few vocations can offer them the sense of purpose and accomplishment that can be reached through a career in Jewish leadership. On a communal level, we desperately need the vision and talent of new generations.

"*Asher nasi yecheta…*" The call to leadership is far from risk-free. Ignoring that call, however, carries the greatest risks of all.

Tzav

צַו

Parsha Summary

From a priestly perspective…

God instructs Moshe to command Aharon and his sons concerning their ongoing role in the Sanctuary's sacrificial rite.

The text returns to a number of korbanot *first introduced in Parshat Vayikra, as God adds details pertinent to the participation of the Kohanim.*

In the course of these instructions, other laws incumbent upon the entire community are communicated, as well. These general edicts include:

◆ *Laws of* pigul, korbanot *disqualified due to erroneous intent*

◆ *Rules applying the concepts of* tuma *and* tahara, *ritual purity and impurity (see Tazria-Metzora 1), to the realm of* korbanot

◆ *Prohibitions concerning the consumption of blood, forbidden fats,* neveilot *(otherwise kosher animals that died without proper slaughter) and* treifot *(otherwise kosher animals that were afflicted by life-threatening wounds or diseases)*

Parshat Tzav closes as God delineates the rituals designed to consecrate Aharon and his sons as Kohanim. These rites culminate with a seven-day inaugural period, leading to an eighth day (described in Parshat Shmini), on which the kehuna *(priesthood) will be officially launched.*

1 Urgent Business

Questions
When and why does the Torah substitute the commandment *tzav* (command) for the more common directive *daber* (speak)? Does this change connote particular contextual urgency or significance?

Why does this substitution specifically occur at the beginning of Parshat Tzav, as God outlines the role of the priests in the sacrificial rite?

Approaches

— A —

Referencing a Midrash in his first comment on the parsha, Rashi quotes the rules that, according to rabbinic tradition, determine the use of the term *tzav* in the Torah text: "*Tzav is used only in cases of urgency, immediacy and continuity* (when the commandment applies intergenerationally)."

Rabbi Shimon maintains: "The Torah must convey specific urgency in cases of *financial loss*."[2]

These rules, however, remain open to interpretation.

Must all three rabbinically proposed criteria (urgency, immediacy and

---

1. Vayikra 6:2.
2. Torat Kohanim 1:1; Rashi, Vayikra 6:2.

continuity) be present for the word *tzav* to be used in the text, or does the term appear even if only one condition is present?

What is the meaning of Rabbi Shimon's interjection? Does he reject the criteria suggested by his colleagues or is he noting an additional requisite condition for the biblical use of the term *tzav*?

— B ———————————————

Rabbi Yehuda Nachshoni delineates a distinction between the use of the verb *l'tzavot*, "to command," within the context of a narrative tale in the biblical text and the use of the verb as an introduction to a divine commandment.

For the verb to appear in a narrative, only one of the rabbinic conditions need be present (e.g., *Va'yetzav Paro l'chol amo*, "And Pharaoh [urgently] commanded his entire nation"[3]). When, however, the verb introduces divine directives, as at the beginning of Parshat Tzav, *all three criteria* listed by the rabbis – urgency, immediacy and constancy – are present.[4]

— C ———————————————

A wide-ranging debate emerges in rabbinic literature concerning Rabbi Shimon's enigmatic declaration, "The Torah must convey specific urgency in cases of financial loss."

The Ramban, for example, postulates that Rabbi Shimon is suggesting an alternative to the three criteria proposed by his colleagues. The term *tzav* is used, at times, in cases of financial loss even when the other conditions are absent. On these occasions, through the language of commandment, the Torah encourages the unhesitating performance of a particular action in spite of the associated cost.[5]

At the opposite end of the spectrum, Rabbi Eliyahu Mizrachi maintains that Rabbi Shimon proposes an additional requisite condition. The term *tzav* will only be used, according to Rabbi Shimon, when the situation reflects urgency, immediacy, continuity *and financial loss*.[6]

---

3. Shmot 1:22.
4. Yehuda Nachshoni, *Hagot B'parshiot HaTorah* (Tel Aviv: Zohar Publishing, 1979), p. 416.
5. Ramban, Vayikra 6:2.
6. Mizrachi, ibid.

— D —

Turning to our parsha, we can easily see how its dramatic opening scene satisfies the first three rabbinic conditions for the use of the term *tzav*. As God instructs Moshe to prepare his brother, Aharon, for the priesthood, He underscores the significance of the moment.

Tzav… Do not hesitate, Moshe. Not a moment is to be lost. The time has come to take the next step in your nation's development through the launching of the priesthood. For all time, Aharon and his descendents will serve as representatives of the people in My sanctified worship. Their singular participation will bring the hopes and strivings of the nation before Me and their teaching will convey to the people My dreams for them. Move quickly and urgently, Moshe, to inaugurate a priestly role that will span the generations.

On the other hand, Rabbi Shimon's position would seem more difficult to defend in the case before us. What monetary loss confronts Aharon and his sons in the fulfillment of their priestly duties? On the contrary, as indicated before (see Vayikra 1, *Approaches* D), the Kohanim benefit materially from the sacrificial rite.

— E —

Some scholars accept the inapplicability of Rabbi Shimon's approach to the opening scene of Parshat Tzav. The Ramban, for example, begins his interpretation of the parsha by declaring: "The teaching of Rabbi Shimon does not apply to this commandment. The children of Aharon, the subjects of the decree, suffer no financial loss. On the contrary, they receive benefit from all the sacrifices…"[7]

Many authorities, however, are unwilling to summarily read Rabbi Shimon's approach out of the parsha. The Ramban himself (in spite of his initial declaration) entertains the possibility that, through the commandment of *tzav*, the Torah references the personal *korbanot* of Aharon and his children which must be offered from their own possessions.[8] Chizkuni, for his part, explains that the risk of financial loss runs throughout the entire sacrificial rite. A priest's failure to execute the Temple rituals properly, this sage maintains, can invalidate a specific *korban* and create the need for a

7. Ramban, ibid.
8. Ibid.

replacement offering.[9] The Maharal envisions an even more pervasive loss emerging for the Kohen as a result of his general ritual obligations. The demands placed upon the Kohen's time by his service within the Temple force him to set aside more lucrative worldly pursuits.[10]

The Levush Ha'ora creatively interweaves concern for all participants in the ritual. The *korbanot* cited at the beginning of the parsha, he says, carry no clear material benefit at all for the owners (the Israelites bringing the *korban*). These sacrifices are Olot (burnt offerings consumed entirely on the altar), and, as free-will offerings, do not even grant atonement for sin. Moved by a spirit of generosity, the Israelites are willing to offer *korbanot* which result in concrete loss with no materially measurable gain. The Torah, therefore, urges alacrity on the part of the Kohanim, lest the priests hesitate and give the owners a chance to reconsider their generous gesture.[11]

—— F ——————————————————————————

Finally, an entirely different, powerfully poignant approach to the issue of loss at the beginning of Parshat Tzav can be discerned through a slight shift in perspective.

Perhaps it is not Aharon, but his brother, Moshe, who confronts the issue of loss at this pivotal juncture.

Parshat Tzav marks the final stages of Aharon's journey towards the priesthood. This journey, which began at the burning bush with Aharon's designation to leadership alongside his brother,[12] was most clearly defined by the appointment of Aharon and his progeny to the *kehuna*, in Parshat Tetzave.[13]

Theory, however, only becomes practice at the beginning of Parshat Tzav, when God sets into motion the steps that will define Aharon's role as a Kohen and inaugurate him and his progeny into that role.

Questions we have raised before (see *Shmot*: Tetzave 2, *Points to Ponder*), therefore, now return with a vengeance. Was Moshe, as some scholars suggest,[14] originally designated to be the Kohen Gadol only to lose that

---

9. Chizkuni, ibid.
10. Gur Aryeh, ibid.
11. Levush Ha'ora, ibid.
12. Shmot 4:14–16.
13. Ibid., 28–29:37.
14. Talmud Bavli Zevachim 102a.

honor due to his continued reluctance at the burning bush? If so, does Moshe regret that loss now, as Aharon prepares in earnest to assume his eternal role? Even if Moshe was never designated for the priesthood, as others maintain,[15] does he, nonetheless, envy his brother when the *kehuna* becomes a reality? As we have previously noted (see *Shmot*: Tetzave 2, *Points to Ponder*), conflicting Midrashic traditions hint at possible divergent emotions that may have coursed through Moshe's heart.

With good reason, therefore, God urges Moshe: *Tzav et Aharon v'et banav*, "Command Aharon and his sons…" *Moshe, the time has come to demonstrate true leadership by relinquishing a portion of your power. Command your brother. Do not hesitate. As I have taught you before, in conjunction with your brother's role (see* Shmot: *Tetzave 1, Approaches C and Points to Ponder), greatness lies in taking a step back and allowing others to shine…*

How telling that both the parsha that predicts Aharon's ascension to the priesthood – Tetzave – and the parsha that marks his last steps towards that goal – Tzav – are characterized by the verb *l'tzavot*. On both occasions, God *commands* Moshe to act with alacrity as he meets the difficult challenge of achieving greatness through personal retreat.

Points to Ponder

Our suggestion that the use of the commandment *tzav* at the parsha's opening may indicate potential loss on Moshe's part rather than on Aharon's underscores the value of attempting to perform an ultimately impossible life exercise: the endeavor to see the world through someone else's eyes.

Years of experience in the rabbinate have convinced me that we each live in our own worlds – worlds that are the product of our unique experience, our individual perspective and our personal predilections. None of us perceives absolute truth because each of us is looking through a subjective prism. The most that each of us can hope for and work towards is that our "own world" remain as close as possible to the "real world." The greater the distance between these two entities, the more difficult life becomes.

By recognizing that others legitimately see things differently than we do, we can often defuse or, at least, lessen the tension surrounding difficult situations.

---

15. Ibid.

I am astounded, for example, by the widely different perceptions often firmly and honestly held by each of the parties in the tragic situation of a dissolving marriage. As each party describes what the marriage was like during the years of its existence, and the part they each played in the process, it quickly becomes clear that they have been living in vastly different worlds. The sooner they acknowledge the legitimate disparity between those worlds, the sooner they gain the ability to get on with their lives, whether together or apart.

The critical events unfolding in Parshat Tzav are certainly experienced very differently by Aharon and Moshe. Perhaps the ability of these very dissimilar brothers to work together was, at least partially, founded on the respect each held for the other's world.

2 Manifest Destiny?

Context

As Parshat Tzav draws to a close, God commands Moshe to instruct Aharon concerning the laws of the *shivat yemei hamiluim*, the seven days of preparation that will lead to the inauguration of the *kehuna* on the eighth day.[1]

These events will launch the ongoing priestly role of Aharon and his progeny across the span of Jewish history.

Questions

Why is the priestly role within Judaism inherited and not "earned"?

Why is honor given, to this day, to a Kohen simply because of his lineage?

Are we not all "equal" in God's eyes? If we are equal, shouldn't Jewish society be a meritocracy?

Approaches

A review of the Torah's outline for Jewish society, from both a historical and a legal perspective, reveals a fascinating tension and interplay between inherited and earned roles and rights.

—— **A** ————————————————————

Certain roles within our tradition are inherited in perpetuity. All male descendents of Aharon are automatically Kohanim, while all male descendents of the tribe of Levi are, of course, Leviim (those who serve within the Temple). Within each Jewish family, firstborn males are accorded specific rights.[2] Jewish men and women have different halachic obligations from

---

1. Vayikra 8:30–36.
2. Devarim 21:17.

43

birth.[3] Once David becomes king all authentic royalty descends from the Davidic dynasty.[4] Even Jewish identity is unalterably inherited through one's mother.[5] According to Jewish law while someone can certainly convert to Judaism, a born or converted Jew cannot "convert out."[6]

— **B** —

On the other hand, other critical roles within Jewish society are clearly earned. Although the Torah is silent on the subject, Midrashic literature clearly reflects the position that God's choice of Avraham is far from arbitrary. Instead, the first patriarch secures his position as the progenitor of the Jewish people only through years of lonely philosophical struggle and search.[7] Moshe, the paradigm of leadership and the progenitor of rabbinic leadership, rises to greatness as a result of his own initiative.[8] Sages, scholars, rabbis and teachers across the ages earn their positions of authority by dint of scholarship and character. More than a few of the scholars of the Mishna and Talmud rise from humble origins, including Shmaya and Avtalyon,[9] Hillel,[10] Rabbi Akiva,[11] Reish Lakish[12] and others.

— **C** —

Most fascinating of all is the tension inherent between these two potential paths of communal participation: what happens when birth roles and earned roles collide.

The pattern established in the patriarchal era, for example, is particularly telling. On the one hand, the concept of birth privilege is already recognized, as can be seen most clearly in the struggle between Yaakov and Esav for the title of firstborn.[13] And yet, in each generation of this historical period, the firstborn loses his rights to a younger sibling. Yitzchak, not

---

3. Mishna Kiddushin 1:7.
4. Rambam, *Mishneh Torah*, Hilchot Melachim 1:7–10.
5. Talmud Bavli Kiddushin 68b.
6. Ibid., Sanhedrin 44a.
7. Zohar 1:86a; Midrash Rabba Bereishit 38:13; Midrash Rabba Bamidbar 14:2.
8. Shmot 2:11–12.
9. Talmud Bavli Gittin 57b.
10. Ibid., Yoma 35b.
11. Ibid., Ketubot 62b; Pesachim 49b; Rambam, introduction to the *Mishneh Torah*.
12. Talmud Bavli Bava Metzia 84a.
13. Bereishit 25:29–34.

Yishmael, is heir to his father's legacy.[14] Yaakov supplants his older brother, Esav, in the struggle for Yitzchak's blessing.[15] Yehuda, Yosef and Levi each receive a dimension of the leadership role which was to rightfully have been Reuven's, as the firstborn.[16] This pattern continues in the generations that follow as Yosef's younger son Ephraim is given precedence over the older Menashe[17] and as Moshe overshadows his older brother, Aharon.

Though the firstborn Israelite males are originally designated for service within the Temple, they lose that privilege through their participation in the sin of the golden calf and the Levites are appointed in their stead.[18] Although not originally designated to serve as a Kohen, Aharon's grandson, Pinchas, rises to that role and, according to some authorities, his descendents serve as Kohanim Gedolim (High Priests), in reward for Pinchas's courageous acts in defense of God's honor.[19]

Even in the less dramatic realm of daily halacha, the law dictates that a sage is given precedence over a Kohen in the distribution of honors, such as leading the Birkat Hamazon (Grace after Meals).[20] Many scholars maintain that such precedence would also be shown to the sage in the order of *aliyot* (ascension to the Torah during the synagogue service), were it not for the need to apply an objective standard in the synagogue, thereby preserving congregational harmony.[21]

Perhaps, however, the greatest proof of the transcendence of earned rights over birthrights can be gleaned from the moment of our nation's birth. As we have noted before, the national era of our people's history begins with the Exodus from Egypt and the Revelation at Sinai. Revelation, in fact, becomes both the moment of the Jewish nation's birth and the defining event for individual affiliation with that nation.

Full descendents of Avraham and Sara, who choose not to leave Egypt at the time of the Exodus, disappear into the mists of history. Even further, a full Hebrew who participates in the Exodus, reaches Sinai, yet refuses

14. Ibid., 21:12.
15. Ibid., 27–28:5.
16. Ibid., 49:1–27; Devarim 33:8–11.
17. Bereishit 48:13–19.
18. Bamidbar 3:11–13; Rashi, Bamidbar 3:2.
19. Bamidbar 25:10–13; Rashi, Bamidbar 25:13; Ibn Ezra, Bamidbar 25:12.
20. Shulchan Aruch, Orach Chaim 201:1–2.
21. Ibid., 135:4; Arba Turim, Orach Chaim 135; Beit Yosef, Orach Chaim 135; Mishna Berura 135:11–12.

to accept God's law, is also lost to his people forever. Conversely, an individual who is not a Hebrew at all, yet is present at Revelation and accepts the Torah (e.g., an Egyptian who joins in the Israelite Exodus), becomes a full member of the Jewish nation. Commitment to God's law, not blood relationship, is the defining factor for individual affiliation with our nation at its birth. (See *Bereishit: Vayeshev 4, Approaches* B, for a fuller discussion of this phenomenon and its implications.)

The verdict of our tradition seems clear. *When a choice must be made between earned role and birth role, earned role triumphs.*

— **D** —————————————————————————————————

The questions raised at the beginning of this study, however, now seem sharper. If, when the two forces collide, earned role trumps birth role, why then does the latter exist at all in Jewish thought and law? Why shouldn't Torah society be, in all of its facets, a meritocracy? Why can't the *kehuna*, for example, be chosen in each generation on the basis of merit rather than bloodline?

New insight into this ancient issue can be gleaned from the story behind a recent remarkable scientific discovery.

Dr. Karl Skorecki, a nephrologist and researcher at the University of Toronto and at the Rambam-Technion Medical Center in Haifa, noted one morning in synagogue that the Kohen called to the Torah was of Sephardic – specifically Moroccan – descent. Skorecki, himself a Kohen of Ashkenazic, Eastern European origin, found himself wondering: "*According to tradition, this [Sephardi] and I have a common ancestor. Could [our shared ancestral line] have been maintained since Sinai, and throughout the long exile of the Jewish people?*"[22]

Motivated by his own work in molecular genetics and by his awareness of the growing application of DNA analysis to the study of history and population diversity, Skorecki decided to test a hypothesis: "if Kohanim are descendents of one man, they should have a common set of genetic markers…that of their common ancestor," Aharon, the first Kohen.[23]

---

22. Yaakov Kleiman, "The DNA Chain of Tradition: The Discovery of the 'Cohen Gene,'" www.cohen-levi.org/jewish_genes_and_genealogy/the_dna_chain_of_tradition. htm.
23. Ibid.

Skorecki undertook a study in conjunction with Dr. Michael Hammer, a leading researcher in molecular genetics at the University of Arizona. The results of this inquiry were nothing short of astounding. As published in the prestigious British science journal *Nature* (January 2, 1997), 98.5 percent of the self-identified Kohanim in a test population of 188 Jewish males carried a specific genetic marker on their Y (male) chromosome. The presence of this genetic marker in the non-Kohen population was significantly lower.

A second study yielded even more striking results. Using an expanded selection of Y chromosome markers, Skorecki and his associates found a particular array of six markers in 97 of 106 Kohanim tested. The chances of these findings happening at random are less than one in 10,000.

The collection of chromosomal markers identified by this study has come to be known as the Cohen Modal Haplotype (CMH) – "the standard genetic signature of the Jewish priestly family."[24]

Commenting on his findings in a 1997 article in the *New York Times*, Skorecki declared: "The simplest, most straightforward explanation is that these men have the Y chromosome of [Aharon].... The study suggests that a 3000-year-old oral tradition [is] correct, [and has] a biological counterpart."[25]

— **E** —————————————————————

Here then, is graphic proof of the value and power of an inherited role. Through pogroms and persecution, wrenching exiles and attempted extermination, a segregated subgroup of honored priests preserves a heritage encoded in its very DNA. Scattered to all corners of the globe, with little or no connection to each other, the Kohanim pass down a tradition from father to son – a tradition of service in a Temple long gone and of an honored role in a Temple yet to come.

What accounts for the success of this faithful transmission? How do the Kohanim maintain their identity with such unerring accuracy across the generations?

The answer would seem to lie in the very character of inherited privilege, a tradition of honor bequeathed across the ages. Interweaving pride,

---

24. Ibid.
25. Quoted in Denise Grady, "Finding Genetic Traces of Jewish Priesthood," *New York Times*, January 7, 1997.

familial loyalty and intergenerational responsibility, such status acquires greater significance specifically because it is inherited. The *kehuna* becomes a precious heirloom, connecting each child to parents, grandparents, great-grandparents and generations long gone.

— **F** ————————————————————————————

The place of both earned role and birth role within Jewish experience now becomes readily apparent. As God launches the journey of His chosen people through history, He weaves two participatory paths into the fabric of their society. Together these paths create a balance essential to the nation's survival.

On the one hand, in each generation, earned opportunities will exist to encourage personal discovery, striving and growth. The realms of Torah scholarship, communal contribution and public leadership will lie open to those who earnestly seek to enter, regardless of personal background.

On the other hand, earned roles alone cannot ensure the perpetuation of all the structures critical to our nation's character. Continuing responsibility must be assigned for the maintenance of institutions ranging from the priesthood to the Jewish home. Only a clear, ongoing division of responsibility, through the establishment of designated birth roles, will preserve the entire tapestry of Jewish life across the centuries.

The dramatic fealty shown by the Kohanim in maintaining their own unique heritage for over three thousand years demonstrates the true, lasting power of inherited roles. This power has helped safeguard the character of our nation from Sinai to this day.

Points to Ponder

Over the past few decades increased educational, professional and personal opportunities have created a call for changes in the traditional role of women in Jewish society. Within the Conservative, Reform and Reconstructionist movements this call has resulted in major transformation. Even in the Modern Orthodox community, however, new phenomena have developed, from women's *tefilla* (prayer) groups to advanced institutions of Judaic scholarship for women, causing controversy among the halachic authorities. The ascendance of women to stations of communal leadership – from synagogue presidencies to professional positions such as *yoatzot halacha* (halachic advisors) – has further fueled the debate.

The uninitiated observer might well wonder what all the fuss is about. Why can't women assume their "rightful" place equal to men in all aspects of Jewish life, without question or challenge?

Our analysis of the critical balance between earned and birth roles in Jewish tradition can help us better understand some of the complexities involved in this ongoing discussion.

Which aspects of a woman's traditional role in Judaism are potentially "earned" and which aspects are "inherited"?

The Mishna distinguishes the inherited role of women in Jewish society from that of men by maintaining that *women are exempt from time-bound positive biblical commandments.*[26] Other areas of law that carry exemptions for women include specific isolated negative biblical commandments,[27] a number of positive rabbinic time-bound mitzvot[28] and certain spheres of testimony[29] and governance.[30]

In actuality, however, the exclusions from this general rule are as significant as the inclusions.[31] Women are, for example, exempt from the mitzvot of tefillin, succa and lulav[32] yet are, for a variety of reasons, obligated in the mitzvot of Kiddush[33], matza[34] and Hakhel (the public reading of the Torah at the end of the *Shmita* year).[35] Exemption, in addition, does not necessarily imply prohibition. With some exceptions, women can accept upon themselves, voluntarily, even those mitzvot from which they are clearly halachically exempt.[36]

Why does Jewish law exempt women from time-bound positive biblical mitzvot? While the Talmud is silent on the issue, numerous suggestions are offered by later commentaries. Does this rule exist, as some would suggest, to allow women to assume primary responsibility for the Jewish home? Perhaps increased public involvement on the part of women in Jewish life

---

26. Mishna Kiddushin 1:7.
27. ibid.
28. Tosafot, Brachot 20b.
29. Shulchan Aruch, Choshen Mishpat 35:14; and in Hagot HaRema.
30. Rambam, *Mishneh Torah*, Hilchot Melachim 1:5.
31. Talmud Bavli Kiddushin 34a.
32. Tosefta Kiddushin 1:10.
33. Talmud Bavli Brachot 20b.
34. Ibid., Pesachim 43b.
35. Devarim 31:12.
36. Tosafot, Eruvin 96a.

would further weaken the home by conveying the message that religious fulfillment can only be found in the public arena? If so, such steps should be taken with great caution. The home is, after all, the single most important educational institution in Jewish experience (see *Bereishit*: Vayechi 4, *Approaches* B and *Points to Ponder*; *Shmot*: Bo 4, *Approaches* A).

On the other hand, the Talmud offers no clear reason for the halachic exemption concerning women. Are we, then, assuming too much by offering the above (or, for that matter, any) rationale? Given the great advances made in women's Jewish education and their changing roles in secular scholarship and the workplace, should Jewish practice lag behind? Major changes can arguably be made in the ritual and communal roles of Jewish women while remaining loyal to the letter of the law. Can we risk the potential disaffection of a large number of today's Jewishly educated, knowledgeable and accomplished women if such changes are not made? Should we not more clearly try to define exactly which aspects of a woman's role are, according to Jewish law, immutably inherited at birth and which aspects can be earned?

Further complicating the debate is the consistent halachic call for privacy and modesty as primary determinants of a woman's role in Jewish life. The rabbis classically explain a famous passage from Tehillim as limiting a woman's potential public participation: "All glorious is the king's daughter within..."[37]

How should this call for social reticence be interpreted today against the backdrop of changing social mores?

A full analysis of the halachic and philosophical issues involved in this discussion remains well beyond the scope of our study. Even a cursory review, however, reveals legitimate concerns on both sides of this controversy that merit careful consideration.

A carefully crafted balance between birth and earned-roles has helped ensure the continuity of Jewish society across the ages. The collision of these roles at the cutting edge of Jewish life today may well shape the course of our people's future.

---

37. Tehillim 45:14; Talmud Bavli Shevuot 30a; Rambam, *Mishneh Torah*, Hilchot Ishut 13:11; and countless other sources.

Shmini

CHAPTER 9:1–11:47

Parsha Summary

Celebration, tragedy, reaction, ritual...

The seven preparatory days for Aharon and his sons draw to a close as the celebratory eighth day – the day on which the kehuna *will be formally launched – arrives.*

God commands the nation to assemble at the Sanctuary's entrance to witness the rituals of investiture through which Aharon and his sons will enter their priestly duties. A heavenly fire descends, consuming the offerings on the altar.

Aharon's moment of personal triumph suddenly turns to wrenching tragedy as his two oldest sons, Nadav and Avihu, offer a "foreign fire" and are themselves consumed by heavenly flames.

Moshe and Aharon react, each in his own way, to the tragedy.

Moshe then commands his brother to refrain from mourning and to continue with the Sanctuary service.

God commands Aharon concerning the prohibition of intoxication during the service within the Sanctuary and concerning other aspects of the Temple rituals.

Parshat Shmini closes with a review of the laws of forbidden foodstuffs and specific laws of tuma *and* tahara, *ritual impurity and purity.*

1 Mysterious Tragedy

Context

Finally, after seven days of preparation, an eighth, celebratory day of investiture dawns for Aharon and his sons. On this day, they will publicly assume the *kehuna*, an honored priestly role to be bequeathed, in perpetuity, to their descendents.

At God's command, the entire nation gathers at the entrance of the Mishkan to witness the rituals of initiation performed by Aharon and his sons. The investiture service reaches a mounting climax as Aharon twice blesses the people (the second time in conjunction with Moshe) and a miraculous fire descends from the heavens, consuming the offerings on the altar.

Suddenly, however, this exalted moment of celebration turns to tragedy and sorrow. The Torah testifies: "And the sons of Aharon, Nadav and Avihu, took, each man, his censer; and they placed in them fire; and they placed upon it incense; and they offered before God a foreign fire which God had not commanded them. And a fire came forth from before God and it consumed them; and they died before God."[1]

Questions

Few episodes in the Torah are as frighteningly mysterious as the story of the demise of Aharon's oldest sons. The questions are basic and stark.

What exactly is the sin of Nadav and Avihu?

Why is this sin so onerous that it merits the overwhelmingly severe punishment of immediate death by God's hand?

---

1. Vayikra 10:1–2.

Approaches

A wide spectrum of opinion emerges among rabbinic sources concerning the nature of the sin and resulting punishment of Nadav and Avihu. At the core of the discussion lies the fundamental mystery: *which aspects of Nadav and Avihu's actions were so onerous, so unforgivable, that they warranted such immediate and harsh divine punishment?*

—A—

At one end of the spectrum stand those scholars who, confronted with the severity of God's reaction, are unwilling to accept this textual narrative at face value. God, they feel, would simply not have punished Nadav and Avihu so harshly over only a ritual-based sin.

A number of Midrashic approaches thus appear in rabbinic literature, each maintaining that the sons of Aharon sinned in a manner suggested by, but far transcending, the straightforward reading of the text.

1. Aharon's sons die because they dare to determine law in the presence of their teacher, Moshe. Erroneously relying upon a source in the text,[2] Nadav and Avihu act contrary to Moshe's instructions.[3]

2. They enter the Temple in a drunken state.[4] Support for this position can be derived from an immediately subsequent passage where God commands the Kohanim not to enter the Temple while drunk, on pain of death.[5]

3. They fail to confer with Moshe, Aharon or with each other. They each act independently and precipitously.[6]

4. They long for the death of Moshe and Aharon in anticipation of the moment when they will inherit the mantle of leadership.[7]

5. They refuse to marry because they feel that no woman is worthy of their exalted status.[8]

6. They [deliberately] fail to have children.[9]

---

2. Vayikra 1:7.
3. Talmud Bavli Eruvin 63a.
4. Midrash Rabba Vayikra, Shmini 12:5.
5. Vayikra 10:8–11; Midrash Rabba Vayikra, Shmini 12:1.
6. Torat Kohanim 10:1.
7. Midrash Rabba Vayikra, Acharei Mot 20:10.
8. Ibid.
9. Ibid., 20:9.

Common to these and to other similar approaches is the belief that only a global, deeply powerful transgression, transcending the ritual backdrop against which it occurred, could possibly have merited the dramatic punishment meted out by God.

— B

At the opposite end of the spectrum, in contrast, stand those commentaries who maintain that the repeated testimony of the text is abundantly clear and sufficient:

+ "And they offered before God *a foreign fire which God had not commanded them.*"[10]
+ "And Nadav and Avihu died before the Lord when they offered *a foreign fire* before the Lord."[11]
+ "And Nadav and Avihu died when they offered *a foreign fire* before the Lord."[12]

Somewhere within this deed itself, these scholars believe, lies the key to the transgression of Aharon's sons. Somehow, the *very act of offering a foreign fire* constitutes an unforgivable sin, a sin that demands swift, harsh punishment.

As the rabbis search the text for clues, a variety of fascinating approaches emerge.

— C

A powerfully imaginative explanation is suggested, for example, by the Ramban and further explicated by later commentaries.

Noting that, according to the text, Nadav and Avihu place the incense directly "*on the fire,*"[13] these scholars suggest a symbolic interpretation. Nadav and Avihu correctly understand that incense is specifically designed to counter the "fire" of *Midat Hadin*, God's seemingly harsh attribute of justice. They fail to realize, however, that every offering in the Sanctuary, including the incense, must be presented to a unified God. Judaism rejects

---

10. Vayikra 1:1.
11. Bamidbar 3:4.
12. Ibid., 26:61.
13. Vayikra 10:1.

not only the existence of multiple gods but also the possibility of multiple independent components of one God. The delineation of separate divine attributes is artificial, a device used by Jewish tradition to assist limited man in understanding an unfathomable, seemingly contradictory Deity (see *Shmot*: *Va'eira 1, Approaches* E). All forces within this world, both those which appear to us as "benevolent" as well as those which appear to us as "punishing," emanate from the same divine source. God's attributes do not operate – and, therefore, cannot be worshiped – independently of each other.

By placing the incense "on the fire," by directing the incense specifically towards the "fire" of God's justice, the sons of Aharon challenge the pillar of Jewish belief, the oneness of God.[14]

Numerous other scholars, moving closer to the realm of *pshat*, focus on the apparent contrast between the singular day of investiture and other days to follow in the Mishkan. On all other days, the Kohanim are clearly commanded to provide fire for the altar as part of their regular functions within the Sanctuary.[15] On this day, however, "earthly" fire is proscribed. God's glory is to be highlighted by the descent of the "heavenly," miraculous fire.

Nadav and Avihu negate this distinction. Ignoring the instructions specific to this exalted day, they bring an earthly "foreign fire." Perhaps, as some suggest, their decision reflects a lack of faith in God's planned intervention.[16] Perhaps they simply fail to understand the unique challenge of the day. One way or the other, *their actions undermine the intended demonstration of God's power and diminish God's glory in the eyes of the people.*[17]

In a brilliant stroke, some commentaries, notably the Rashbam, the Bechor Shor and the Chizkuni, take the *pshat* one step further by interweaving the various pieces of the narrative into one cohesive whole. The fire that destroys Nadav and Avihu, these scholars maintain, is the very same heavenly fire sent by God to consume the offerings on the altar. Emerging from the Holy of Holies, this miraculous fire passes by the incense altar. There it encounters and kills Nadav and Avihu, who, ignoring Moshe's instructions,

---

14. Ramban (as interpreted by Racanti), Vayikra 10:1; Rabbeinu Bachya, ibid. (in his third approach).
15. Vayikra 1:7.
16. Rabbeinu Bachya, Vayikra 10:1 (in his first approach).
17. Rashbam, Vayikra 10:1; Bechor Shor, ibid.

have unknowingly entered the fire's path. The fire then proceeds on its intended course to the external altar where it consumes the offerings.[18]

This approach does not, by any means, completely solve the mystery of Nadav and Avihu's fate. Perhaps, however, their death becomes somewhat easier to accept if we believe that *their own actions physically place them in harm's way.*

—— **D** ————————————————————————————————

An additional textual source and a puzzling declaration in the Midrash serve as foundations for an entirely different rabbinic approach to the sin of Nadav and Avihu.

Based on the verse "And the Lord spoke to Moshe after the death of Aharon's two sons, *when they drew near to the Lord,* and they died,"[19] the Yalkut Shimoni comments: "And when the sons of Aharon joyously perceived that a new heavenly fire had descended from heaven and consumed the offerings on the altar, *they immediately acted to add 'love upon love'* [by bringing their own fire to the altar as well]."[20]

According to the commentaries who build on these sources, Aharon's older sons are righteous individuals who do not consciously sin either before or on this fateful celebratory day. Their failure, instead, ironically stems from a spontaneous act of religious passion. Moved by the power of God's Presence, awestruck by the pageantry of the moment, Nadav and Avihu reflexively set out on a path of their own design in an attempt to draw near to an immanent God. In doing so, they turn their back on the true path of religious worship as outlined in the Torah.[21]

This approach is most effectively summarized in the words of Nehama Leibowitz:

> We find ourselves learning that Nadav and Avihu did not incur formal guilt through transgression of any of the commandments associated with the ritual service. [Their sin instead rose from] a desire to draw near, to cling to the Creator; *not, however, according to the dictates of the Lord but according to the dictates of their hearts.*

————————————

18. Rashbam, Vayikra 10:2; Bechor Shor, ibid.; Chizkuni, ibid.
19. Vayikra 16:1.
20. Yalkut Shimoni, Shmini 524.
21. Naphtali Herz Wessely, *Biur,* Vayikra 16:1.

[Nadav and Avihu's actions thus represent a rejection of obedience to God's will –] of the yoke of the kingdom of heaven – the acceptance of which is the goal of the entire Torah.

The worship of the Lord is based neither upon fleeting moments of personal ecstasy nor upon the periodic, albeit sincere, dedication of one's soul – but, rather, upon the acceptance of the yoke of heaven, Torah and mitzvot.[22]

Within Judaism, the path towards sanctity is clearly delineated. God's presence in our lives is assured only through our ongoing acceptance of and obedience to His will.

One final note to this approach is added by the Ohr Hachaim as he comments on the passage in Parshat Acharei Mot: "And the Lord spoke to Moshe after the death of Aharon's two sons, *when they drew near to the Lord, and they died.*"[23]

The text wants us to understand, the Ohr Hachaim maintains, that Nadav and Avihu died *before* they could achieve their goal. They did not attain "closeness to God" through their deaths.[24]

The story of Aharon's oldest sons thus emerges as a cautionary tale, warning against the potential excesses of religious zeal.

One could erroneously conclude that Nadav and Avihu's actions were commendable, that their supreme personal sacrifice was a small price to pay for the unimaginable prize of a close encounter with God. The Torah therefore emphasizes that Nadav and Avihu's journey was aborted short of their goal. A fundamental flaw in their approach doomed the endeavor from the start. "Religious escapism" is not a Jewish value. God does not desire the literal or figurative sacrifice of our earthly existence in our search for His presence. Once again, the Torah strikes its oft-repeated refrain. Our task is to find God while rooted in our own reality, to encounter the Divine by living in and sanctifying the physical world.

The Ohr Hachaim's approach to this event is consistent with his observations concerning the dialogue between God and Moshe directly before Revelation (see *Shmot: Yitro 3, Approaches* A). How fascinating that it is

---

22. Nehama Leibowitz, *Studies in Vayikra* (Jerusalem: World Zionist Organization, 1980), p. 103.
23. Vayikra 16:1.
24. Ohr Hachaim, Vayikra 16:1.

specifically this scholar, known for his kabbalistic leanings, who warns that God is not to be found "by breaking through and attempting to draw near"[25] in the search for a transcendent moment of spiritual ecstasy.

Points to Ponder

Ritual plays a central, multifaceted role in Jewish experience. When properly practiced and understood, ritual observance

1. creates an ongoing connection between daily life and the Divine;

2. regularly reminds us of pivotal ideas and concepts that are easily forgotten;

3. forges a uniform, uniting observance that transcends time and place.

Specifically because of its all-important, complex role, Jewish ritual must be carefully calibrated in each generation. At the core of this task lies the fundamental tension between constancy and innovation in Jewish ritual law.

On the one hand, the most basic symbolic mitzvot, such as mezuza or tefillin, must remain constant and unchanging. Their immutable character is essential to the role they play in the transmission of *mesora*. As the Torah testifies in a familiar passage from the first paragraph of the Shma: "And you shall teach them thoroughly to your children and you shall speak of them while you sit in your home, when you walk on the way, and when you retire and when you rise. *And you shall bind them as a sign upon your arms and as symbols between your eyes.*"[26]

The text's sudden leap from the general commandments of learning and teaching Torah to the mitzva of tefillin underscores the pivotal role played by symbolic mitzvot in the intergenerational transmission of tradition. *You will only succeed in the teaching of your children*, the Torah states, *when that teaching is accompanied by concrete, practical mitzvot such as tefillin.*

Ideas, by their very nature, change across time. Rituals, however, remain constant. While a parent's personal vision of Judaism will be different from that of even his observant child, their tefillin are the same. *Shared concrete observance of symbolic mitzvot ensures a continuity of purpose that withstands changing times, circumstances and world outlooks.*

---

25. Ibid.
26. Devarim 6:7–8.

On the other hand, newly created ritual is constantly being added to the fabric of Jewish tradition across time. Rites as basic as the kindling of Shabbat and festival candles; the laws of Chanuka and Purim; the standardized prayers; and so much more have been added across the ages through rabbinic legislation and even through the adoption of communal custom.

The balance between constancy and change, central to halacha as a whole, thus acquires heightened significance in the area of symbolic mitzvot. For while new Jewish rituals must certainly develop over time in response to changing needs and circumstance, unfettered change actually undermines the role ritual plays in the preservation of Jewish practice and thought. We are therefore challenged, as we so often are in Jewish experience, to find a way to "keep things the same" even as we allow for change. This challenge is reflected in our own time, as the Jewish community struggles to define appropriate permanent ritual to mark the overwhelming phenomena that have shaped our world, from the horrors of the Shoah to the miraculous establishment of the State of Israel.

We can now understand an additional tension built into the scene of Nadav and Avihu's tragic death.

The investiture of the *kehuna* launches, in earnest, one of the primary ritual streams of Jewish history. Finally with the *kehuna* in place, the Temple service is ready to begin – a service that will serve as the centerpiece of Jewish worship for centuries and as the paradigm of that worship for many more.

At this critical moment, in full view of the entire nation, Nadav and Avihu challenge the system. Dissatisfied with the investiture rites mandated by God and communicated by Moshe, they decide to follow a ritual path of their own design.

Had Nadav and Avihu been allowed to proceed unimpeded, ritual anarchy could well have resulted. At this most critical moment in the development of Jewish tradition, the message conveyed to all present would have been: *Creative ritual is completely acceptable; follow your hearts; determine your own mode of expression; the path towards God can be designed by you. There is no need for uniformity of thought or practice as you individually search for spirituality in your lives.*

Only an emphatic and immediate response from God could salvage the moment and set the Jewish nation firmly upon its nuanced spiritual path. While allowing the necessary room for individual religious search and discovery, communal rules of worship had to be established, boundaries enforced. The people had to be taught that one could not create new ritual at will. The challenge raised by Nadav and Avihu had to be answered in forceful fashion.

The discussion and debate concerning Nadav and Avihu's fate, reflected in our study, will certainly persist for years to come. Questions concerning the nature of their sin, the extent of their punishment and the lessons to be learned will continue to captivate and mystify future students of the text. One truth, however, is clear. At a critical moment in our history, God's emphatic actions preserve the delicate balance between ritual constancy and innovation, a balance essential to the perpetuation of our tradition.

2 Mysterious Reactions

Context

Immediately following the sudden, devastating deaths of Nadav and Avihu, the following interchange takes place between Moshe and Aharon:

> And Moshe said to Aharon: Of this did God speak when He said, "I will be sanctified among those who are nearest to me, and before the entire nation shall I be glorified."
> And Aharon was silent.[1]

Questions

What is the meaning of Moshe's reaction, "*Of this did God speak when He said...*"?

Is Moshe citing an earlier divine prediction of Nadav and Avihu's death? If so, what is the source of that prediction? Was the tragic, violent death of Nadav and Avihu somehow preordained even before their sin?

Is Moshe's response to the death of Aharon's sons designed to address his brother's pain? If so, in what way are Moshe's words comforting?

What is the significance of Aharon's silence?

Approaches

—— A ——

Confronted with Moshe's mysterious reference to a prior prediction of Nadav and Avihu's death, Rashi raises the obvious question: "Where did [God] say this?"

---

1. Vayikra 10:3–4.

In answer, Rashi cites a Talmudic Midrash which sees a foreshadowing of Nadav and Avihu's fate in the divine proclamation, recorded in the book of Shmot, which presages the inauguration of the Sanctuary service: "And I will make Myself known there to the people of Israel and I will be sanctified in My Glory."[2]

Moshe understands the unusual phrase "and I will be sanctified *in My glory*" to mean: *and I will be sanctified through those who glorify Me.* He therefore immediately interprets God's words as a dire prediction: *the inauguration of the Sanctuary service will be sanctified by the ultimate sacrifice of those individuals "closest to God."*

Moshe secretly harbors this premonition until, in the aftermath of the death of Nadav and Avihu, he turns to Aharon and says: "Aharon, my brother, I have known that the Temple would be sanctified by [the sacrifice of] those closest to God. And I assumed that it would either be me or you. Now I know that they [Nadav and Avihu] are greater than me or you."[3]

According to this Talmudic Midrash, Moshe comforts his brother by underscoring the overwhelming spiritual greatness of Aharon's sons. He hopes, as those comforting mourners often do, that Aharon will find solace in the contemplation of the lives, rather than the deaths, of those for whom he mourns.

—— **B** ————————————————————————————

Rashi's grandson, the Rashbam, who, as we have repeatedly seen, consistently prefers the path of *pshat*, strenuously objects: "The aggadic explanation that Moshe consoled Aharon by pointing to a divine prediction that God would be sanctified through [the sacrifice] of those who glorify him… is not an acceptable interpretation of the text. [Could we possibly believe that] God would announce to Moshe: Create for me a Mishkan and on that very day the greatest among you will die?"[4]

The Midrash, the Rashbam seems to imply, skirts dangerously close to the concept of human sacrifice, a phenomenon which the Torah clearly defines as anathema to God.[5] How, asks this scholar and those who follow

———————————

2. Shmot 29:43.
3. Talmud Bavli Zevachim 115b.
4. Rashbam, Vayikra 10:3.
5. Devarim 12:31.

his lead, could God demand the lives of Nadav and Avihu as part of the Sanctuary's sanctification?

If the Midrashic claim of a divine foreshadowing of Nadav and Avihu's death is rejected, however, our original question returns. What is the meaning of Moshe's assertion: "Of this did God speak when he said…"?

The Rashbam's revolutionary answer to this question will be reviewed below.

—— C ————————————————————————

The Ramban also rejects, albeit in less strenuous terms than the Rashbam, the Midrashic interpretation quoted by Rashi.

Choosing a different direction, the Ramban reinterprets Moshe's statement by noting that the word *daber*, "speak," is often used in the text to reflect God's internal decisions and decrees, as opposed to actual speech. Moshe does not say to Aharon "Of this did God *speak*," but rather, "This is what God *decided*…"

According to the Ramban, Moshe's statement to Aharon is to be understood as follows.

"This is what God decided: 'I will be sanctified by those who are nearest to Me.'" *Even those most involved in My service must observe the mandated boundaries. Even they cannot enter sanctified areas of the Sanctuary at will, in improper fashion or at the wrong time.*

'And before the entire nation shall I be sanctified.' *From the example of those closest to Me the entire nation will learn to treat My Sanctuary with honor."*

Aharon's silent response to Moshe's statement, continues the Ramban, indicates that the High Priest's initial reaction to the tragedy was far from silent. Aharon at first cries bitterly and loudly, only to fall silent after hearing Moshe's words.[6]

The Ramban seems to suggest that Moshe's successful consolation of his brother centers upon the notion that the death of Nadav and Avihu at least served a purpose. *Through the death of your sons,* Moshe says to his brother, *the people have learned an invaluable lesson. They will now know, beyond the shadow of a doubt, that no one is exempt from the requirement of treating the Sanctuary with respect.*

———————

6. Ramban, Vayikra 10:3.

The idea of finding purpose in the death of Nadav and Avihu, suggested by the Ramban, is set forward in even clearer terms by other commentaries.

The Da'at Zekeinim Miba'alei Hatosafot, for example, interpret Moshe's statement of God's intent – "I will be sanctified among those who are nearest to Me, and before the entire nation shall I be glorified" – as follows:

Through the death of these near ones [Nadav and Avihu], I [God] will be sanctified and exalted in the eyes of the entire people. [The nation] will draw the inference that, if I have punished those near to Me in such fashion, how much more careful must the people as a whole be in guarding their own behavior; and they will fear Me.[7]

While the Midrash sees Moshe's consolation as centering on the quality of Nadav and Avihu's lives, these commentaries view Moshe's consolation as centering on the quality of their death. *Your sons*, Moshe says to his brother, *died a death that sanctified God's name.*

As logical as this approach appears to be, however, it marks a dramatic departure from the traditional concept of a "death that sanctifies God's name." This sad label typically applies to tragic situations (all too common in our turbulent history) when Jews are forced to sacrifice their lives in defense of their beliefs and practices, or even simply as a consequence of their Jewish identity. Such deaths are considered to be *al Kiddush Hashem*, "for the sanctification of God." In the case before us, however, Nadav and Avihu are, at best, punished for their errant behavior in failing to follow God's instructions. By labeling their death under these circumstances as "sanctified," simply because their demise serves an educational purpose, these commentaries seem to take the concept of *Kiddush Hashem* in a new, somewhat troubling direction.

— **D** —————————————————————————————

Perhaps because of this issue, the Rashbam, who so emphatically dismissed the Midrashic approach, also rejects the suggestions of the Ramban and Tosafists.

In a dramatic example of looking at the text with "new eyes," this scholar offers a radically different approach from almost all other commentaries. Most scholars, like those cited above, connect Moshe's comments to

---

7. Da'at Zekeinim Miba'alei Hatosafot, Vayikra 10:3.

the immediate past, viewing his words as an attempt to comfort his brother in the face of overwhelming tragedy.

The Rashbam instead maintains that Moshe's words actually reference the immediate future and are *not words of consolation, but of challenge.*

In the next few sentences, God will command Aharon to refrain from *aveilut*, the traditional practices of mourning over his sons.[8] Such public grief is inappropriate on the part of a Kohen Gadol actively involved in the Sanctuary service. Perhaps this stricture can best be understood by considering the similar, more familiar halachic phenomenon that emerges when a public festival and private mourning coincide. According to Jewish law, if one begins mourning before a festival, the holiday completely dissipates that period of mourning. If the festival occurs before *aveilut* begins, the bereavement process is suspended until after the festival.[9] Festival joy and mourning simply cannot coexist. Similarly, a Kohen Gadol involved in the service of God must set aside his personal grief in order to continue his duties.[10]

According to the Rashbam, Moshe's words to his brother reflect just this challenge. The fateful interchange between Moshe and Aharon in the aftermath of the death of Nadav and Avihu is meant to be understood as follows.

"And Moshe said to Aharon: Of this did God speak when he said, 'I will be sanctified among those who are nearest to Me, and before the entire nation shall I be glorified.'" *My brother*, argues Moshe, *the difficult challenge before you reflects God's stated law. Public demonstrations of mourning are prohibited on the part of a Kohen Gadol involved in the Sanctuary service.*

By following this law, by courageously refraining from mourning despite your overwhelming grief, you will publicly sanctify God's name. Your willingness to continue the service will fulfill God's mandate that He be "publicly sanctified through the actions of those nearest to him and, thereby, glorified before the entire nation."

"And Aharon was silent." *Summoning all his strength, Aharon refrains from openly mourning over his sons.*[11]

---

8. Vayikra 10:6–7.
9. Shulchan Aruch, Orach Chaim 548:1, 7.
10. Vayikra 21:12.
11. Rashbam, Vayikra 10:3.

In brilliant fashion, the Rashbam thus avoids the problems potentially inherent in the text. In this scholar's view, there was no divine prediction of Nadav and Avihu's demise. Moshe is not attempting to rationalize the death of Nadav and Avihu nor is he consoling his brother in the face of inconsolable loss. Instead, Moshe urges Aharon to meet the challenge of the moment, to rise above his own personal pain in the fulfillment of sacred communal responsibilities.

Courageously, Aharon complies.

Points to Ponder

Va'yidom Aharon, "And Aharon was silent."

Our world grows increasingly uncomfortable with silence.

Televisions, radios, cell phones, iPods and computers fill the airwaves with endless chatter, negating the possibility of quiet contemplation; lapses in conversation so disturb us that we feel compelled to say something, anything, to fill the void; comfortable silence, calm solitude disappear as increasingly we turn up the volume in our homes, offices and cars.

"Rabbi Shimon [the son of Gamliel] stated: 'All my life have I grown up among the sages, and I have found nothing better for man than silence.'"[12]

How different is our raucous world from the ideal contemplative environment envisioned by Rabbi Shimon, an environment designed to encourage introspection, self-examination and spiritual growth. How far we have traveled from the wilderness solitude in which our nation was born and which shaped the lives of so many of our leaders and prophets.

Furthermore, we have forgotten that silence can sometimes be the most effective, meaningful communication of all.

Consider, for example, the halachic dictate that, upon visiting a mourner, one should wait for the mourner to speak first.[13] An unforgettable personal experience taught me the true purpose and power of this law.

Upon hearing of the tragic, untimely death of a grandson of Rabbi Moshe Feinstein, I determined to pay a shiva call (condolence visit) even though I did not know the parents well. I entered a room to find the child's father sitting on the floor surrounded by roughly fifty men (Jewish law mandates that during the seven-day period of mourning the mourner

---

12. Pirkei Avot 1:17.
13. Shulchan Aruch, Yoreh Deah 376:1.

must sit on a low surface[14]). For forty-five minutes, no one said a word. The mourner did not feel like speaking and, in accordance with the law, no visitor spoke first. The silence was punctuated only when, every few moments, a visitor rose, approached the mourner, recited the traditional formula "May God comfort you among the mourners of Zion and Jerusalem" and left, to be replaced by another visitor.

After forty-five minutes of silence, I rose, recited the formula myself and left.

I had never before, nor have I ever since, experienced a more moving shiva visit. The eloquent message communicated through our silence could not have been clearer: *We are with you*, we silently said to the mourner, *as best we can be, in your sorrow. There is no need to speak if you do not wish to speak. We will sit silently with you and allow our presence to speak for itself.*

Perhaps, then, Aharon's silence in the aftermath of his children's sudden, violent death does not indicate an acceptance of Moshe's words but a rejection.

Confronted with his brother's attempts at consolation and rationalization (if we accept the position of the commentaries other than the Rashbam), Aharon wordlessly responds: *Moshe, there are times when words do not suffice, when they are, in fact, hurtful. I reject your attempt to explain the inexplicable. No words of comfort will assuage my heart's deep pain. I am willing to accept God's justice, but I know that I will never fully understand. For me, in the face of overwhelming loss there is only one meaningful response: silence.*

Va'yidom Aharon, "And Aharon was silent."

Sometimes silence is the most profound communication of all.

---

14. Ibid., 387:1; Shach 387:1.

3 Sanctuary Sobriety

Context

In the shadow of Nadav and Avihu's tragic death, God turns to their father, Aharon, and commands:

> Do not drink wine or intoxicating beverage, you and your sons with you, when you come into the Tent of Meeting, and you will not die; this is an eternal decree for your generations. In order to distinguish between the sacred and the profane and between the impure and the pure, and to teach the children of Israel all of the statutes that God has spoken to them through Moshe.[1]

While the text seems to clearly prohibit the consumption of any alcoholic beverage during the Kohen's fulfillment of his functions as priest and educator, the Talmud, after extensive debate, limits the full biblical prohibition to the ingestion of "intoxicating amounts" of wine.[2] In further discussion, many halachists delineate additional, less severe penalties both for the consumption of other intoxicating beverages and for smaller amounts of wine.[3] Finally, most scholars extend the requirement of sobriety during the teaching and application of the law to all teachers and not only to the Kohanim.[4]

Moving beyond the technical aspects of the law, numerous commentaries focus on its potential motivation. The Torah's concern, they say, centers on the debilitating effects of alcohol. An individual who is inebriated to any degree will neither be able to properly execute the Sanctuary service nor appropriately engage in halachic discussion and decision making. The Torah therefore prohibits the consumption of wine as a safeguard against possible intoxication.[5]

---

1. Vayikra 10:9–11.
2. Talmud Bavli Kritot 13b; in accordance with the position of Rabbi Elazar.
3. Rambam, *Mishneh Torah*, Hilchot Biat HaMikdash 1:1–2.
4. Ibid., 1:3; Rashi, Vayikra 10:11.
5. Ramban, Shmot 10:9; Ibn Ezra, Shmot 10:9; Sforno, Shmot 10:10–11.

Questions

Why are these commandments necessary?

Given the intricate detail of the Sanctuary service; given the clear re-peated divine warnings concerning the potential consequences of error in that service; given the overwhelming specter of Nadav and Avihu's death as an apparent result of ritual deviation; given the fact that proper halachic decisions clearly require one's full faculties; why would anyone assume that these functions could be performed in a state of intoxication? Why must the Torah state the obvious?

To go one step further, if the Torah's fundamental concern is potential error in the Sanctuary service or in halachic deliberation, why frame the prohibition as a ban upon alcoholic beverages? Why not simply reiterate a general warning that these disciplines must be approached with awe, rev-erence and caution?

Finally, if this law is based on the potentially debilitating effects of al-cohol, why is a difference drawn in the Talmud between wine and other intoxicating beverages? Shouldn't all substances that could potentially lead to inebriation be equally prohibited?

Approaches

— A

An astute observation made by a museum guide during one of my first trips to Israel can help us frame an answer to these questions.

"You can deduce," he said, "common practice within a society from the legal edicts enacted by its government."

"Centuries from now," he continued to explain, "when the ruins of this museum are excavated, archaeologists will not find signs in the rubble stat-ing 'No bicycle riding.' Since it is not current common practice in our day to ride bicycles through museums, legal postings prohibiting such behavior are not necessary and will not be part of the archaeological record.

"Excavators will, however, find 'No smoking' signs. This discovery will lead them to correctly surmise that smoking was likely to occur in public buildings during the twentieth to twenty-first centuries and that the ad-ministrators of this museum moved to prevent such activity."

———— B ————————————————————————————————————

This comment may well shed light on the Torah's concern for the sobriety of the Kohanim.

God finds it necessary to prohibit the consumption of wine during ritual and intellectual religious activity in response to "common practice" of the time.

The use of alcohol and other psychoactive drugs was an integral component of the religious rites of many ancient cultures. Rather than viewing inebriation and similar "escapist" behaviors as impediments to spiritual search, these societies considered the use of psychoactive substances an essential prerequisite of that very search.

Archaeological evidence, in fact, traces the use of psychoactive drugs in every age and on every continent from prehistoric times to the present. In modern times, the term *entheogen* (meaning literally "generating the divine within") has been coined to refer to vision-producing drugs taken to bring on a spiritual experience.[6] The use of such substances, many have believed across the ages, enables man to loosen the shackles of his earthly existence and truly encounter the Divine.

In direct opposition to this approach, normative Judaism preaches an "earthly" encounter with our Creator. As we have consistently seen (see *Shmot*: Shmot 3, *Approaches* D, E; Yitro 2, *Approaches* C, D), one of the Torah's primary messages is that God is to be found and experienced in this world, with our feet firmly planted on the ground. The Sforno maintains that Moshe, our greatest prophet, achieved his greatness specifically because of his ability to relate to God without relinquishing his physical senses.[7]

The ban on alcoholic consumption in specific settings, therefore, does not emerge solely from apprehension over alcohol's potentially debilitating effects. A much more fundamental philosophical issue is reflected in this prohibition.

God's message to His people is once again clear: *I am not to be found in the mists at the summit of Sinai. I am not to be encountered in esoteric visions or "out of body" experiences. You are to find Me in your world through*

———————————

6. R. Gordon Wasson, *The Wondrous Mushroom: Mycolatry in Mesoamerica* (New York: McGraw-Hill, 1980), xiv.

7. Sforno, Shmot 33:11.

performance of My mitzvot, through the sober study, application and living of My law.

— **C** —

We can now also understand, as well, the distinction made in the law between wine and other intoxicating substances. Wine, even more than other psychoactive materials, has long occupied a particular place in religious ritual. This fact is evidenced at both extremes within Jewish law. On the one hand, because of the unique status of wine in pagan culture, the Torah mandates the prohibition of *yayin nesech* (wine that has been used for idolatrous purposes and is, therefore, prohibited to all Jews at all times). On the other hand, wine, in moderation, finds its positive place within Jewish practice, used to mark special occasions and events.

Had the Torah's only concern been for potential error on the part of the Kohanim, all intoxicating beverages would have been treated equally. By singling wine out for special attention, however, the Torah communicates that there is more to this prohibition than meets the eye. Wine used properly and in moderation, the Torah teaches, like all of God's physical creations, enhances our appreciation of the Divine. When used to escape reality, however, all psychoactive substances undermine our spiritual search, which is predicated on creating a union in our lives between heaven and earth.

— **D** —

At the dawn of our history, as the spiritual search of our nation begins, God again reiterates the distinction between Judaism and the surrounding cultures. Others may find their spiritual path predicated upon an escape from the realities of the physical world. Our path, however, is based upon the embrace and sanctification of that very world.

4 Considering Kashrut

Context

As Parshat Shmini draws to a close, the Torah abruptly turns its attention to a set of laws that fall into the halachic category popularly known as kashrut.[1]

The text delineates, among other laws, the categories of animals, fish and fowl that are halachically permitted or prohibited for consumption.

To be considered kosher, an animal must possess split hooves and chew its cud, while a fish must possess both fins and scales. Prohibited birds are listed individually in the text without the delineation of defining characteristics.

After outlining a series of additional regulations, Parshat Shmini ends with the following broad exhortation:

> For I am the Lord your God, and you shall sanctify yourselves and you shall be holy, for I am holy.... For I am the Lord your God Who raises you from the land of Egypt in order to be for you a God; and you shall be holy for I am holy. This is the law of the animal and the bird and all living creature that swarms in the water and for every creature that teems on the ground. To distinguish between the impure and pure and between the creature that may be eaten and the creature that may not be eaten.[2]

---

1. The word *kosher* simply means "fit" and does not apply only to permitted foods but can, of course, be used in reference to other items such as mezuzot, tefillin and even articles that do not fall into the category of mitzvot. The use of the term specifically as a general heading for permitted foods is, thus, "popular usage."
2. Vayikra 11:1–47.

Questions

Is there any logical rhyme or reason to these laws of kashrut which occupy such a critical, prominent place in the life of every observant Jew?

Why does the Torah append these laws, in seemingly arbitrary fashion, to the end of Parshat Shmini? Does the placement of these regulations provide a hint towards their significance?

Before answering these questions, two general observations must be made.

A. The laws of kashrut do not emerge from the biblical text monolithically. In addition to the regulations before us, numerous strictures recorded in various passages in the Torah play a role in determining the status of specific foodstuffs. These restrictions are further expanded upon through rabbinic legislation.

The parameters found in the Torah include (but are not limited to):

1. The bans on the consumption of blood[3] and forbidden fats[4] of even kosher animals

2. The ban on the consumption of the sciatic nerve of a kosher animal[5]

3. The prohibitions concerning the cooking of a mixture of kosher meat and milk, the consumption of such a cooked mixture, and the derivation of benefit from such a cooked mixture[6]

4. The requirement for the proper slaughter of a kosher animal[7]

5. The ban on wine that had been used for idolatrous purposes[8]

In isolated cases, the Torah does provide historical[9] or ethical[10] rationales for the laws in question. On the whole, however, the text is conspicuously silent.

---

3. Ibid., 7:26–27, 17:10–12; Devarim 12:16, 23–25.
4. Vayikra 7:23–25.
5. Bereishit 32:33.
6. Shmot 23:19, 34:26; Devarim 14:21.
7. Devarim 12:21; Talmud Bavli Chulin 28a.
8. Devarim 32:38.
9. Bereishit 32:33 (the prohibition concerning the consumption of the sciatic nerve).
10. Vayikra 17:11; Devarim 12:23, 15:23 (the prohibition concerning the consumption of blood).

B. Due to the Torah's silence, most specific laws of kashrut fall into the legal category of *chukim*, laws for which no reason is given in the Torah text.

Faced with the challenges presented by *chukim* in general, the rabbis debate whether or not one is allowed to posit potential reasons for these seemingly "reasonless" regulations. (For a full discussion of this and other issues surrounding *chukim*, see *Shmot*: Teruma 3.)

In this study we will adopt the position that one is allowed to suggest reasons for specific *chukim*, as we sample some of the suggested interpretations for the practical yet enigmatic laws that close Parshat Shmini.

Approaches

— **A** —

In her opening comments on this section, Nehama Leibowitz distinguishes between the Torah's regulations concerning permitted/prohibited food sources and seemingly similar laws found in other ancient cultures. While other traditions demonize the forbidden creatures themselves, seeing them as representing forces contrary to God's will, no such value judgments are rendered in Jewish law. The halachic ban on specific food sources is simply that: a restriction on human behavior. The animals designated as forbidden within the Torah are not inherently evil; they are simply forbidden for consumption by Jews.[11]

This distinction mirrors the much greater divide between superstitious and religious practice; between belief in arbitrary, dangerous forces vying for governance of the world and loyalty to a unified, thinking God Who makes demands upon human behavior. (See *Bereishit*: Bereishit 3 for a full analysis of this distinction, which traces back to the Garden of Eden.)

In light of Leibowitz's observations, however, our primary question gains even greater traction. If the creatures forbidden by the Torah are not "inherently evil," why would God prohibit their consumption?

— **B** —

A number of prominent classical scholars, including the Rambam, the

---

11. Nehama Leibowitz, *Iyunim Chadashim B'sefer Vayikra* (Jerusalem: Hasochnut Hayehudit, 1970), pp. 119–121.

Ramban and the Ba'al Hachinuch, maintain that the foods prohibited by the Torah are physically injurious to human health.[12]

"If there are some among [these foods]," argues the Ba'al Hachinuch, "whose potential for harm is known neither to us nor to medical scholars, do not be concerned. The 'True Physician' [God], Who warned us of them, is wiser than you or they."[13]

Even the Rashbam, staunch defender of textual *pshat*, offers this health-based explanation as the "literal interpretation of the text and as a response to heretics."[14]

— C —

Other authorities, however, vehemently oppose the notion that the laws of kashrut could possibly be based upon health concerns.

"Heaven forbid that I should believe so," claims the Abravanel, as he raises three primary objections to health-based explanations for the laws of kashrut:

1. Such interpretations reduce the stature of the Torah by lowering it to the level of a simple medical tome.

2. The foods prohibited by Jewish law are regularly consumed by non-Jews to no adverse physical effect.

3. Countless other dangerous substances abound in our environment, yet are not included in the Torah's list of forbidden foods.[15]

In the face of these and other arguments, a number of scholars shift the focus of concern. The foodstuffs prohibited by the Torah, they maintain, are indeed potentially damaging to man. *The threat posed by these substances, however, plays out in the spiritual, rather than in the physical, realm.*

As the Abravanel clearly states:

[Through the ban on specific foods] the Torah does not seek to heal the bodies of man nor to ensure their physical well-being…but rather to safeguard the health of the soul and to cure its infirmities.

12. Rambam, *Moreh Nevuchim* 3:48; Sefer Hachinuch, mitzva 73; Ramban, Vayikra 11:11.
13. Sefer Hachinuch, mitzva 73.
14. Rashbam, Vayikra 11:3.
15. Abravanel, Vayikra 11.

[The text], therefore, bans those foods which defile and desecrate man's pure soul…, creating in him an evil disposition…, giving rise to a spirit of impurity, desecrating both thought and action.

One by one, with minor variations, commentaries such as the Sforno[16] and the Kli Yakar[17] fall in line with this approach. The creatures prohibited for consumption by Torah law, they maintain, all share one common feature. Their ingestion as food somehow damages man's moral fiber and spiritual fabric.

Even the Ramban, who is willing to accept the idea that forbidden animals are damaging to man's physical health (see above), nonetheless sees spiritual danger as a primary motive for prohibiting their consumption.[18]

—— **D** ——

Building on the notion that the substances forbidden by the Torah are injurious to man's spiritual welfare, the Sforno offers a fascinating rationale for the seemingly arbitrary placement of these laws towards the end of Parshat Shmini.

In order to understand the textual flow, this scholar maintains, we must return to the book of Shmot, to the sin of the golden calf. There, in the very shadow of Sinai, we find that God withdraws from His people in response to their overwhelming failure. The Israelites become a nation bereft, unable to relate to their God directly, as they did before their sin.

In the course of his prayers, however, Moshe discerns the mechanisms through which the Israelites can once again achieve direct communion with the Divine. The Mishkan, its utensils, priestly servants and sanctified offerings will draw God back into the midst of His people.

A journey of reconciliation thus begins, framed by God's detailed commandments concerning the construction and operation of the Mishkan, the nation's ready response, the building of the Mishkan, the transmission of the laws of the *korbanot*, the preparations for the investiture of the *kehuna* and the launching of the Sanctuary service. In the opening segments of Parshat Shmini, this transformative process reaches its dramatic climax,

---

16. Sforno, Vayikra 11:2.
17. Kli Yakar, Vayikra 11:1.
18. Ramban, Vayikra 11:13.

as the Kohanim enter their sanctified role and a heavenly fire consumes the offerings upon the altar.

Suddenly these events are tragically marred by the violent death of Nadav and Avihu at God's hand. Moshe's goal, however, has been achieved. *God has returned to His people.*

Noting this success, Moshe now moves to prepare the Israelites for God's constant presence in their lives. He commands them to consume only those foods that will enable them to "bask in the light of eternal life" and he instructs them to refrain from ingesting those substances that would impede their spiritual growth.[19]

Through the eyes of the Sforno, the Torah laws concerning permitted and prohibited foodstuffs are transformed from technical regulations into an essential component in the dramatic reconciliation between God and His people.

— E —

Finally, a number of commentaries propose what is, perhaps, the most basic rationale of all for the laws of permitted and prohibited foodstuffs. The foods banned by the Torah, they maintain, are not prohibited because of specific characteristics in the substances themselves. Instead, God commands these regulations because He knows that *the very act of selective abstinence, in the area of sustenance, will benefit the Israelites in manifold ways.*

According to these scholars, the laws of permitted and prohibited foodstuffs are designed to:

1. Help maintain a clear separation between the Jewish people and surrounding cultures.

2. Train each Jew towards a disciplined lifestyle marked by the acceptance of God's will.

3. Connect the ordinary act of eating to Jewish law, thereby injecting God-awareness into the daily life of each Jew.

4. Cultivate the people's recognition of their own powers of self-control.[20]

From the perspective of these scholars, the regulations of permitted and prohibited foodstuffs help maintain an essential equilibrium within

---

19. Sforno, Vayikra 11:2.
20. Akeidat Yitzchak Vayikra, sha'ar 60; Shmuel David Luzzatto, *Hamishtadel.*

the life of each Jew. As we have consistently noted (see *Bereishit*: Bereishit 1, *Approaches* D, E), the Torah preaches that our physical surroundings are a divine gift, to be appreciated and enjoyed. Man's embrace of the material world, however, must be balanced by a sense of limits, humility and personal perspective. To live a sanctified life, we must always be in control of, rather than controlled by, our passions. Through continued abstinence from those foods prohibited by the Torah, the Jew learns to control his own desires by bending them to God's will.

—— **F** ——————————————————

When all is said and done, the Torah's silence concerning many of the laws of kashrut leaves these regulations squarely in the realm of *chukim*. We may never fully understand, for example, why a deer is kosher while a horse is not; why shellfish are forbidden yet turkeys allowed.

As the above study demonstrates, many scholars find the struggle to comprehend these and other mysterious edicts of the Torah worthwhile, potentially yielding insights that can enrich our observance of the law. Success or failure in our search for meaning, however, can have no ultimate bearing on our observance of the law. *The revelation of God's will in the Torah is, in and of itself, enough to command the observant Jew's obedience – even when God's ultimate purposes remain unknown.*

Points to Ponder

Sometimes it's simply a matter of perspective…

With a short, incisive observation, the Chatam Sofer offers an approach to the laws of permitted/prohibited foodstuffs that turns things around one hundred eighty degrees.

The novel idea raised by the text, the Chatam Sofer suggests, is not what is forbidden to us but, rather, what is permitted.

This section of law opens with the statement "These are the creatures *which you shall eat*…," and then continues with a list of foods that are *allowed* for consumption. With these passages, the Torah informs us that God grants us permission to eat "permitted foods." Without this divine authorization, apparently, even these foods would not be allowed. The Torah thus reminds us that man acquires the right to benefit from the world only through God's acquiescence.[21]

In our age of "entitlement" we would do well to consider the Chatam Sofer's perspective. Man should not begin with the assumption that the world is fundamentally "his" and that God then sets limitations.

The opposite is true: *The world is a gift from God. Man is "entitled" only to that which God allows.*

21. Chatam Sofer, *Torat Moshe*, Shmini, quoted in Leibowitz, *Iyunim Chadashim B'sefer Vayikra*, 127.

Tazria-Metzora   תזריע-מצורע

CHAPTER 12:1–15:33   פרק יב:א-טו:לג

Parsha Summary

Purity and impurity, in various shapes and sizes...

    At the end of Parshat Shmini, the Torah opened the door on the mystifying realm of tuma *and* tahara, *ritual impurity and purity. Now, with the parshiot of Tazria and Metzora, we enter that realm full force.*

    After a brief section reviewing the laws of tumat yoledet *(impurity resulting from childbirth), Parshat Tazria quickly turns its attention to the primary topic of these two parshiot: the diagnosis and treatment of* tuma *brought about by the plague of* tzara'at, *biblical leprosy.*

    In great depth, the Torah reviews a wide variety of physical ailments, conveying critical information to the Kohanim who will be responsible for the identification and management of afflictions falling into the category of tzara'at. *Included in this review are afflictions affecting persons, garments and dwellings.*

    Parshat Metzora closes with additional laws concerning zav, *impure bodily emissions, and* niddut, *laws surrounding a woman's monthly cycle.*

1 Navigating a Strange World

Context

With the opening of the parshiot of Tazria and Metzora, we are thrust headlong into an alien world, the world of *tuma* and *tahara*, ritual impurity and purity.

The world laid out within these parshiot is populated by the some of the most baffling phenomena within the Torah, including *tumat yoledet*, impurity resulting from childbirth; *tzara'at*, biblical leprosy affecting individuals, garments and houses; *zav*, impure bodily emissions; *niddut*, laws surrounding a woman's monthly cycle; and more.[1]

Questions

Confronted with this bewildering array of foreign concepts, the natural tendency is to "shut down," to conclude that these ideas address a different time, a different place, a different population. Reinforcing this conclusion is the fact that many (although, as we will see, not all) of the laws of purity and impurity do not apply in our day in the absence of the Temple.

And yet, the Torah is an eternal document meant to speak to all times and generations…

While each of the individual phenomena described within the parshiot of Tazria and Metzora can be analyzed in isolation, and while the laws of *tuma* and *tahara* throughout the Torah are unimaginably complex, this study will take a global approach.

Once again, we are dealing with *chukim*, laws for which no reason is given in the Torah. As we have indicated elsewhere (most notably in our previous study), such laws are meant to be observed even if their reasons

---

1. Vayikra 12–15.

are not understood. The fundamental purpose of these laws may, in fact, be the training of loyalty to God in the face of mystery.

For the purpose of this study, however, we will again adopt the philosophical position that encourages analysis of possible rationales behind *chukim*. Adherents of this position maintain that such analysis potentially enriches our observance of the mitzvot.

The question before us, therefore, is: *What, if any, rational explanation can be suggested for the overall existence of the halachic states of tuma and tahara? What lessons can be derived from these mystifying concepts?*

Approaches

— **A** —————————————————————————————

As a first step in our search, we must overcome the immediate problems presented by the biblical terms *tuma* and *tahara*.

No appropriate English translation exists for these Hebrew words. The usually suggested translations, "pure and impure," or "clean and unclean," carry value judgments that, as we will see, are not necessarily applicable to all types of *tuma* and *tahara*.

Jewish tradition, in addition, uses the terms *tuma* and *tahara* in a wide-ranging and sometimes even confusing manner. On the one hand, in their legal application, these terms refer to the specific halachic constructs of ritual "purity and impurity." On the other hand, these same expressions are also used symbolically throughout biblical and rabbinic literature to represent a number of different positive and negative phenomena.

To cite a few examples:

1. Animals, fish and fowl halachically permitted for consumption are labeled by the Torah as *tahor* while prohibited creatures are referred to as *tamei*, even though no ritual purity or impurity is conveyed upon their consumption.[2]

2. When God warns the Israelites against following the corrupt ways of other nations He repeatedly uses the terminology of *tuma* and *tahara* in his exhortations.[3]

---

2. Ibid., 11:1–23.
3. Ibid., 18:24–28.

3. The holiest day of the year, Yom Kippur, carries not only the obligation of personal atonement but also the mandate of *Lifnei Hashem tit'haru*, "Before the Lord you shall [spiritually] *purify* yourselves."[4]

Any attempt to analyze the laws of *tuma* and *tahara* must set aside the judgmental overlays placed upon these terms and focus solely on the evidence presented by the laws themselves.

— **B** ———————————————————————————

The highest form of ritual impurity in Jewish law is created by contact with death. Such *tuma* is referred to within halachic literature as *avi avot hatumah*[5], literally the "father of all fathers of *tuma*," and results in the temporary exclusion of the affected individual from the Temple compound.[6]

This central correlation between death and impurity, however, is difficult to understand. *Kavod hameit*, honor and care for the deceased, is one of the most powerful mandates of Jewish law.[7] The obligation to assist in the burial of a *meit mitzva*, an individual who leaves no one behind to care for his mortal remains, supersedes almost all other religious obligations.[8] In community after community, individuals who regularly prepare the dead for burial are held in the highest esteem and earn the honorific title *chevra kadisha*, "sacred society."

If the obligation to care for the dead is so clearly central to Jewish thought and law, why should contact with death result in a state of ritual impurity, causing the affected individual's temporary exclusion from the Temple's confines?

— **C** ———————————————————————————

Two possible approaches can be suggested.

1. Tumat hameit, *ritual impurity conveyed through contact with death, underscores Judaism's fundamental focus on life.*

The Jewish nation is born into a world preoccupied with the mysterious reality of death. From the pyramids of Egypt to pagan burial rites, in culture after culture, much of religious ritual focuses on preparations for

---

4. Ibid., 16:30.
5. Rashi, Bamidbar 19:22 and elsewhere.
6. Bamidbar 19:13.
7. Talmud Bavli Smachot 10:1.
8. Rambam, *Mishneh Torah*, Hilchot Megilla V'Chanuka 1:1; Hilchot Nezirut 7:11–13; Hilchot Eivel 3:9–10.

man's journey into an unknown afterlife and on communion with those souls who have already departed on that journey.

In stark contrast, God's Revelation to the Israelites centers upon life in the "here and now." While Jewish tradition certainly maintains a steadfast belief in life after death and in the immortality of the human soul,[9] these concepts are nowhere to be found openly in the Torah. Attempts to contact the dead are expressly forbidden in the text.[10] An individual's mortal remains are to be treated with dignity, yet deification of the departed is clearly prohibited. Kohanim are specifically constrained from any contact with the dead except under specific circumstances,[11] and the Kohen Gadol is even more severely circumscribed.[12] Over and over again, the Torah exhorts the Jew to focus on the sanctification of his life in this world and to leave the mysteries of the unknown to God.[13]

Perhaps, then, the laws of *tuma* and *tahara* are designed at their most basic level to distance Jewish ritual worship from the arena of death. By temporarily excluding anyone who comes into contact with a dead body from the Sanctuary, the Torah conveys a clear message: *Unlike those around you, your traditions center on life, not death. Your priests are neither dark mystics nor sorcerers attempting to plumb the depths of a netherworld but divinely appointed guides on the path to more meaningful lives. The Sanctuary, its vessels and its service are designed to assist in the consecration of your earthly existence.*

Heaven awaits those among you who succeed in your spiritual quest. You will only succeed, however, if you are not preoccupied with heaven.

Emphasis upon life in this world continues to distinguish Judaism from other faith traditions to this day. The prominence placed upon the hereafter by the teachings of Christianity and Islam is largely absent from normative Jewish discourse. Like so much else of Jewish law, the laws of *tuma* and *tahara* remind the Jew to concentrate on the quality of his life in the "here and now," and to leave his ultimate reward in God's hands.

2. *The laws of* tuma *ritualize the challenge of responsiveness to an outside world.*

---

9. Ibid., Hilchot Tshuva 8:1–2.
10. Devarim 18:11.
11. Vayikra 21:1–4.
12. Ibid., 21:10–12.
13. Vayikra 18:5; Devarim 10:12; Devarim 30:11–16; and elsewhere.

Even the most powerful events and circumstances in our environment easily become rote if they are repeated often enough. Vicious crimes no longer startle us when we read of them on a daily basis in the newspaper. Wartime casualty counts are eventually ignored when they are publicly announced week after week. The litany of the world's ongoing woes – famine, disease, ethnic slaughter – becomes background noise, scarcely affecting us in any meaningful way.

Encounters with death are direct and constant in many walks of life. Physicians, nurses, hospital and nursing home workers, funeral directors, soldiers and others face a daily onslaught to their senses that can easily cause the profound to become pedestrian. Under this onslaught, life easily loses its majesty and death its mystery.

The Torah does not want us to become so callous that we fail to be affected by the events and circumstances that touch our lives. God, therefore, mandates the ritually limited state of *tuma* in response to contact with death. By doing so, He effectively states: *Your encounter with death may well have been unavoidable, even laudatory (as in the case of a* meit mitzva*; see above). You should not, however, emerge from that profound encounter unchanged. To ensure that this is so, I will limit your access to ritual observance for a period of time. Hopefully, this formalized state of limitation will heighten your psychic responsiveness to the world, as well.*

Like all religious rituals, the phenomenon of *tuma* is designed to convey an overarching life lesson. The quality of our lives is in large measure determined by the ways in which we respond to all events entering our sphere.

— **D** —————————————————————————

Clearly, neither of these approaches fully explains the myriad intricate laws that fall under the Torah's rubric of *tuma* and *tahara*. Each approach, however, suggests possible lessons that can be gleaned from the central core of these mysterious mandates.

Points to Ponder

Two disparate observations emerge from our study.

A. While the majority of edicts falling under the rubric of *tuma/tahara* do not apply in the absence of the Temple, one major area of law remains fully functional to this day: the mandates of *taharat hamishpacha*, family purity.

In brief overview, Jewish law dictates a monthly minimum twelve-day physical separation between husband and wife, correlating to the wife's menstrual period and seven days following. During these days, the woman is considered *temeia* and marital relations are prohibited. At the end of this period of separation, upon the woman's immersion in a mikva, full marital relations can be resumed.[14]

For centuries, *taharat hamishpacha* remained a major pillar of the ritual life of observant Jews.

With the advent of the modern era, however, this area of law fell upon hard times. "Sophisticated" American and European Jews rebelled against edicts that they found both archaic and intrusive. Misunderstanding and misinterpretation of the basic concepts abounded, spurred by the inability to translate the terms *tuma* and *tahara* in a way that avoided value judgments. Many women (understandably) rejected the notion that "impurity" or "uncleanness" could be caused by the natural rhythms of their lives, with the tragic consequence that they consequently turned their backs on the observances of their mothers and grandmothers.

Recent years have seen increased observance of the laws of *taharat hamishpacha* among young observant couples, in no small measure due to concentrated efforts on the part of religious leaders to reeducate the community concerning the importance and value of these laws. Numerous scholars, for example, have opined on potential ways in which adherence to the mandates of *taharat hamishpacha* can benefit a marriage, including injecting a monthly sense of renewal into the husband-wife relationship, ensuring that a couple learns to relate to each other on levels beyond the physical, cultivating a husband's sensitivity towards his wife during a vulnerable time of the month, sanctifying the physical bond between husband and wife, and more.

These suggestions, of course, should not be misconstrued. The demanding laws of *taharat hamishpacha* are far from a cure-all for marital discord. Perhaps the best way to sum up their potential effect on a marriage would be to say: *the laws of* taharat hamishpacha *will not make a bad marriage good, but they can make a good marriage better.*

---

14. Shulchan Aruch, Yoreh Deah, 183–200.

Nonetheless, while these observations may well assist in making the laws of *taharat hamishpacha* more palatable and attractive, the fundamental objections raised above still remain. Why should a woman automatically be considered *temeia* at certain times of the month through no fault of her own? Can these laws be explained in a way that does not offend modern sensibilities?

We arrive at one possible approach if we consider the following points based upon ideas raised in our study:

1. *Tuma* is not necessarily a negative state but, rather, a halachically *limited state* which is mandated in response to a powerful stimulus.

2. A woman who experiences her menstrual period is, thereby, neither "impure" nor "unclean." Instead, she enters the halachically limited state of *tuma*. In her case, this state is caused by a potent, recurring event that regularly touches her life with intimations of mortality.

3. Each month, during menstruation, a potential life passes through a woman's body. Rather than going unnoticed, this profound event should affect her life and her husband's, as well. The law therefore mandates, with no judgment attached, a period of limitation, of physical separation between husband and wife. Only after these days of separation have passed, and the woman's experience has been properly noted and acknowledged, can full marital relations be resumed.

4. Far from demeaning the woman's natural cycle, the laws of *taharat hamishpacha* thus underscore her miraculous nature as the potential bearer of life. Observance of these laws also sanctifies the physical union between husband and wife by reminding them of their unique role as partners with God in creation.

B. A telling Talmudic narrative reminds us that our approach to death can teach us a great deal about how we should approach life.

The Talmud recalls a time in Jewish history when the expense of burying the dead was a greater burden upon the survivors than the grief of the death itself. So onerous, in fact, did this cost become, that people began to abandon the bodies of their loved ones and flee.

Finally, the great sage, Rabban Gamliel, noted the serious problem and determined to treat his own fate in humble fashion. Prior to his death, he instructed his attendants that he be brought to the grave in simple linen shrouds. Upon perceiving Rabban Gamliel's actions, the entire nation followed suit and established the universal custom of burial in linen shrouds.[15]

Rabban Gamliel's courageous act, in reaction to gratuitous funeral expenses, enabled the community to regain perspective in the face of death. In contrast to other cultures who exalt the earthly remains of deceased individuals, Judaism requires that the body be treated with simple respect. Like a Torah scroll or other holy item that becomes invalid, the body is a sanctified object whose holy purpose (housing the human spirit) has now been lost. As such, it is neither to be actively destroyed nor unnaturally preserved but, instead, buried in a fashion that allows for a return to its elements. Expensive caskets, mausoleums, embalming of bodies and other attempts to hold on to the physical beings of our beloved departed are, from a Jewish perspective, wasted expenditures. Rabban Gamliel's actions, performed at a time when the Jewish community had lost its way concerning death, created a uniform burial process that lasts to this day. Rich or poor, scholars or laborers, upon death all are equal; all are buried in the same linen shrouds and placed in simple wooden coffins or directly in the earth.

While Rabban Gamliel's approach to death remains with us to this day, however, his lesson concerning life has unfortunately not yet been fully assimilated.

Today, the observant Jew does not spend exorbitantly in the face of death. He does, however, spend exorbitantly in the face of lifecycle events. In so many communities, bar mitzvas, bat mitzvas, weddings, etc., have been transformed into lavish celebrations entailing enormous unnecessary waste, as families seize these opportunities to demonstrate the extent of their material wealth and financial success. Some, unable to afford the cost of these events, place themselves in debt in a desperate attempt to "keep up with the Cohens." *How can I deny my child what all other children have?* becomes the litany often heard by rabbis attempting to counsel a saner approach. Increasingly, the religious significance of these rites of passage is lost in the wanton extravagance. The situation resembles the Talmudic description of funeral costs in the days of Rabban Gamliel, when the cost of burial was more burdensome to the survivors than the death of their loved one.

---

15. Talmud Bavli Moed Katan 27b; Ketubot 8b.

As many observers have noted, it is well past time to regain our perspective concerning not only the cost, but the very meaning, of these events. *Humility and modesty in the face of death should teach us humility and modesty in the face of life, as well.*

2 *Simcha* or Sin?

Context

Parshat Tazria opens with one of the strangest examples of biblical ritual "impurity": *tumat yoledet*, *tuma* resulting from childbirth.

The Torah relates that, following the birth of a male child, a child-bearing mother enters a seven-day period of *tuma*, while following the birth of a female child, a fourteen-day period of *tuma* is mandated. In each case, these days of *tuma* are then followed by much lengthier periods (thirty-three days after the birth of a male child and sixty-six days after the birth of a female child) of modified separation from sanctified objects.

Finally, at the close of each extended period, the mother brings a burnt offering and a sin offering to the Temple to mark her full re-entry into society.[1]

Questions

Bearing a child is clearly one of the most highly sanctified acts possible; the first divine blessing/commandment given to man while still in the Garden of Eden;[2] the clearest demonstration of man's partnership with God. Why, then, does a woman automatically incur a state of *tuma* as a result of childbirth?

What is the significance of the different separation periods mandated in response to the birth of a male and female child, respectively? Aren't all children of equal value?

Finally, and most problematically, what is the significance of the *korbanot* brought by a *yoledet*, a childbearing mother? In particular, why does the Torah instruct a woman to bring a sin offering in the aftermath of

---

1. Vayikra 12:1–8.
2. Bereishit 1:28.

childbirth? What possible "sin" could be associated with the glorious act of bringing a new life into the world?

Approaches

——**A**————————————————————————————————

The most basic, and in some ways the most problematic, approach to the perplexing issues surrounding the *tumat yoledet* is offered by a group of scholars including Rabbeinu Bachya and the Kli Yakar. These commentaries view both the *tuma* resulting from childbirth and the sin offering in its aftermath as a reflection of the primal sin of Chava, the first woman.[3] In response to Chava's role in the consumption of the forbidden fruit of the Tree of Knowledge of Good and Evil, God condemns her and her female progeny to the travails of childbirth.[4]

While giving birth to a child is, therefore, a glorious mitzva, the pain and difficulty associated with the process is the product of sin.

This approach, however, gives rise to serious issues concerning the nature of divine reward and punishment. As we have noted before, Judaism clearly rejects the Christian notion of "original sin" (see *Bereishit*: Lech Lecha 4, *Approaches* A). We are not guilty, in perpetuity, of the sin committed by Adam and Chava. On this issue the Torah is clear: "Fathers shall not die because of their children, nor shall children die because of their fathers. Each individual will die in his own sin."[5] We are each held culpable only for our own failings and not for the failings of others, past, present or future.[6] How, then, can these scholars suggest that each childbearing woman across history must somehow atone for a crime committed by her ancestor, at the beginning of time?

The key to understanding this approach may well lie in a distinction that we have noted previously (see ibid.). While Judaism absolutely rejects the Christian concept of "original sin," we cannot deny the reality of "intergenerational reverberation."

---

3. Rabbeinu Bachya, Vayikra 12:7; Kli Yakar, Vayikra 12:8.
4. Bereishit 3:16.
5. Devarim 24:16.
6. See *Bereishit*: Lech Lecha 4, *Approaches* A for discussion concerning reconciliation of this concept with a seemingly contradictory biblical text.

We are not responsible, in any way, for the transgression committed by Adam and Chava at the beginning of time. We are, however, affected by that sin's ramifications. This is not a punishment, but a reality of life. Had Adam and Chava not sinned, we would now be living a very different existence in the Garden of Eden.

Similarly, we are all concretely connected to each other across the generations. Such overarching life issues as where we are born, to whom, into what environment – and, in fact, whether or not we are born at all – are determined not only by God, but also by our parents and by those who came before them as well. Even more importantly, our decisions and actions today will critically affect the lives of our children and their progeny tomorrow.

At the decisive moment of childbirth, therefore, the Torah graphically reminds the new parents, through a series of rituals, of the phenomenon of "intergenerational reverberation." The mother's state of *tuma*, her consequent period of physical separation from her husband, the offerings she brings in the aftermath of these events, all result from actions committed by her primal ancestor, millennia earlier. The Torah's message could not be clearer: *We are each partially a product of what came before. How careful, then, must new parents be with their own continuing decisions and actions – for those very decisions and actions will help shape the lives of generations to come.*

—— **B** ————————————————————————————

An entirely different approach is suggested by Rabbi Shimshon Raphael Hirsch. This scholar notes that the Torah sets the stage for the passage describing *tumat yoledet* with the unusual phrase *isha ki tazria*, "when a woman yields seed…"[7]

By choosing the verb *lizroa*, "to yield seed," in describing human conception – as opposed to the usual biblical term, *lit'hor*, "to conceive" – the Torah stresses the universal, physical character of childbirth. This verb is used on only one other occasion in the text: in conjunction with the creation of the earth's vegetation, which is described as *mazria zera l'mineihu*, "yielding seed to its kind."[8]

---

7. Vayikra 12:2.
8. Bereishit 1:11–12.

"The highest and noblest occupation," says Hirsch, "on which the whole future of the human race is built…is of purely physical nature. Man originates, grows and exists like a plant…"[9] At the moment of childbirth, the childbearing mother, involved in "the most sublime procedure of her earthly calling,"[10] is forced to painfully submit to the laws of nature. As her child enters the world, she becomes one with all the other creatures of creation, governed by processes beyond her control.

Tellingly, the Torah specifically chooses this moment, the moment when a new soul's arrival into the world is bounded by natural law, to underscore man's unique ability to transcend that law. After childbirth, the childbearing mother confronts an immediate challenge. By deciding to follow Torah law, she embarks upon a conscious journey from *tuma* to *tahara*. Step-by-step, she is guided past the physical constraints of natural law towards a renewed awareness of her own spiritual potential. Her freely chosen journey towards complete religious involvement reminds all that man, once born, is a morally free agent.[11]

—— **C** ——

An additional perspective on *tumat yoledet* can be suggested, based upon our prior observations concerning the general theme of *tuma* (see Tazria-Metzora 1).

The state of *tuma* often seems to occur in response to an individual's encounter with a profound event or experience. God does not want us to pass through life unaffected by what crosses our path. By mandating a ritually limited state following such encounters, the Torah creates a forced response. The period of *tuma* teaches us that something has changed, that we must be responsive to all experiences that touch our lives.

Few events are as potentially life altering as childbirth. The Torah therefore establishes a period of *tuma* to encourage the mother to assimilate the many complex truths with which she has come face-to-face: from the reality of her own mortality to her sublime partnership with God in creation, and finally to the responsibilities she now bears towards her newborn child.

---

9. Rabbi Shimshon Raphael Hirsch, Vayikra 12:2.
10. Ibid.
11. Ibid.

The childbearing mother's world has changed forever. The Torah insists that she recognize that fact.

— **D** ———————————————————————————————

Widely disparate views are suggested by the commentaries in their attempts to explain the varying lengths of the *tuma* cycles mandated after the birth of male and female infants, respectively. At one end of the spectrum are those who suggest biological bases for these variations. The disparity, they say, is rooted either in the dissimilar time periods required for the formation of male and female fetuses in utero[12] or in the different number of days needed for the mother's body to recuperate after their birth.[13]

At the opposite end of the spectrum are those scholars who suggest that the *tuma* variations are philosophically based. Rabbi Shimshon Raphael Hirsch, for example, believes that the extended period of *tuma* after the birth of a girl reflects the greater responsibility the mother will shoulder in training that child towards the responsibilities of womanhood: "at the birth of each fresh daughter, [the mother] has *doubly to arm herself*, for the child and for herself, to tread the lofty path of purity and morality up to the heights preached by the Sanctuary of God."[14]

Noting that the commandment of circumcision is abruptly inserted in the midst of the passage concerning *tumat yoledet*, Rabbi David Zvi Hoffman connects that commandment to the conclusion of the mother's *tuma* period. The *tuma* cycles for all childbearing mothers should, by all rights, be equivalent, whether they bear a male or female infant. The length of the period for a mother who gives birth to a boy, however, is shortened by the advent of the child's circumcision – either to allow the mother to be *tehora* to her husband during that joyous occasion or because, somehow, the child's circumcision actually serves to counteract the mother's *tuma*.[15]

---

12. Chizkuni, Vayikra 12:4; Ibn Ezra, Vayikra 12:4; Ramban, Vayikra 12:4, based on position of Rabbi Yishmael quoted in Talmud Bavli Nidda 30b.
13. Ramban, Vayikra 12:4; Sforno, Vayikra 12:2–5.
14. Rabbi Shimshon Raphael Hirsch, Vayikra 12:4–5.
15. Rabbi David Tzvi Hoffman, Vayikra 12:3. Note: Today's observance, as defined by rabbinic law, mandates a separation period well beyond the biblically mandated period of *tuma*, so that a woman is never *tehora* to her husband within the biblically specified timeframe; today there is therefore no practical difference between the observed period of *tuma* following the birth of either gender, and the difference is purely symbolic.

This fundamental connection between the newborn's circumcision and the ending of his mother's seven-day *tuma* period is enigmatically foreshadowed by the Targum Yonatan, who states: "On the eighth day she [the mother] becomes permitted [to her husband] and on that day [the child's] foreskin is severed."[16]

E

The final mystery surrounding the *yoledet* centers on the two *korbanot* that she offers at the end of her extended period of limitation: The *Korban Olah*, the burnt offering, and the *Korban Chatat*, the sin offering. What, ask the scholars, is the significance of these *korbanot*, particularly the sin offering? Once again we find ourselves wondering: what transgression could possibly be associated with the glorious event of childbirth?

We have already reviewed one answer to this question: the sin offering of each childbearing mother relates to the transgression of her primal ancestor, Chava, in the Garden of Eden (see above, *Approaches* A).

Recognizing, however, the problems inherent in this approach (see *Approaches* A), numerous commentaries seek alternative explanations for the *korbanot* of the *yoledet*. The Abravanel, for example, maintains that the burnt offering serves to reconnect the childbearing mother to the God Who has redeemed her from the travails of childbirth. Ironically, however, those very travails, in and of themselves, indicate the need for a sin offering. The Talmud maintains that "That there is no suffering [in this world] without sin."[17] The child's mother, therefore, offers a *Korban Chatat* for any sin that she may have unknowingly committed and which might have been reflected in the pain of the birthing process.[18]

Going a step further, a Talmudic dialogue actually identifies a specific sin on the part of the childbearing mother which is targeted by the sin offering:

> The students of Rabbi Shimon Bar Yochai asked their teacher: "Why does the Torah command the childbearing mother to bring a *korban*?"
>
> He responded: "Because when she bends down to give birth, she swears [as a result of her pain] that she will no longer be available to

---

16. Targum Yonatan, Vayikra 12:3.
17. Talmud Bavli Shabbat 55a.
18. Abravanel, Vayikra 12:1–8.

her husband. The Torah, therefore, mandates her to bring a *korban* [to atone for a vow that she will not keep]."[19]

While perhaps a bit tongue-in-cheek, Rabbi Shimon Bar Yochai's response underscores an important point concerning the power of speech. By all rights, we could argue that anything a woman says under the duress of childbirth should be ignored or excused. Words, however, once uttered, must be reckoned with. Too often, we claim the privilege of being "contextually understood"; anything we say out of anger or under pressure, we feel, should not be taken seriously. *I did not really mean what I said*, we argue, *and everyone should know that.*

Fully intended or not, however, words strike their targets with a power all their own. The object of our anger often feels: *I know he was angry, but he wouldn't have said it if it didn't carry some truth, if he didn't really mean it on some level.*

Let the mother bring her *korban*, therefore, says Rabbi Shimon Bar Yochai, to atone for her words, even those words that arguably could have been "excused."

Points to Ponder

Many years ago, an alternative, somewhat out-of-the-box approach to the *korbanot* of the *yoledet* occurred to me. I offer this interpretation for your consideration, as an original "Midrash" (suggested by a lover of *pshat*).

The Talmud notes a surprising fact. With one exception, whenever a *Korban Olah*, a burnt offering, and a *Korban Chatat*, a sin offering, are simultaneously commanded in the Torah text, the Chatat always precedes the Olah. This would seem logical. After all, a petitioner must address the past before turning to the future. An Olah, symbolic of a renewed relationship with God, should only be offered after the slate of past misdeeds is first cleared through the offering of a Chatat.

The one exception to the usual sequence is here, when the Torah lists the *korbanot* of a *yoledet*. In this case, the Olah is listed first. This sequential shift would seem to indicate that, in this instance alone, the burnt offering precedes the sin offering.

To make matters even more complicated, however, the Talmud goes on

---

19. Talmud Bavli Nidda 31b.

to explain that the reverse listing of the *korbanot* in the case of the *yoledet* is only that: a reverse listing. In actuality, the *korbanot* were brought in their usual order (the Chatat before the Olah), even in the case of the *yoledet*.[20]

Why does the Torah reverse the order of the *Korban Olah* and the *Korban Chatat* only in the case of the childbearing mother, especially if this reversal exists only in the text and not in practice?

Perhaps, the Torah symbolically changes the sequence of the *korbanot* on this one occasion because this is the only case where a sin offering is brought not for a sin that occurred in the past but for one that is bound to occur in the future.

The moment of childbirth is a moment of rarefied personal perspective. Although it was over thirty years ago, I clearly remember the first time I held my oldest child in my arms, as if it happened yesterday. In spite of the many who had told me of the power of that moment, I was still completely unprepared.

In that instant, you recognize with unerring clarity that nothing in the world is more important to you than this child, than this precious gift that God has bestowed upon you.

But then…

Three months later, at two o'clock in the morning, when, more tired than you have ever been in your life, you are changing the diaper of a screaming infant; when, three years later, you are again running in circles after a recalcitrant toddler; when, fifteen years later, your teenage son or daughter rolls his or her eyes at you in that frustrating way, as only a teenager can…

At those moments, somehow, that child doesn't seem quite so precious. You lose sight of the clear instant when you held a new life in your hands, when nothing was more important than the life and welfare of that newborn child.

The Korban Chatat *of the yoledet is listed second because it addresses the future rather than the past.* This particular sin offering is brought for all the inevitable moments when the crystal perspective accompanying childbirth will be lost, for all the times when this precious life will not be appreciated as dearly as it was at the moment of its arrival.

And maybe, in this one instance, the *Korban Chatat* will perform its

---

20. Talmud Bavli Zevachim 90a.

task proactively. Perhaps the offering will serve as a reminder to work a little harder on the retention of perspective, so that we do not lose sight of the most precious gifts granted to us by a loving God.

3 Disease or Divine Reckoning?

Context

The bulk of the parshiot of Tazria and Metzora deal with a description of the dramatic effects of *tzara'at*, often defined (for want of a better term) as biblical leprosy.

The Torah delineates in fine detail the specifics of this mysterious affliction – which affects individuals, clothes and dwellings – and the steps to be taken under the guidance of the Kohanim towards its diagnosis and treatment.[1]

Questions

What exactly is *tzara'at*, biblical leprosy? Is this affliction a natural, physical illness or a supernatural phenomenon?

Given the myriad diseases that affect humankind, why does the Torah devote so much text to a description of this specific malady, its diagnosis and treatment?

Approaches

The mystery of *tzara'at* gives rise to a wide-ranging series of observations among the commentaries.

—— **A** ——

At one end of the spectrum lie those scholars who view *tzara'at* as a contagious physical illness with dangerous potential for spread to the entire population.

The Abravanel, for example, explains the Torah's concern for "afflicted" clothing in distinctly natural terms. Unlike strong materials such as metal, clothing will readily absorb bodily decay upon close personal contact. The

---

1. Vayikra 13–14.

Torah is, therefore, concerned that *tzara'at* will spread from a *metzora* (an individual afflicted with *tzara'at*) to his garments. To prevent further contagion, therefore, all suspicious stains and growths on clothing must be examined by a Kohen.[2]

For his part, the Ralbag interprets the puzzling phenomena of clothing and dwelling afflictions according to scientific theory of his day. Foreign moisture or heat entering an item, he claims, causes an imbalance in that item's natural stasis and leads to the item's disintegration. This destructive process is evidenced at an early stage through the appearance of red or green growth (colors associated in the text with *tzara'at*).[3]

Although the Meshech Chochma initially categorizes the theme of *tzara'at* as one of the "secrets of the Torah," he then avers: "Nonetheless, one can say that these afflictions are contagious diseases." The treatment of the illness itself, this scholar maintains, is ample evidence of its communicable nature. The *metzora* experiences enforced isolation and is required to actively alert others to his condition. Any physical interaction with infected individuals is extremely dangerous. The Torah, therefore, assigns the task of such interaction (the diagnosis and treatment of the ill) to the sons of Aharon who, in their role as Kohanim, are separate from the rest of the people and are granted extraordinary divine protection.[4]

Finally, Rabbeinu Bachya discerns concern for communicable disease in the Torah's mandate that the *metzora*, at the end of his period of isolation, let loose a bird offering "on the face of the field." The release of the bird into a place absent of human habitation, he maintains, represents an implicit prayer that the *metzora*'s erstwhile contagion should not spread to others.[5]

— **B** —

At the opposite end of the spectrum are those commentaries who eschew any natural explanation for the *tzara'at* afflictions discussed in the parshiot of Tazria and Metzora.

---

2. Abravanel, Vayikra 13:47–59.
3. Ralbag, Vayikra 13:47–59.
4. Meshech Chochma, Vayikra 13:2.
5. Rabbeinu Bachya, Vayikra 15:53.

These scholars point to a number of details of *tzaraat* outlined in the Written and Oral Law that are clearly inconsistent with the characteristics of communicable diseases, including:

1. The Kohen diagnoses *tzaraat* based only on examination of those parts of the body which he can readily see. No careful examination is required in the folds of the body.[6]

2. When *tzaraat* is suspected in a dwelling, the Torah orders the Kohen to remove everything from the house before conducting his examination.[7] If *tzaraat* is a communicable disease, such a procedure would expose the public to potentially infected material.

3. Examinations of potential *tzaraat* are not performed by the Kohanim on Shabbat, holidays, or upon a bridegroom during the seven days of celebration following his wedding.[8]

4. The laws of *tzaraat* only apply to dwellings in the Land of Israel and only after the land has been divided into individual holdings. These laws do not apply to homes owned by non-Jews or to dwellings of any ownership in the city of Yerushalayim.[9]

5. The laws of *tzaraat* do not apply to non-Jews. A lesion contracted by a convert before his conversion to Judaism is of no consequence.[10]

6. Under certain circumstances, if lesions cover an individual's entire body he is not considered contaminated.[11]

7. After the nation's entry into the land, a *metzora* is only to be excluded from walled cities (as determined by the city's status at the time of the conquest of the land). He is to be allowed to remain in unwalled cities and to roam freely through the rest of the countryside.[12]

---

6. Vayikra 12:12.
7. Ibid., 14:36.
8. Talmud Bavli, Moed Katan 7b; Mishna Negaim 1:4, based upon Vayikra 13:14.
9. Talmud Bavli, Yoma 12a.
10. Torat Kohanim 13:1–2; Midrash Hagadol Vayikra 13:2.
11. Vayikra 13:12–13. Note: So counterintuitive is this specific phenomenon that some commentaries compare it to the law of the Red Heifer, considered the ultimate mystery of the Torah. Other scholars, however, explain that the spread of such lesions indicates that the affliction is in its final stages and is no longer communicable to others (see Ibn Ezra, Vayikra 13:13).
12. Mishna Keilim 1:7.

According to Rabbi Shimshon Raphael Hirsch, these and other details "show the absolute folly" of any attempt to interpret Torah laws as rules and regulations created for health or sanitary purposes.[13]

— C —

If the afflictions described in the parshiot of Tazria and Metzora, however, are not natural diseases, what exactly are they? What message is God sending the people through the visitation of these frightening supernatural phenomena? What crimes perpetrated by individuals within the nation could possibly trigger such severe divine reckoning?

— D —

The Talmud lists, in the name of Rabbi Yonatan, seven sins that cause the affliction of *tzara'at*: evil or damaging speech, murder, perjury, sexual immorality, arrogance, robbery and miserliness. [14]

In similar (albeit more poetic) fashion the Midrash cites six phenomena, drawn from the book of Mishlei,[15] that trigger the illness: haughty eyes, a lying tongue, hands that spill innocent blood, a heart that ponders thoughts of violence, feet always ready to run for evil purpose, false testimony (that results in the spreading of lies) and the sowing of discord between brothers.[16]

Of these associations between crime and punishment, however, only one seems to capture the rabbinic imagination completely. Over and over again, the rabbis link the punishment of *tzara'at* to the related crimes of *motzi shem ra*, slander (literally, the bringing out of a "bad name"), and *lashon hara*, evil or damaging speech.[17] Within a halachic context, *motzi shem ra* refers to true slander, e.g., the spreading of false information about another individual, while *lashon hara* refers to the vocalization of any damaging information, even if true. Both of these actions are considered grave transgressions within Jewish law.

The rabbis find support for the link between these sins of speech and the affliction of *tzara'at* in a series of clues, including:

---

13. Rabbi Shimshon Raphael Hirsch, Vayikra 13:59.
14. Talmud Bavli Arachin 16a.
15. Mishlei 6:16–19.
16. Midrash Rabba Vayikra 16:1.
17. Talmud Bavli Arachin 15b.

1. The term *metzora* itself can be broken down and linguistically connected to the expression *motzi shem ra* (slander).[18]

2. Moshe is temporarily struck with *tzara'at* at the burning bush when he casts aspersions on the Israelites by doubting their willingness to respond to God's call for the Exodus.[19]

3. Miriam is punished with *tzara'at* when she maligns her brother, Moshe.[20]

4. The practical response to *tzara'at* (seclusion from the community) results in a punishment that fits the crime. The *metzora* must distance himself through isolation from society because his words created distance between husband and wife, between a man and his friend.[21]

5. The bird offerings brought by the *metzora* at the end of his period of seclusion mirror the nature of his sin. He injured others through the "chatter" of slander and gossip. His purification is, therefore, effectuated through the means of "chirping, twittering" birds.[22]

— **E** —

A much deeper philosophical current, however, courses through the rabbinic assertion of a connection between sins of speech and the affliction of *tzara'at*. To the minds of the rabbis, few crimes are as damaging to both victim and perpetrator as the crimes of slander and damaging speech.

The foundation for this viewpoint is laid early on in a seemingly strange interpretation offered by the classical translator of biblical text, Onkelos. Commenting on the seminal phrase concerning the man's creation, "And He breathed into his [man's] nostrils the breath of life, and man became a *living being*,"[23] Onkelos translates, "…and man became a *speaking spirit*."[24]

Why does Onkelos cast the Torah's overarching statement of man's creation in such a seemingly narrow light? Why single out the power of speech as the one faculty that distinguishes the human being at the moment

---

18. Talmud Bavli, ibid.; Rabbeinu Bachya, introduction to Parshat Metzora; Da'at Zekeinim Miba'alei Hatosafot, Rabbeinu Bachya and numerous other commentaries on Vayikra 14:1.
19. Shmot 4:6; Rashi, ibid.
20. Bamidbar 12:9.
21. Talmud Bavli Arachin 16b.
22. Ibid.
23. Bereishit 2:7.
24. Targum Onkelos, Bereishit 2:7.

of his conception? Aren't man's true distinctions his soul, his intellect and his power of reasoned thought?

A brilliant insight into the approach of Onkelos is offered by Rabbi Yitzchak Arama in an extensive discussion on Parshat Metzora. While man's intellect does set him apart from the beast, this scholar notes, his intellect is only fully revealed and actualized through verbal communication. *Speech is the God-given tool through which an individual's heart and mind are reflected to an outside world.*

The fundamental connection between verbal communication and man's inner being is underscored by King Shlomo in the book of Mishlei: "The plans of the heart belong to man, but the answer of the tongue comes from the Lord."[25]

Because speech is so reflective of man's unique character, the obligations associated with verbal communication carry great significance. An individual who misuses his power of speech degrades himself through the very skill meant to mirror his greatness. So foundational is this transgression, that the perpetrator can no longer lay claim to the majestic title of "a speaking spirit." Improper speech, says Arama, can be compared to "using royal garments to clean the trash heap."[26]

From this perspective, the sins of *motzi shem ra* and *lashon hara* acquire another, devastating layer of significance. Much of the literature concerning these transgressions focuses upon the obvious victim, the target of the verbal attack. This focus is certainly understandable. The damage potentially caused to others by an individual's unthinking and deliberately cruel speech cannot be overstated (see Kedoshim 4b).

Arama, however, together with other scholars, directs our attention towards another victim of these grievous transgressions: *the perpetrator himself.*

Created in God's image – granted reason, intellect and the ability to actualize that intellect positively in the surrounding world – the perpetrator diminishes his own stature and demeans his human essence. Far from the "speaking spirit" that God created him to be, he reveals himself as a meanspirited creature, oblivious to – or even relishing – the pain his words cause to others.

---

25. Mishlei 16:1.
26. Akeidat Yitzchak Vayikra, sha'ar 62.

God, therefore, specifically punishes sins committed through speech with the plague of *tzara'at*, an affliction that mirrors what the perpetrator has done to himself. Through his grave actions, the *metzora* has fallen from his place at the pinnacle of God's creation. No longer a "living being," no longer a "speaking spirit," he suffers from an illness so severe that the rabbis claim, "A *metzora* is considered dead." [27]

Ostracized from society, he must experience an isolating period of spiritual repair before he can begin, through true repentance, to reclaim his greatness.

Our tradition hopes that, perhaps then, chastened and humbled, the *metzora* will realize the truth of the psalmist's assertion: "Who is the man who desires life? Guard your tongue from [speaking] evil and your lips from uttering falsehood."[28]

Points to Ponder

The possible connection between sins of speech and the plague of *tzara'at* raises serious issues concerning the application of divine justice to our lives. Are we to view the misfortunes that confront us, from illness to accident, as heaven-sent retribution for our sins? Does God punish us today, as He did in biblical times, through the direct visitation of calamity?

The answer that emerges from sources in our tradition seems complex, if not contradictory.

On the one hand, the Torah repeatedly speaks of the calamities destined to befall the Jewish nation as a result of their transgressions. The second paragraph of the Shma Yisrael, recited twice daily by observant Jews, for example, clearly states that the granting of natural bounty in the Land of Israel is contingent upon the actions of the Jewish nation.[29] So direct is the connection between pain and wrongdoing in this world that the rabbis declare: "There is no suffering without sin"[30] (see Tazria-Metzora 2, *Approaches* E).

On the other hand, the relationship between affliction and sin in our experience is deeply elusive. The issue of theodicy, divine justice, lies at

---

27. Midrash Rabba Shmot 1:34.
28. Tehillim 34:13–14.
29. Devarim 11:13–21.
30. Talmud Bavli Shabbat 55a.

the core of all Jewish questioning, from the time of Avraham to our day.[31] Even Moshe, whose communion with God was more direct than that of any other individual in human history, is denied insight into the mystery of theodicy[32] (see *Shmot*: Ki Tissa 5, *Approaches* E).

Anyone who has witnessed the suffering of an innocent child can eloquently testify to our inability to decipher God's ways.

What, then, should our approach be when calamity strikes? Are we meant to view the misfortunes that confront us during our lifetimes as punishment for our sins or as seemingly arbitrary phenomena beyond our ken?

While a full analysis of the overarching philosophical issues emerging from this question are well beyond the scope of our discussion, a lesson emerging from the dawn of our history can be particularly instructive. (See *Bereishit*: Vayeira 3, *Approaches* E, F, and *Points to Ponder* for a fuller discussion.)

Avraham responds to two critical challenges in strikingly different ways.

Confronted with the divinely ordained destruction of the evil cities of Sodom and Amora, the patriarch openly bargains with God in their defense.[33] Challenged, on the other hand, with the *Akeida* (the God-commanded sacrifice of his son Yitzchak) Avraham emerges from the text as silent and totally compliant.[34]

Where is the patriarch's sense of justice in the face of his innocent son's looming death? How can the man who argued so eloquently on behalf of Sodom and Amora remain silent when confronted with the *Akeida* and the apparent destruction of his own prophetic dreams of nationhood?

The key to Avraham's behavior may well lie in the vast difference between the two events that confront him.

The fate of the cities of Sodom and Amora is firmly rooted in the realm of *din*, justice. God informs Avraham: *The inhabitants of the cities of Sodom and Amora are evil; therefore, they deserve to perish.* When God relates to man in the sphere of *din* everything makes sense; there is a clear cause and

---

31. Bereishit 18:22–33.
32. Talmud Bavli Brachot 7a.
33. Bereishit 18:22–33.
34. Ibid., 22:1–3.

effect. Within this realm, we are invited to argue and struggle with our Creator. Avraham can thus rise and confront God in defense of the cities.

The *Akeida*, on the other hand, takes place in the realm of *nissayon*, trial. When God brings us into the sphere of *nissayon*, arguments and struggle are futile. In this arena, there is no clear cause and effect. In contrast to God's decree concerning Sodom and Amora, no clear reason is given for the *Akeida*. God is hidden from view and there is no readily perceived logic to His actions.

Man's challenge within the realm of *nissayon* is solely to pass the trial, to respond to God's will with dignity and constancy of faith. That is why Avraham is silent in the face of the *Akeida*. He realizes that he has entered the world of *nissayon*, and that his challenges have changed.

Through prophetic vision, Avraham was able to distinguish between the two realms of *din* and *nissayon* and react to each appropriately. We, however, are unable to make this distinction. We have no way of knowing, nor are we meant to know, whether a particular life challenge is a punishment, a trial, or a combination thereof. We therefore react on both levels at once. In times of crisis, we struggle, pray, plead and argue for justice. We allow difficult experience to catalyze our personal repentance and charge our spiritual growth. And, then, when all the prayers are exhausted, when our soul-searching has ended, we turn to God and accept His unfathomable will.

Acharei Mot אחרי מות

פרק ט״ז:א׳-י״ח:ל

Parsha Summary

A sanctified day, sanctified rituals, a sacred people…

God commands Moshe to instruct Aharon concerning the service to take place in the Sanctuary on the sanctified day of Yom Kippur.

Central to the Yom Kippur Temple service, among other ritual offerings, is the mysterious rite of the se'ir hamishtaleiach, *"the sent goat."* Within this ceremony, the High Priest selects two similar he-goats, upon which lots are drawn: one lot inscribed *"for the Lord"* and one lot inscribed *"for Azazel."* The he-goat designated *"for the Lord"* is slaughtered as a sin offering. Later in the service, Aharon recites a communal confession over the second he-goat and this animal, *"bearing the iniquities"* of the Israelites, is sent to *"Azazel, in the wilderness."*

The discussion of the Yom Kippur ritual is highlighted by the description of the sacred day as a time of atonement for the people of Israel across the ages.

The parsha then turns to a series of general admonitions, including:

1. The requirement that sanctified offerings be limited to the area of the Sanctuary

2. The prohibition concerning consumption of blood

3. The requirement to cover the blood of a slaughtered animal

4. The prohibition concerning the consumption of animals that are not properly slaughtered

5. Detailed laws prohibiting immorality and listing the arayot, forbidden sexual relationships

1 The Sent Goat

Context

God commands Moshe to instruct his brother, Aharon, concerning the Sanctuary service to take place on Yom Kippur, the holiest day of the Jewish calendar year.

At the center of this Yom Kippur service lies the mysterious ritual of the *se'ir hamishtaleiach*, "the sent goat":

> And from among the children of Israel he [Aharon] shall take two he-goats as a sin offering…and stand them before the Lord, at the entrance of the Tent of Meeting.
>
> Aharon shall place lots upon the two he-goats: one lot for the Lord and one lot for Azazel.
>
> And Aharon shall bring near the he-goat upon which the lot for the Lord has been drawn and shall make it a sin offering. And the he-goat, upon which the lot for Azazel has been drawn, shall be stood alive before the Lord, to affect atonement upon it, to send it to Azazel, in the wilderness.[1]

Further in the parsha, the text continues:

> And Aharon will place his two hands upon the living he-goat and shall confess upon it all of the iniquities of the children of Israel and all of their rebellious sins in all of their sins, and he shall place them upon the head of the he-goat and he shall send it at the hand of a designated man to the wilderness.
>
> And the he-goat shall bear upon it all of their iniquities to a desert land, and he shall send the he-goat into the wilderness.[2]

---

1. Vayikra 16:5–10.
2. Ibid., 16:21–22.

Questions

How are we to understand this strange, even troubling ritual of the "sent goat" which serves as the centerpiece of the service on the holiest day of the year, at the holiest spot on earth, under the direction of the Kohen Gadol, acting as the representative of the entire nation?

The questions are manifold.

What is the significance of the simultaneous selection of two goats? This question becomes even more intriguing in light of the Mishnaic dictate that the goats chosen should be as similar as possible in stature and appearance.

Why are lots drawn to determine the fate of each goat? Why not simply designate, without resorting to a ceremony of chance?

What is the implication of the confession uttered by the Kohen Gadol over the "sent goat" on behalf of the entire nation? What role does this confession play in the atonement of Yom Kippur? Isn't atonement a private, personal process best experienced individually rather than communally? [Note: These questions will be dealt with in the following study.]

Above all, the very concept of the *se'ir hamishtaleiach* itself raises a series of troubling concerns.

Are the sins of the people truly transferred to the "head of the goat," as the text seems to indicate? Does the animal really become a ritual "scapegoat" for our sins? Such an idea seems completely antithetical to Jewish law and its prohibition of all superstitious practice.[3] Over and over again, the Torah speaks of the doctrine of personal responsibility. We are each responsible for our actions, good or bad. Atonement for sins can only be effected through a wrenching process of *tshuva*, return, which entails *recognition* of past transgressions, *remorse* over those transgressions and a *commitment* to future change. To suggest now that the *tshuva* process can somehow be short-circuited through a magical act of transference of sins seems to fly in the face of all that we believe.

Furthermore, where is this goat being "sent"? What is the definition of the term *Azazel*? Why does the Torah mandate that a portion of this ritual be performed off of the Temple Mount? To whom or to what is this animal being offered? It seems totally inconceivable that Jewish tradition, founded

---

3.   Vayikra 19:26.

on the absolute principle of a single unified God, could suddenly embrace a ritual including an off-site offering to another unknown force.

Approaches

The Talmud identifies the *se'ir hamishtaleiach* as a classical legal mystery, one of five halachic phenomena that earn Satan's scorn due to their illogical nature. From this perspective, the sent goat ritual is a clear example of a *chok*, a law for which no reason is given in the Torah (see *Shmot*: Teruma 3, *Approaches* A).

Once we enter the realm of *chukim*, this Talmudic source concludes, any attempt at real understanding is pointless. We are challenged, instead, to observe the law even when (or, perhaps, particularly when) the law's purpose remains elusive: "I, the Lord have established [these laws] and you have no right to question them."[4]

Other rabbinic sources, however; while accepting the sent goat ritual's classification as a *chok*, nonetheless find value in the struggle to understand (see Shmot: Teruma 3, *Approaches* B–F).

A review of their search for answers will take us on a journey to the extremes of rabbinic opinion, from the mystical to the rational. Some of the suggestions offered will seem radical. One classical opinion will venture, in fact, so dangerously close to the edge of acceptability that its proponent will record it only in code, lest it be misinterpreted by those unready to read it.

The potential lessons that can be gleaned, however, from the struggle to understand this central Yom Kippur rite make the journey more than worthwhile.

First, however, a historical note, underscoring the depth of the problems.

Later events may well reflect the dangers of misinterpretation associated with the "sent goat" ritual. The Mishna records that, centuries after the inception of the ritual, Babylonian Jews attending the Temple service (the Talmud corrects this to "the Alexandrian Jews") began to pull at the hair of the individual accompanying the "sent goat" and shout: "Take [our sins] and leave! Take [our sins] and leave!"

---

4. Talmud Bavli Yoma 67b.

Uncomfortable with the desecration of the Temple service resulting from the people's literal interpretation of the sent goat ritual, the rabbis mandated the construction of an elevated pathway leading from the Temple grounds to the outskirts of Jerusalem. The goat was then led on this pathway, out of the reach of onlookers.[5]

These developments only serve to strengthen our previously raised questions. What explanations can be offered for a ritual which, at face value, seems to contradict so many basic principles of Jewish belief?

— A

Our analysis best begins, perhaps, with an attempt to define the term *Azazel*. Who, or what, does this word – describing the ultimate destination of the "sent goat" – signify?

The broadest consensus among the authorities develops around the definition of Azazel as a geographic location. Numerous scholars, including Rashi, adopt the Tannaitic position that the word *Azazel* (built on the root word *az*, strong or bold) connotes a wilderness site of exceptional strength and harshness.[6] The goat, they maintain, was led to a desolate mountain in the wilderness where it met its fate, falling over the edge of a sharp precipice.[7]

What possible reason, however, could there be for this procedure? If the sent goat was to be a sacrifice, why was it not offered in the usual manner on the Temple Mount?

— B

Prominent among the rationalists concerning the *se'ir hamishtaleiach* is, of course, the Rambam who, as is his wont, offers an intellectual-philosophical explanation for this strange ritual.

This scholar notes a general pattern in connection with the sin offerings offered as part of the Temple ritual. Unlike burnt offerings, which are consumed in the fire of the Sanctuary's altar, sin offerings brought as atonement for severe transgressions are burned outside the Israelite camp. This ritual distinction, the Rambam suggests, mirrors a deeper philosophical

---

5. Ibid., 66a–b.
6. Talmud Bavli Yoma 67b.
7. Ibid., 67a–b.

divide. Far from creating the symbolic "sweet savor to God" of the celebratory burnt offerings, the burning of a sin offering reflects the destruction
of the negative. Through this ritual, the supplicant makes known his desire that the sin which necessitated the sacrifice be erased, destroyed and
eradicated from memory. The Torah, therefore, mandates that specific sin
offerings be consumed, not on the altar, but outside the camp. Atonement
can only be achieved if the people distance themselves from the sins associated with the burning of these offerings.

When it comes to the *se'ir hamishtaleiach*, the Rambam continues, our
tradition goes one step further. So severe are the year-long communal sins
represented by this offering, that it is sent as far from the camp as possible,
to the desolate wilderness of Azazel.

Above all, concludes the Rambam, the Torah's reference to the placing
of the sins of the nation on the *se'ir hamishtaleiach* cannot be taken literally. "Sins are not physical burdens which can be removed from one man's
back and placed upon the back of another."[8] *Rather, the drama of the sent
goat ritual is designed to strike fear and awe in the hearts of onlookers and
move them towards the difficult task of personal* tshuva. The message of the
ritual is clear: as the goat embarks on its final journey into the distant wilderness, symbolically accompanied by the sins of the people, all present
should cleanse and distance themselves from past failures and transgressions by committing themselves to concrete future change.[9]

Other commentaries suggest additional educational layers to the rituals surrounding the *se'ir hamishtaleiach*.

Haktav V'hakabala, for example, references a phrase concerning
idolatry that appears later in Parshat Acharei Mot: "And they shall no longer slaughter their offerings to the demons (literally the "he-goats") after
whom they stray…"[10] Idolatrous practice at the time included the worship
of wilderness demons which often took the form of goats. The dramatic
destruction of the sent goat is thus designed to convey to the nation the
emptiness and the abhorrent nature of idol worship. As the people witness
the graphic, violent end of the sent goat, the detritus of idolatry will dis-
sipate from their souls and they will cleave to their Creator. By prompting

---

8. Rambam, *Moreh Nevuchim* 3:46.
9. Ibid.
10. Vayikra 17:7.

the nation to return to their God, maintains *Haktav V'hakabala*, the *se'ir hamishtaleiach* will thus functionally "bear upon it all of their iniquities."[11]

Moving in a different yet equally rational direction, the Abravanel, the Akeidat Yitzchak and others view the rituals surrounding the *se'ir hamishtaleiach* as symbolic of the eternal struggle between two twin brothers, Yaakov and Esav, and their progeny. These two towering historical figures emerge from the same womb at the same time. One brother, however, is fated to serve the Lord as the ancestor of his chosen people while the other is destined to a violent, turbulent existence. So too, two goats, preferably of equal stature and appearance, are selected during the Temple service on Yom Kippur. Through the drawing of lots, God's will is evidenced as their fates are determined. One goat is chosen to ascend the Temple's altar as a holy sacrifice while the other is sent to its destruction in a wild, desolate, barren land. From this perspective, the ritual of the sent goat is specifically fashioned to remind the Israelites, on the holiest day of the year, of their unique destiny and responsibility as the descendents of Yaakov, God's chosen people.[12]

Finally, perhaps the most obvious *pshat*-based explanation for the ritual of the *se'ir hamishtaleiach* is further offered by the Abravanel and the Akeidat Yitzchak, and elaborated upon extensively by Rabbi Shimshon Raphael Hirsch. The rituals within the Sanctuary on Yom Kippur reflect a fundamental truth central to the very fabric of creation. In order to afford man with free choice, for every good God creates, He necessarily fashions a concomitant evil. The challenge facing each individual witnessing the dramatic ritual of the sent goat is dramatically clear: *Which path will you choose? Will you dedicate your life to the sanctified worship of the Lord; will you "ascend His altar," or will you, God forbid, allow your base impulses to lead you down the destructive path "to Azazel"?*[13]

— C —

At the opposite end of the interpretive spectrum from the rationalists are those who approach the entire ritual of the *se'ir hamishtaleiach* in mystical,

---

11. *Haktav V'hakabala*, Vayikra 17:22.
12. Abravanel, Vayikra 16:1–22.
13. Abravanel, ibid.; Akeidat Yitzchak Vayikra, sha'ar 63; Rabbi Shimshon Raphael Hirsch, Vayikra 16:10.

Midrashic terms. Many of their suggestions, however, seem to raise serious philosophical difficulties.

One tradition in the Talmud and Midrash, for example, links the Yom
Kippur Temple ritual to a most puzzling passage in the Torah, found towards the end of Parshat Bereishit. At the close of a ten-generation genea-
logical table leading from Adam to Noach, and immediately before the
announcement of God's decision to punish the world through the great
flood, the text states:

> And it came to pass when man began to multiply on the face of the
> earth and daughters were born to them; and *the sons of the gods* [alter-
> natively, sons of the rulers] saw that the daughters of man were good
> and they took for themselves as wives from whomever they chose. The
> giants were upon the land in those days and also afterward, when the
> sons of the gods [or sons of the rulers] consorted with the daughters
> of man, who bore to them. They were the mighty who, from old, were
> men of name.[14]

Clearly, this baffling passage calls for a full analysis, which is beyond the
scope of our current study. Suffice to say, numerous interpretations (again,
from the rational to the mystical) are offered by the commentaries.

One approach to the text, however, recorded in the Talmud and Midrash, identifies the "sons of the gods" as Aza and Azael (in other sources,
Shemchazei and Azael), two angels who convince God to send them into
the corruption of human society in order to prove their own steadfast-
ness. Upon their descent to earth, however, these angels immediately rebel
against God's will and, in the process, introduce further sexual licentious-
ness into human experience. The Temple offerings on Yom Kippur – and
particularly the *se'ir hamishtaleiach* – are offered to atone for the sins of
these angels (note the similarity between *Azael* and *Azazel*) and the subsequent sexual immorality that has followed, across the centuries. [15]

Among the unanswered problems raised by this Midrashic tale is
the portrayal of angels as independent beings with free choice. This de-
piction directly contradicts Judaism's general understanding of angels as

---

14. Bereishit 6:1–2.
15. Talmud Bavli Yoma 67b; Rashi, ibid.; Midrash Rabba Devarim.

messengers of God with no free will of their own (see *Bereishit: Vayeitzei 4, Approaches* A).

An explanation, perhaps, emerges if we view this Midrash in figurative rather than in literal terms. The rabbis use Midrashic technique to underscore the grave dangers surrounding potential sins of a sexual nature. So great are the temptations that even "angels" can ultimately fall prey; and so pervasive is the problem in the human sphere that the central Temple ritual on Yom Kippur is dedicated to the atonement of such sins. This Midrash finds support, not only in the many laws within Jewish tradition designed to prevent sexual offenses, but also in a Yom Kippur practice which continues to this day. The Torah portion chosen for recitation on Yom Kippur afternoon is specifically the section from Parshat Acharei Mot that catalogues the Torah's prohibitions of sexual immorality.[16]

—— **D** ——————————————————————————

Another Midrashic approach to the *se'ir hamishtaleiach* is so potentially explosive that one of its scholarly proponents is only willing to allude to it "in code." After outlining a number of ideas concerning this mysterious ritual, the Ibn Ezra makes the following baffling statement: "If you have the ability to decipher the secret that is found after the word Azazel, you will know its secret and the secret of its name.... And I will reveal a small portion of the secret in a riddle: 'When you are thirty-three years old, you will know it.'"[17]

A brief, reassuring message to those readers who are thirty-three years old or older and do not understand this declaration: *don't worry, you are in good company.*

Scholars across the ages have struggled to break the Ibn Ezra's code. Among the many solutions offered, the most widely accepted is that of the Ramban, who, tongue in cheek, opens his explanation as follows: "Behold, Rabbi Avraham (Ibn Ezra) is a trustworthy soul who keeps a secret; and I am the talebearer who will reveal his secret; for [it really is no secret,] our rabbis have already revealed it on many occasions."[18]

---

16. Talmud Bavli Megilla 31a.
17. Ibn Ezra, Vayikra 16:8.
18. Ramban, ibid.

The Ramban goes on to disclose the key to the Ibn Ezra's riddle: if you count *thirty-three sentences* in the text from the first mention of the word *Azazel*, you arrive at a statement that we have already encountered in this study: "And they shall no longer slaughter their offerings to the demons [literally the "he-goats"] after whom they stray…"[19]

Apparently, the Israelites actively worshiped demons, angels and other perceived supernatural "forces." The Torah, therefore, expressly prohibits this pointless veneration. Angelic or demonic "forces" are not independent entities worthy of worship. They are simply manifestations of God's will (see *Bereishit*: Vayeitzei 4, *Approaches* A).

As the Ramban continues his analysis of the Ibn Ezra, however, it becomes abundantly clear why the latter might have been hesitant to openly state his position. There is, it seems, an exception to the rule prohibiting gifts to supernatural forces other than God:

> On Yom Kippur, however, *the Holy One Blessed Be He commanded that we send a goat to the wilderness, to the "force" that rules in desolate places*…and from whose power devolves…bloodshed, warfare, violence, strife and destruction…and under whose authority are the demons referred to by the rabbis as *mazikim*, "destroyers," and in the biblical text as *se'irim*, "he-goats."[20]

Recognizing the startling nature of his own words, the Ramban immediately explains that the *se'ir hamishtaleiach* is by no means to be understood as an independent offering of our own initiative to this "force" of the wilderness. Such an act would be totally contrary to Torah law and thought – *an open contradiction of our belief in one unified God*. The gift to Azazel must instead be viewed as fulfillment of God's will, best compared to a gift of food given by the supplier of a banquet to a servant at the host's request. The supplier grants nothing directly to the servant, nor does he honor the servant at all. All substance and honor is given only to the host through adherence to the host's directives. So, too, we send the goat to Azazel only in fulfillment of God's command.

---

19. Vayikra 17:7.
20. Ramban, ibid.

This approach, maintains the Ramban, also explains the use of lots in the selection between the two goats. Had the Kohen chosen the goat to be sent to Azazel, it would have been as if he were worshiping the "force" of the wilderness and offering directly in its name. The ritual as outlined in the Torah, however, calls for both goats to be stood before the Sanctuary. Both animals are offerings to God, Who then makes His will known through the drawing of lots. God, not the Kohen, determines the fate of each of the offerings. God selects the gift for Azazel.

In spite of the Ramban's earnest attempts to buffer the blow, however, his explanation of the Ibn Ezra's approach to the *se'ir hamishtaleiach* strikes with unsettling force. How can we accept a Torah mandate that not only treats angels as independent powers, but enjoins us to extend a "gift" to one such power on the holiest day of the Jewish calendar year? Even if the bequest to Azazel is indirect, this Sanctuary ritual seems to undermine the very essence of our belief in one, and only one, heavenly force.

Perhaps, once again, a solution lies in finding the moral message embedded at the core of this mysterious approach. Yom Kippur, the holiest day of the Jewish year, carries one overarching imperative: *tshuva*, "return," or, to be more specific, positive behavioral change. *Commitment to such change, however, is doomed to failure without a fundamental recognition of the power of evil and sin.* Year after year, the best of intentions, eloquently expressed over the High Holidays, fall prey to the temptations of the "real world." Our high expectations for ourselves, forged in the rising emotional tide that crests with the cadences of Ne'ila (the dramatic closing Yom Kippur prayer), are soon dashed against the shoals of everyday pressures that inevitably stunt our spiritual growth.

Our tradition thus attempts to forestall this eventuality through the message of the sent goat. A gift is given to the "destructive force" of the desert in an apparent effort to direct the power of even that "force" towards our betterment.

And, through this symbolic act, a powerful, personal message is conveyed to all present…

Do not let this holiest of days pass without attaining a healthy respect for the potentially destructive forces that inhabit your world. Above all, recognize the strength of your own personal yetzer hara, *your evil inclination, and its unerring ability to undermine your valiant attempts at self-betterment. Denial of its existence has not worked for you in the past and will not work for you in the future. Attempted sublimation of the* yetzer hara *is, in fact, the surest way to grant it greater power over your actions.*

Adopt, therefore, a different tack. Acknowledge your "adversary"; respect its strength; then turn that strength to your benefit. Channel the energy that could lead you astray and direct it towards good.

The ritual of the *se'ir hamishtaleiach* thus emerges as a dramatic re-iteration of a fundamental truth which, according to Jewish tradition, is embedded in the fabric of the world's creation (see *Bereishit*: Bereishit 1, *Approaches* F).

No aspect of man's divinely created makeup is inherently evil. Good and evil are instead defined in concrete terms, by how our potential is used. The very internal forces that are so often destructive – lust, ambition, the drive for control and power – can, when properly acknowledged, controlled and harnessed, lead us to the greatest good and accomplishment.

In our search for a proper life path, "Azazel" can and must become our ally.

Points to Ponder

Our analysis of the "sent goat" ritual underscores a fundamental truth concerning Torah study, which cannot be stated often enough: even the most difficult, esoteric concepts within our tradition can, upon diligent study, yield extraordinary lessons of immediate relevance to our lives. The treasures of meaning are there for the taking. All that is required is the will and the energy.

2 Communal Confession

Context

As indicated in the previous study, the communal *vidui*, confession, recited by the Kohen Gadol over the *se'ir hamishtaleiach* is a central feature of this Yom Kippur Temple ritual:

> And Aharon shall place his two hands upon the living he-goat and he shall *confess upon it all of the iniquities* of the children of Israel and all of their rebellious sins in all of their sins, and he shall place them upon the head of the he-goat and he shall send it at the hand of a designated man to the wilderness.[1]

Questions

What is the implication of the confession uttered by the Kohen Gadol over the "sent goat" on behalf of the entire nation?

What role does this communal confession play in the atonement divinely granted on Yom Kippur? Aren't confession and *tshuva* private, personal processes best experienced individually rather than communally?

How can an understanding of this *vidui* and of the phenomenon of confession, in general, shed further light on the mysterious ritual of the *se'ir hamishtaleiach* and on the pivotal concept of *tshuva*?

[Note: Although the term *tshuva* is popularly translated as "repentance," the proper interpretation of the term is "return." Repentance is only one step in the wrenching process of *tshuva*, which entails *recognition* of past transgressions, *remorse* over those transgressions and a *commitment* to future change (see also above, Acharei Mot 1, *Context*). Properly experienced, *tshuva* results in true behavioral change as we "return" to God and to our

---

1. Vayikra 16:21.

124

proper life path. For the sake of textual clarity, however, we will at times make use of the popular translation "repentance" in this study.]

Approaches

This study departs from our usual structure. Rather than examining a wide range of approaches to a particular issue, we will explore the thoughts of one towering sage as interpreted, centuries later, by another.

During my rabbinic studies at Yeshiva University, I was privileged to attend the *shiurim* (Talmudic classes) of Rabbi Joseph Dov Soloveitchik, known to me and to so many others simply as the Rav. These many years later, I still find the experience difficult to describe. Never before, nor ever since, have I been as challenged intellectually as I was by the Rav.

In the Rav's *shiur*, a phenomenon occurred that only occurs when Torah study is experienced at its best. The centuries melted away. With us in the classroom we felt the personal presence of the very sages, from time immemorial, whose writings we studied and with whom we "dialogued."

Particularly striking, however, was the Rav's relationship to the Rambam. I use the term *relationship* consciously. Although centuries separated these scholars, the Rav spoke of the Rambam as if he was speaking of, and even to, a cherished mentor and colleague. He analyzed every word of the Rambam's legal code, the *Mishneh Torah*, maintaining that "Maimonides was very exact in his use of words as far as we know and did not indulge in flowery language. In light of this, we should be as scrupulous as possible when studying his code, the *Mishneh Torah*, in trying to learn the true significance of each word we read."[2]

What follows is a brief introduction to the Rambam's thoughts surrounding the *se'ir hamishtaleiach*, as seen through the Rav's eyes. This information is culled both from *On Repentance: The Thought and Oral Discourses of Rabbi Joseph Dov Soloveitchik*, edited by Pinchas Peli (Jason Aronson, 1996), as well as from my own personal recollections.

A

Before turning to the specific *vidui* associated with the *se'ir hamishtaleiach*, we must first examine the Rambam's approach to the general phenomenon

---

2. Pinchas H. Peli, *On Repentance: The Thought and Oral Discourses of Rabbi Joseph Dov Soloveitchik* (Northvale, NJ: Jason Aronson, 1996).

of confession and its place in Jewish thought and law. The Rambam opens his review of the laws of *tshuva* with the following halacha:

> With regard to all the precepts in the Torah, whether positive commandments or negative ones, if a person transgresses one of them, either willfully or unknowingly, when he does *tshuva* and returns from his sin, it is his duty to confess before God, blessed be He...*and this confession is an affirmative precept* [my italics]...[3]

Numerous later authorities raise two questions concerning the Rambam's formulation of the *tshuva* process. Firstly, they ask, why doesn't the Rambam depict *tshuva* in obligatory terms, choosing instead to state "*when* he [the sinner] does *tshuva*"? Secondly, the Rambam's delineation of confession as a positive biblical precept seems counterintuitive. At first glance, they argue, confession would appear to be only a means to an end, a first step on the path towards the mitzva of full *tshuva*. Why, then, does the Rambam list confession itself as a mitzva?

Based on the Rambam's words, therefore, some authorities arrive at a startling conclusion: while the Rambam believes that confession is a biblical obligation, *he does not consider* tshuva *a mitzva at all*. Return to God, they maintain, is in Maimonides' view a self-understood rather than a commanded act. Intuitively, no member of the community of Israel would choose to remain immersed in sin without desiring to repent. God, therefore, affords us the opportunity to "restart" our lives through the gift of *tshuva*.[4]

The Rav strenuously disagrees: "Can one really contemplate the possibility that confession be considered a precept while repentance is not? What would be the significance of confession without repentance?"[5]

Numerous sources within the Torah, the Rav adds, plainly define *tshuva* as a mitzva.[6] Furthermore, the Rambam's own language on a number of occasions supports this view.[7] Most tellingly, the very heading of the section in his *Mishneh Torah* that summarizes the laws of *tshuva* reads:

---

3. Rambam, *Mishneh Torah*, Hilchot Tshuva 1:1.
4. Minchat Chinuch, mitzva 364.
5. Peli, *On Repentance*, p. 70.
6. Devarim 4:30, 30:1–3.
7. Rambam, *Mishneh Torah*, Hilchot Tshuva 2:7, 7:5.

"The Laws of Return: One positive precept – that *the sinner shall repent of his sin before the Lord and confess.*"[8]

Clearly, the Rambam views repentance – and not confession alone – as a mitzva. Why, then, does the Rambam, as noted above, focus so distinctly on the obligation of confession, going so far as to label confession itself *an affirmative precept*?

The answer, suggests the Rav, lies in the Rambam's general categorization of biblical mitzvot into two distinct groups.

1. *Those mitzvot whose fulfillment and practice are identical.* One both performs and fulfills each of these mitzvot through a single physical act. Examples of this group include the taking of the four species on the holiday of Succot, the sacrifice of the *korban* Pesach and the counting of the Omer.

2. *Those mitzvot whose practice and fulfillment are not identical.* In these cases, "The precept cannot be fulfilled through the performance of... external acts alone; its true fulfillment lies within the realm of the heart."[9] The physical act connected to each of these mitzvot is designed to give rise to powerful inner feelings, thoughts and realizations. Only through these internal phenomena is the mitzva "fulfilled."

Laws of mourning and rejoicing, the recitation of the Shma and the mitzva of prayer are all included in this second group of mitzvot, *as is, maintains the Rav, the mitzva of tshuva.* The verbal confession is the obligatory physical act designed to give rise to a heartfelt feeling of return.

The Rambam's language in the *Mishneh Torah*, continues the Rav, now emerges as true to form. Whenever the Rambam deals with a mitzva whose performance is marked by external deed but whose fulfillment can only take place within the heart, he distinguishes between the two aspects of the mitzva in his codification of the law. In describing the laws themselves, the Rambam details only the actual performance, the concrete act associated with the mitzva. In his section headings, however, he defines the mitzva in its entirety, citing both physical performance and internal fulfillment.

The first halacha in the Rambam's laws of *tshuva* thus focuses upon the physical action through which the mitzva of return is performed: the concrete act of verbal confession. As mentioned above, however, this entire

8. Ibid.
9. Peli, *On Repentance*, p. 71.

section of law is introduced by a heading that reflects both tangible performance and psychic fulfillment: "The Laws of Return: One positive precept – that the sinner shall *repent of his sin* (fulfillment) before the Lord *and confess* (performance)."

—— **B** ————————————————————————————

A deeper question now emerges. Why does the Rambam consider the act of verbal confession so critical to the mitzva of the Return? Why can't *tshuva* take place solely in one's heart?

The Rav lists two main reasons why the Torah obligates a penitent to make confession.

1. Confession serves to complete the *tshuva* process. Verbalization forces the penitent to crystallize both his remorse over the past and his commitment to future change:

> Feelings, emotions, thoughts and ideas become clear, and are grasped only after they are expressed in sentences mirroring a logical and grammatical structure. As long as one's thoughts remain repressed, as long as one has not brought them into the open…they are not truly yours; they are foreign and elusive…. Repentance contemplated, and not verbalized, is [therefore] valueless.[10]

2. By forcing us to admit the facts, confession robs us of the ability to fool ourselves. Through verbalization we compel ourselves to examine not only our sins, but the nature of our sins. Acts that we might have written off as unintentional are scrutinized anew and we are compelled to admit motivations that we would have rather ignored:

> Confession compels man – in a state of terrible torment – to admit facts as they really are, to give clear expression to the truth…[t]o look ourselves straight in the eye, to overcome the mechanism of self defense; to smash asunder the artificial barriers, to go against our natural inclination to run and hide, to tear down the screen, to put into words what our hearts have already determined…"[11]

---

10. Ibid., pp. 91–92.
11. Ibid., p.95.

At this level, the Rav maintains, confession becomes a wrenching act of personal "sacrifice" which moves man beyond remorse to shame. The penitent's will is broken as he is forced to act against his very nature:

> Just as the sacrifice is burnt upon the altar so do we burn down, by our active confession, our well-barricaded complacency, our overblown pride, our artificial existence.... Only then, after the purifying catharsis of confession, does one return, in circular motion, to God who is there before man sins, to our Father who is in heaven, who cleanses us whenever we approach Him for purification.[12]

— **C** —————————————————————

Having briefly reviewed the general role of confession in the process of return, we can now turn our attention to the specific *vidui* pronounced by the Kohen Gadol over the *se'ir hamishtaleiach*.

Again, in the first chapter of his laws of *tshuva*, the Rambam writes:

> Since the *se'ir hamishtaleiach* brings acquittal for all of Israel, the High Priest confesses over it in the name of all Israel....
>
> The *se'ir hamishtaleiach* brings acquittal for all the sins mentioned in the Torah, the venial and the grave, those committed with premeditation and those done unintentionally, those which become known to their doer and those which do not – all are granted acquittal by means of the *se'ir hamishtaleiach*, provided only that the sinner has repented.
>
> If, however, he has not repented, the scapegoat can bring acquittal only for the lighter sins.[13]

In a lengthy analysis of this passage, the Rav raises a series of critical questions, including the following.

1. What innovation does the Rambam introduce with his initial declaration, "Since the *se'ir hamishtaleiach* brings acquittal for all of Israel, the High Priest confesses over it in the name of all Israel"? The classification

---

12. Ibid., pp.95–96.
13. Rambam, *Mishneh Torah*, Hilchot Tshuva 1:2.

of the sent goat as a communal sacrifice is obvious and emerges from the Torah text itself.

2. Immediately before his passage dealing with the *se'ir hamishtaleiach*, the Rambam lists a litany of potential means of atonement which are effective only when accompanied by repentance. How can he now suddenly claim that the ritual of the *se'ir hamishtaleiach* effects atonement for specific sins *even in the absence of such repentance*?

3. What is the delineating line between "lighter" sins for which the *se'ir hamishtaleiach* is automatically effective and more severe sins which require *tshuva* as well?

— **D** —————————————————————————

The Rav answers these questions with one bold, imaginative stroke. Based on sources in the Written and Oral Law, he posits that on Yom Kippur two essential types of atonement are potentially granted to man: *individual and communal*.

Individual expiation is open to each and every Jew who is strong enough to undergo a full, heartfelt process of return. Such acquittal is achieved in solitary fashion as the penitent plumbs the depths of his own heart and soul.

Communal atonement, however, is different. This expiation is granted globally to *Knesset Yisrael*, the community of Israel, "in its entirety and as a separate mystical kind of self, as a separate entity in its own right."[14] Once granted to the collective, this acquittal is automatically afforded to each individual who remains linked to *Knesset Yisrael* through an unbreakable bond.

Each Jew, therefore, must travel along two separate paths in order to achieve a full measure of atonement on this holiest of days.

On the one hand, man must travel alone and in solitary fashion along the path to individual repentance. At the same time, however, "'Repentant Man' will not reach his goal and the completion of his mission – salvation – as a lonely man of faith, but only as part of the community of Israel."[15]

———————

14. Peli, *On Repentance*, p. 106.
15. Ibid., p. 42.

—— **F** ————————————————————————————

True to his essence as a giant of Jewish law, the Rav roots the two elements of Jewish identity, the individual and the communal, in two fundamental contracts between God and His people.

The first of these agreements, the inherited covenant from our forefathers, is sealed at Sinai and reiterated in the Wilderness of Moav. This global contract, enacted with our ancestors at the dawn of our national history, is handed down in perpetuity to all who remain bound to the Jewish collective.

The second covenant, on the other hand, is spelled out in the book of Devarim where Moshe states, "Not with you alone do I seal this covenant and this oath, but with whoever is here, standing with us today before the Lord, our God; and with whoever is not here with us today."[16] This contract, enacted not only with the generation to whom Moshe speaks but with each Jew in each generation until the end of time, is the source of the "sanctity of self," the independent sanctity of each individual Jew across the ages.

A double bond thus ties each Jew to God – as an individual and as a member of the people, *Knesset Yisrael*, the seed of Avraham. This double bond, in turn, gives rise to two essential avenues of *tshuva* which lie before man on Yom Kippur. On this holiest of days, each Jew must certainly travel the long road of individual repentance. At the same time, however, each individual must ensure the health of his bond with the Jewish collective. Only by traveling along both these paths will the individual achieve his full atonement.

—— **G** ————————————————————————————

In light of the Rav's observations, the Rambam's comments concerning the confession associated with the *se'ir hamishtaleiach* become abundantly clear.

When the Rambam states, "Since the *se'ir hamishtaleiach* brings acquittal for all of Israel, the High Priest confesses over it in the name of all Israel," he is *actually defining the nature of atonement* granted by the ritual of the sent goat.

The *se'ir hamishtaleiach*, in the Rambam's opinion, represents the path of communal atonement, the global path afforded as a whole to *Knesset*

———————————

16. Devarim 29:13–14.

Yisrael. During this ritual, therefore, the Kohen Gadol, acting as the representative of the Jewish collective, recites a confession "in the name of all Israel." The completed ritual then affords atonement to every individual linked to *Knesset Yisrael.*

The *se'ir hamishtaleiach* does not, however, address the path of personal atonement. That path continues to stretch before each individual and can only be traversed alone, through wrenching self-scrutiny and commitment to behavioral change.

In the absence of the Temple ritual, the day of Yom Kippur itself, according to the Rav, provides the opportunity for both requisite paths of atonement. He brings support for this position from the blessing found in the Yom Kippur liturgy, "Blessed art Thou…, Who pardons and forgives *our transgressions and the transgressions of His people, the House of Israel*"[17] and from the Rambam's statement "The Day of Atonement is a time of repentance for all, *for individuals and for multitudes*, and is the moment of pardon and forgiveness *for Israel.*"[18] The dual language in both sources indicates that the Day of Atonement provides two requisite paths of expiation – for individuals and for the collective, *Knesset Yisrael*, as a single entity.

The Rambam's claim that the *se'ir hamishtaleiach* grants atonement even in the absence of repentance is also understandable in light of the communal nature of the atonement granted by this ritual. An individual's inclusion in this expiation is not dependent upon his personal *tshuva* but upon his bond with the Jewish collective, *Knesset Yisrael.* The atonement afforded by the *se'ir hamishtaleiach* is, therefore, effective in the absence of personal repentance.

Finally, the Rambam's distinction between grave and "lighter" sins also becomes clear. The delineation between these two categories of transgressions is determined by whether or not a specific sin carries the punishment of *karet*, spiritual excision from the community. Sins carrying such a penalty cannot be communally atoned for in the absence of *tshuva* for one simple reason: the individual guilty of such a crime *has effectively cut himself off from the community, Knesset Yisrael.* This breach must be repaired. Only by reconnecting with the collective through personal return can the individual expect to partake of the communal atonement afforded

---

17. Yom Kippur Amida.
18. Rambam, *Mishneh Torah*, Hilchot Tshuva 2:7.

through the *se'ir hamishtaleiach*. That is why Rambam states that, in the absence of *tshuva*, "the sent goat can bring acquittal only for the lighter [i.e., non-*karet*-incurring] sins."

———**H**————————————————————————

And thus, an exquisite tapestry of legal and philosophical concepts is woven by two towering giants, separated by centuries. Intricate halachic nuance and towering theological concept merge as, together, the Rambam and the Rav uncover the critical balance between individual and communal identity lying at the core of the holiest day of the Jewish year.

Points to Ponder

A few words must be shared concerning the Rav's understanding of the concept of *Knesset Yisrael* and its central place in Jewish thought.

In the Rav's worldview, belonging to the collective is essential – not only to the Jew's definition as "Repentant Man," but to his very definition as a Jew:

[Each Jew's] whole endeavor as an individual is worthless to him until he renews his connection with the covenantal community and reintegrates in it....

The individual Jew constitutes an integral part of *Knesset Israel*. This is not a free and voluntary association; it is an ontological-essential one. As *Knesset Israel* is not a sum total or arithmetic combination of such and such individuals, but a metaphysical personality of singular essence and possessing an individual judicial personality, so the individual Jew does not have an independent existence but is a limb of *Knesset Israel*....

A Jew who has lost his faith in *Knesset Israel* even though he may, in his own little corner, sanctify and purify himself through severities and restrictions – this Jew remains incorrigible and totally unequipped to partake of the Day of Atonement which encompasses the whole of *Knesset Israel* in all its parts and in all its generations....

A Jew who lives as part of *Knesset Israel* and is ready to lay down his life for it, who is pained by its hurt and is happy at its joy, wages its battles, groans at its failures, and celebrates its victories.... A Jew who believes in *Knesset Israel* is a Jew who finds himself with an indissoluble bond not only to the People of Israel of his generation but to *Knesset Israel* through all the generations.[19]

During his lifetime (1903–1993), the Rav expressed deep concern over the spiritual survival of Diaspora Jewry and the physical safety of the Jewish community in Israel. He maintained, however, that faith in *Knesset Yisrael* mandates against despair, requiring each Jew to believe in the continued existence of our people until the coming of the Messiah.

One can't help but wonder, however, how much more fearful the Rav would be today, witnessing not only an exacerbation of the crises he noted in his lifetime, but also the growing pressures within the Jewish community upon the very integrity of *Knesset Yisrael*.

Fragmented for years, we have become a people increasingly divided against ourselves as the fault lines between us, both in Israel and the diaspora, grow into seemingly unbridgeable chasms. Charedi, Zionist, Secular, Conservative, Reform, Orthodox, Settlers, Peace Activists – we continue to retreat into homogeneous groups, seeking the safety of those who share our ideas and our own life outlook.

And the groupings grow even narrower…

Even within the Orthodox community, for example, do Charedi and Religious Zionist Jews feel kinship with or antipathy towards each other as they pass on the street? Do Modern Orthodox Jews and Satmar Chasidim truly see themselves as part of the same people, with the same dreams?

There was a time when the good of the collective "trumped" the particularistic concerns of each insular group. In spite of disagreements, there were lines that we simply wouldn't cross against each other. That vision of the good of the whole, today, seems increasingly threatened.

I can hear the Rav's voice whispering in my ear of the importance of *Knesset Yisrael*. His vision of shared origin and shared destiny is one that we lose, God forbid, at our peril.

---

19. Soloveitchik, "The Lonely Man of Faith," *Tradition* 7, no.2 (summer 1965): 125; quoted in Peli, *On Repentance*, pp. 42–43.

3 A Timely Man

Context

An individual is designated to assume custody of the sent goat and lead it to its final destination in the wilderness. This individual is referred to by the text simply as an *ish iti*, a "designated man" (literally "a timely man").[1]

So significant is the role of the "designated man" in the process of communal atonement that a series of way stations are set up along his route into the wilderness. At each station, the *ish iti* is offered the option of breaking his Yom Kippur fast, that he may retain the strength necessary to successfully complete his mission (the Talmud, however, testifies that no *ish iti* ever actually ate on Yom Kippur).

According to biblical law, any Israelite can serve as the *ish iti*; the High Priests, however, eventually mandate that only Kohanim assume this role.[2]

Questions

Given the pivotal function performed by the *ish iti* in the attainment of communal atonement, the Torah's silence concerning the requisite qualifications for his role is bewildering.

Shouldn't the individual who completes the central Yom Kippur ritual of the *se'ir hamishtaleiach* be required to be righteous, holy, ritually observant? Why aren't these, or for that matter, any real requirements spelled out? Why is the Torah satisfied simply with the designation *ish iti*?

Furthermore, exactly what does the term *ish iti* signify? What innovative criteria is the Torah establishing through the reference to "a designated

---

1. Vayikra 16:21.
2. Talmud Bavli Yoma 66a–67b.

135

man"? Wouldn't any individual chosen for this task, by definition, automatically be considered "designated"?

Approaches

The approaches of the rabbis to the title *ish iti* range from the mystical to the utilitarian. Almost all who comment, however, base their suggestions on the literal interpretation of the words *ish iti*, "a timely man."

—— **A** ——————————————————————————

One source in the Talmud, for example, views the designation as situationally – rather than personally – descriptive. The term *ish iti* conveys that the critical role of the "designated man" must be fulfilled *at all times*; even on Shabbat and even if the task calls for the overriding of specific Shabbat laws.[3]

Choosing an entirely different path, the Chizkuni offers a startling mystical interpretation. Invariably, this scholar says, the individual designated to accompany the sent goat to its final destination does not survive the following year. The Torah, therefore, mandates that an *ish iti* be deliberately chosen – an individual whose *time to die* has arrived. In this way, only someone who is already destined to perish during the coming year will be appointed to this doomed role. The Kohanim were able to determine such a candidate, continues the Chizkuni, through their facility in the process of astrological divination.[4]

The Chizkuni's approach, however, is deeply troubling on two counts: both because of the arbitrariness of the *ish iti*'s fate and because of the reliance of the Kohanim upon divination, an art that is clearly prohibited by the Torah.[5]

Interestingly, while the Chizkuni claims Midrashic foundation for his disquieting suggestion, later scholars are unable to locate any Midrashic source.[6]

———————————

3. Ibid., 66b. Note: This rabbinic observation is difficult to understand. Any law that would potentially desecrate Shabbat would desecrate Yom Kippur, as well. Why then focus on the circumstance when Shabbat and Yom Kippur coincide? The Talmud addresses the issue in technical terms.
4. Chizkuni, Vayikra 16:21.
5. Vayikra 19:26.
6. Torat Chaim Chumash (Jerusalem: Mossad Harav Kook, 1990), footnote on Chizkuni, Vayikra 16:21.

——— **B** ———————————————————————————————————————

Those commentaries, such as the Rashbam, who generally view the text through the lens of *pshat*, maintain a straightforward, utilitarian approach to the term *ish iti*. The only prerequisites for this role, they claim, are knowledge of wilderness pathways and a consequent preparedness to depart for Azazel at a moment's notice.[7] In the eyes of these *pashtanim*, the designated man, unlike the Kohen, is neither a role model for nor a representative of the people before God. He is simply a facilitator.

Once the ceremonial requirements of the sent goat ritual have been completed by the Kohen, all that remains is to get the job done as expeditiously as possible. Someone must ensure that the sent goat reaches its final destination without delay. The only essential criterion for this role, the role of "designated man," is that the candidate be the best man for the job.

——— **C** ———————————————————————————————————————

Yet another Talmudic source, quoted in Rashi, sees an additional requirement embedded in the term *ish iti*. To be a "timely man" one must be *muchan l'kach miyom etmol*, "prepared for the task from the previous day."

This source, at face value, strengthens the utilitarian position of the *pashtanim*. Pre-appointment is apparently necessary to ensure that the "designated man" will be ready to respond to the call of duty at a moment's notice.

——— **D** ———————————————————————————————————————

The requirement of "readiness" on the part of the *ish iti*, however, can be achieved even without pre-appointment. Why does the Talmud specifically insist that the "designated man" be prepared for his mission "from the previous day"?

A tantalizing possibility emerges if we consider the Talmudic mandate *muchan l'kach miyom etmol* in broader terms. Perhaps the rabbis are defining a singular character trait in the selection of the *ish iti*, a personal quality which they believe to be of inestimable value for any individual traveling along the path towards true *tshuva*.

---

7. Rashbam, Vayikra 16:21.

Consider, for a moment… How different would our lives be if we were truly *muchan l'kach miyom etmol*, if somehow we could train ourselves to perceive the seeds of the future, each day, in our actions and in the world around us? What would have truly changed had we been prepared yesterday for today? What will change now if we are prepared today for tomorrow?

The rabbis, as always, said it well: "Who is truly wise? He who sees that which is a-borning."[8]

— **E** —

We can now begin to understand the single prerequisite that the rabbis mandate for the man who brings the Yom Kippur process of communal atonement to its conclusion. He must be, literally and figuratively, *muchan l'kach miyom etmol*.

Each Yom Kippur, after all, we inevitably confront our "regrets."

If only I had been more aware… If only I could have known where my words or my actions would lead… I would certainly have spoken more carefully… I would certainly have acted differently… if only I had known…

Essential to the process of *tshuva*, then, is increased awareness of the ultimate impact of our deeds. If we can somehow perceive the potential future results of our words or actions, we will be more able to carefully calibrate our current reactions and interactions, sparing ourselves and those around us untold measures of pain.

To sensitize the nation towards this task of self-awareness, the Torah mandates only one symbolic requirement for the *ish iti*. The individual who completes the communal process of atonement on the holiest day of the year must simply be *muchan l'kach miyom etmol*, prepared for the task from the previous day.

Points to Ponder

My father, of blessed memory, passed away a short time before Rosh Hashana 5758. That year, I sorrowfully prepared my High Holiday sermons armed with a new understanding of the grieving process. Although I had certainly counseled many mourners before, only through my own loss did I truly begin to comprehend man's journey through the "valley of the shadow of death."

---

8. Talmud Bavli Tamid 32a.

I spoke that Yom Kippur, before the Yizkor prayer (the memorial prayer) of the *ish iti* and of his requirement to be *muchan l'kach miyom etmol*.

By way of illustration, I cited the connection drawn by Rav Soloveitchik between the dual experiences of mourning and *tshuva*. Noting the similarity between the laws of shiva (the seven-day mourning period mandated by Jewish law) and the laws of Yom Kippur, the Rav arrives at a dramatic conclusion: *mourning, in Jewish law, is largely an act of tshuva.*

> Man is always a latecomer as far as the formation of value judgments is concerned. His axiology [value system] or appreciation of persons, things and events is always a product of hindsight. In retrospection man discovers the precise value of something which, or somebody who was, but is no longer with us…. While the somebody was near, while I could communicate with the somebody, I was unaware of him…. He comes into existence and turns into somebody important and precious at the very moment he departs from me and is lost in the mist of remoteness. Only after he has gone do I begin to ask: Who was he? What did he mean to me?[9]

With the Rav's observations as backdrop, I continued to speak in personal terms of my own *tshuva* process and of the lessons we can all learn from the "designated man":

> If only I had recognized what I had when I had it… If only I could have predicted the deep pain and emptiness I now feel with my father gone… I would never have taken his presence for granted while he was with me…
>
> If only we could all be, like the *ish iti, muchan l'kach miyom etmol,* truly prepared for life experiences – cognizant of what would be and how we would feel today – yesterday.

---

9. Rabbi Joseph B. Soloveitchik, *Out of the Whirlwind,* edited by David Schatz, Joel B. Wolowelsky and Reuven Ziegler (Hoboken, NJ: Ktav Publishing House, 2003).

Kedoshim

CHAPTER 19:1–20:27

פרק יט:א-כ:כז

Parsha Summary

Striving for sanctity, in thought, in word, in deed…

An abrupt change in content and tone is found in the text as God turns to the ethical, moral and ritual precepts designed to shape the character and personal behavior of the Jewish nation.

God commands Moshe to gather the people and command them: "Holy shall you be, for holy am I, the Lord, your God." This general exhortation toward sanctity introduces a parsha so significant that the rabbis claim, centuries later, "Most of the fundamental teachings of the Torah are derived therefrom."

Included in Parshat Kedoshim are such towering ethical edicts as:

1. "You shall fear, every man, his mother and his father; and you shall keep My Sabbaths; I am the Lord your God."

2. "You shall not steal; you shall not deny falsely; you shall not lie to one another."

3. "You shall not curse the deaf; and before the blind you shall not place a stumbling block; and you shall fear your God; I am the Lord."

4. "You shall not travel as a gossipmonger among your people; you shall not stand idly by the blood of your fellow; I am the Lord."

5. "You shall not hate your brother in your heart; you shall surely rebuke your fellow, and not bear sin because of him."

6. "You shall not take revenge and you shall not bear a grudge against the members of your people; and you shall love your fellow as yourself; I am the Lord."

Included, as well, are mysterious ritual laws such as:

1. Kilayim *and* shaatnez: *prohibitions concerning the crossbreeding of animals, specific agricultural mixtures and the combination of certain fibers in clothing*

2. Orla *and* neta reva'i: *the prohibition against consumption of the first*

three years' produce of a fruit tree and the obligation to bring the fourth year's fruit to Jerusalem for consumption

*   3. Edicts prohibiting sorcery and superstitious beliefs*

*   4. Edicts prohibiting men from totally cutting off their sideburns and shaving with a razor*

*   Parshat Kedoshim closes with a series of warnings against immoral acts and with an elucidation of the punishments for the forbidden relationships first outlined at the end of Parshat Acharei Mot.*

1 All Together Now...

Context

The rabbis note a surprising departure from the norm in the introductory sentence of Parshat Kedoshim: "And the Lord spoke to Moshe, saying: 'Speak to the *entire assembly of the children of Israel* and say to them...'"[1]

This phrase clearly contrasts with the usual formula used to introduce countless passages of Torah text: "And the Lord spoke to Moshe, saying: 'Speak to the *children of Israel* and say to them...'"

The variation leads the Midrash to conclude that, at God's command, Parshat Kedoshim was taught to the Israelites by Moshe in an exceptional way.

Normally, the rabbis explain, the Torah was transmitted to the Israelites in a hierarchical manner:

> Moshe learned from the Almighty himself. Aharon then entered and Moshe recited the lesson for him. Aharon moved aside and sat to Moshe's left. His [Aharon's] sons entered and Moshe recited the lesson for them. They moved aside, Elazar sitting on Moshe's right and Itamar on Aharon's left. The Elders entered and Moshe recited the lesson for them. They moved aside and seated themselves to the side. Then all the people entered and Moshe recited the lesson for them. This way the people heard [the lesson] once, the Elders twice, Aharon's sons three times and Aharon four times.[2]

---

1. Vayikra 19:1–2.
2. Rashi, Shmot 34:32, based on Talmud Bavli Eruvin 54b.

The phrase "Speak to the *entire assembly of the children of Israel*," however, indicates that, in the case of Parshat Kedoshim, the method of transmission was changed. Parshat Kedoshim is of such singular importance, the rabbis maintain, that it was taught *b'hakhel*, "in full assembly," to the entire nation at once.

At God's command, all the Israelites heard this portion of the law together, directly from Moshe, because "most of the fundamental teachings of the Torah are derived therefrom."[3]

Questions

The rabbinic claim concerning the transmission of Parshat Kedoshim seems counterintuitive. To quote an oft-used Talmudic admonition: *mima nafshach* (either way you look at it), it doesn't make sense!

If, on the one hand, the hierarchical method of Torah transmission is the most effective, this method should certainly have been employed in the communication of Parshat Kedoshim, one of the most important sections of Torah law.

If, on the other hand, full assembly is the most effective form of Torah transmission, why was this method not employed in the communication of the entire Torah?

Approaches

—— **A** ——

A case can be made, from a pedagogical perspective, that the issue at hand is not the particular mode of transmission but the impact that can be achieved through variation in educational technique.

By commanding Moshe to assemble the entire nation together for the transmission of one particular section of the law, God automatically alerts the Israelites to the significance of that section. *I am changing the way things are done*, He effectively says, *because, this time, something is different.*

The usual method of Torah transmission, as efficient as it may be, is suspended this one time so that the people will never forget the parsha from which "most of the fundamental teachings of the Torah are derived."

---

3. Rashi, Vayikra 19:2, based on Torat Kohanim, Kedoshim 1:1.

—— **B** ————————————————————————————

Numerous scholars, however, are not content to leave matters at that level.

Concrete connections, they insist, can be made between the contents of Parshat Kedoshim and the specific method of full assembly, chosen for this parsha's transmission.

Rabbi Eliyahu Mizrachi, for example, maintains that God gathers the nation in full assembly in order to minimize potential misunderstanding and dispute concerning this pivotal section of Jewish law. Had the fundamental regulations of Parshat Kedoshim been communicated to separate groups, one faction within the nation could easily have disputed another faction's recollection of the law. Dangerously competing versions of what God actually said might well have proliferated.

By insisting that all the Israelites hear these pivotal edicts together, God ensures uniformity in the transmission of the law and greatly minimizes the possibility of variation.[4]

Rabbi Aharon Ibn Chaim, a medieval commentary on the Midrash, chooses a different path. Torah edicts, he says, are generally designed to be understood on different levels by different people, each according to his ability and training. The usual hierarchical mode of Torah transmission took these natural variations into consideration; each group within the nation was trained through the method most appropriate to its level. Deep philosophical currents within the law were transmitted to the scholars, while universal practical considerations were communicated to all.

The concrete regulations of Parshat Kedoshim, however, are unique. Meant to be understood equally by all, they were transmitted to the entire nation on the same level, at once.[5]

The eighteenth-century Chassidic scholar Rabbi Kalonymus Kalman Halevi Epstein perceives within the requirement for full assembly a reflection of the critical concept of communal affiliation. Defending the Chassidic practice of *hitbodedut*, personal isolation, Epstein explains that, at times, an individual must distance himself from society in order to escape its evil influences. Such personal retreat, however, is self-limiting. True sanctity can only be achieved through reconnection with a Torah

---

4. Mizrachi, Vayikra 19:2.
5. Korban Aharon, Vayikra 19:2.

community, through shared experience with others who are also seeking to serve God.

Parshat Kedoshim, the parsha in which God directly challenges the Israelites to "be holy," is therefore transmitted in full assembly. Lest anyone think otherwise, God reminds each individual within the nation that his personal search for sanctity will ultimately require full participation with those around him.[6]

— C

Perhaps, however, the boldest suggestion concerning the transmission of Parshat Kedoshim is introduced by the sixteenth-century scholar Rabbi Moshe Alshich. The Alshich maintains that this parsha is taught in full assembly in order to convey to all those present their equal ability to achieve a life of holiness:

> Certain individuals are gravely mistaken when they claim, "Not all are worthy of this, only one or two in each generation." …That is not so! There is no one within the community of Israel who will fail to succeed, if he wishes to ascend in Torah and piety to the point where he reaches the state of holiness…[7]

God commands Moshe, therefore, to set aside the divisions that normally characterize his teaching of Torah text. This time, the nation will stand together, as equals, when they hear the command *Kedoshim tihiyu*, "Holy shall you be…"[8]

— D

At first glance, however, the Alshich's interpretation seems impossibly utopian. Is it really true that in the realm of sanctity all individuals are created equal? Our own life impressions would clearly indicate otherwise. Religious scholarship, philosophical acumen, even an "aptitude for piety" are possessed by different people in varying degrees. Can any of us, after all, truly

---

6. Maor Va'shemesh, Vayikra 19:2.
7. Torat Moshe, Vayikra 19:2.
8. Vayikra 19:2.

expect to be a Moshe or an Aharon? How can the Alshich seriously suggest that all individuals have an equal ability to achieve holiness?

The key to this approach may well lie in the balance between role and relationship in Jewish thought, a balance reflected in the two different modes of Torah transmission that we have encountered in the course of this study:

1. *In the area of* role *(see Tzav 2), clearly, we are not all created equal.*

As noted previously, many life positions within Jewish experience are automatically assigned at birth. Men and women, for example, are obligated differently under Jewish law. Specific leadership roles, such as the priesthood and the monarchy, are inherited. Arbitrarily assigned, these birth roles are not open to personal choice.

To go a step further, even earned roles, technically open to all, are not, on a practical level, *equally* open to all. Here, biological genetic factors rather than ritual genetic factors are the primary determinants. While all can aspire to Torah learning, for example, not everyone can become a *gadol hador*, the luminary of a generation. Our lives are defined not only by our hopes, aspirations and efforts, but also by the predetermined personal DNA with which we enter the world. Other factors such as the environment into which we are born, the historical period in which we live and the choices made by those who precede us all help determine the specific roles that we ultimately play within our nation's story.

The hierarchical mode of Torah transmission, generally used in the original communication of the law, was structured to preserve and emphasize the critical roles assigned to, or earned by, individuals within Israelite society at the time. The Kohanim, the Leviim and the Elders, who served as ritual representatives of and teachers to the people, thus received a different level of training than the bulk of the nation.

Only if each individual Israelite, at the dawn of our history, acknowledged and embraced his specific role could a structure of communal responsibility be established that would enable the Jewish nation to endure across the generations.

2. *In the area of* relationship *to our Creator, we are all potentially equal.*

Every relationship within human experience is unique, a product of the participants and their singular personalities. Our relationship with God is no exception.

Each of us relates to God as we are: soft or strong, scholar or novice, spiritual or cerebral. In the realm of this relationship, the only yardstick by which we are judged is ourselves. Whatever our life role may be, the strength of our connection to God is determined by how well we fulfill that role and by the personal qualities we demonstrate as we fulfill it.

This is the realm of sanctity, a realm in which we are all potentially equal – the greatest rabbi and the unlearned tradesman, the High Priest in the Sanctuary and the farmer in the field. Sanctity is attained through God's presence in our lives, through the forging of a relationship with the Divine that is unique and specific to each of us.

The Rambam underscores this universal potential for holiness in his review of the laws of *tshuva*: "Every man possesses the capacity to be as righteous as Moshe or as wicked as Yeravam [who rebelled against the Davidic dynasty after Shlomo's death]."[9]

Maimonides does not claim that we can each *be a Moshe* but, rather, that we can each be *as righteous as Moshe*. Just as Moshe reached his potential for holiness, so, too – judged against the backdrop of our own abilities, character and environment – we can each aspire to reach ours.

At the moment of the transmission of Parshat Kedoshim, God commands Moshe to eschew the communal hierarchy and to gather the nation in 'full assembly': *As they hear the commandment "Holy shall you be…," let the cobbler stand shoulder to shoulder with the High Priest; let the blacksmith stand with the Elders; let the unlearned stand with the scholar; that they may know that the search for holiness knows no favorites, that a relationship with their Creator is equally open to all.*

---

9. Rambam, *Mishneh Torah*, Hilchot Tshuva 5:2.

2 Between Children and Parents

Context

After commanding the nation to "be holy," God delineates a series of wide-ranging, important practical laws. The first of these mitzvot reads as follows: "You shall fear,[1] every man, his mother and his father; and you shall keep my Sabbaths; I am the Lord your God."[2]

Questions

Two technical textual questions become immediately obvious upon confronting this text.

In the Ten Declarations of the Sinaitic Revelation, God commanded: "Honor *thy father and thy mother*" (Shmot 20:12). Why, here, does the text invert the parental order and state: "You shall fear, every man, *his mother and his father...*" (Vayikra 19:3).

Even more puzzling is the overall sentence structure before us. Why does the Torah list both the directive to fear one's parents and the directive to honor God's Sabbaths in the same sentence? What is the connection between these two disparate commandments?

If we strike a bit deeper, more basic questions emerge as well.

Why does the Torah open the critical list of laws of Parshat Kedoshim specifically with the exhortations to fear one's parents and to observe God's Sabbaths?

What are the practical halachic parameters of the edict to fear one's parents? Exactly how does this commandment differ from the earlier directive, "Honor your father and your mother," found in the Ten Declarations?

---

1. Though we will be translating *"yirah"* as "fear," this term potentially conveys a spectrum of emotions from "fear" to "awe."
2. Vayikra 19:3.

Approaches

─── **A** ──────────────────────────────────

The two obvious textual questions are immediately addressed by the scholars of the Talmud.

God inverts the parental order within these commandments, the rabbis maintain, in response to a child's natural inclinations. Children tend to honor their mothers more than their fathers and to fear their fathers more than their mothers. To overcome these tendencies, the Torah deliberately "swims against the tide."

In the regulation of honor, the text lists the father first, while in the edict of fear, the mother is recorded first. In this way, the Torah exhorts children to love and to fear their parents equally.[3]

Concerning the mysterious connection established in the text between God's Sabbaths and the parent-child relationship, the rabbis explain that the Torah is actually setting halachic boundaries. A child is obligated, they say, to fear and obey his parents *unless* they instruct him to break God's law (e.g., to desecrate the Sabbath). In such a circumstance, God's standing orders overrule parental directives. Thus, the sentence concludes with the phrase, "I am the Lord your God," implying *both you and your father are obligated to honor Me.*[4]

─── **B** ──────────────────────────────────

The broader question concerning the placement of these edicts at the beginning of Parshat Kedoshim may well be connected to a fascinating pattern noted by the Mishnaic sage Rabbi Levi. Many laws of this parsha, he maintains, are actually a restatement or a reformulation of the Ten Declarations of Sinai,[5] as follows:

───────────

3. Talmud Bavli Kiddushin 30b–31a.
4. Rashi, Vayikra 19:3, referencing Talmud Bavli Yevamot 5b.
5. Midrash Rabba Vayikra 24:5.

Ten Declarations	Parshat Kedoshim
1. I am the Lord your God[6]	I am the Lord your God[7]
2. You shall have no other gods before Me[8]	And molten gods you shall not make for yourselves[9]
3. Do not take the name of the Lord your God in vain[10]	You shall not swear falsely by My name[11]
4. Remember the Sabbath day to keep it holy[12]	And you shall keep My Sabbaths[13]
5. Honor your father and your mother[14]	You shall fear, every man, his mother and his father[15]
6. Do not murder[16]	You shall not stand idly by the blood of your neighbor[17]
7. Do not commit adultery[18]	Both the adulterer and the adulteress shall surely be put to death[19]
8. Do not steal[20]	You shall not steal[21]
9. Do not bear false witness against your friend[22]	You shall not go as a gossipmonger among your people[23]
10. Do not covet...[24]	Love your fellow as yourself[25]

Building on Rabbi Levi's observation, Rabbi David Tzvi Hoffman offers a rationale for the placement of the laws of parental respect at the head of the edicts of Parshat Kedoshim. Man instinctively fears and respects other

---

6.   Shmot 20:2.
7.   Vayikra 19:3.
8.   Shmot 20:3.
9.   Vayikra 19:4.
10. Shmot 20:7.
11. Vayikra 19:12.
12. Shmot 20:8.
13. Vayikra 19:3.
14. Shmot 20:12.
15. Vayikra 19:3.
16. Shmot 20:13.
17. Vayikra 19:16.
18. Shmot 20:13.
19. Vayikra 20:10.
20. Shmot 20:13.
21. Vayikra 19:11.
22. Shmot 20:13.
23. Vayikra 19:16.
24. Shmot 20:14.
25. Vayikra 19:18.

men, says Hoffman, more than he fears and respects an intangible God. The parsha thus opens with the singular human relationship that fashions a child's entrée into his heritage. Parents are God's representatives within a child's world. Not only do they partner in the physical creation of the child, but they are the bearers of the divinely inspired tradition, values and practices that are meant to shape his life (see Yitro 4, *Approaches* B). If a child learns to revere his parents, the Torah implicitly states, he will ultimately learn to revere God.

For similar reasons, continues Hoffman, the Torah immediately moves from the parent-child relationship to the theme of Shabbat: "And you shall keep My Sabbaths." Observance of Shabbat, the concrete sign of God's role as Creator and of His covenant with the Jewish people, serves as a first step on the journey towards a full appreciation of God's sanctity.[26]

Nehama Leibowitz explains Hoffman's position as follows: the Ten Declarations of Sinai are ordered *conceptually*, with the foundational commandment "I am the Lord your God" listed first. The edicts of Parshat Kedoshim, on the other hand, are arranged *educationally*, demonstrating how a personal relationship with God can be attained.[27] In Leibowitz's opinion, the Ten Declarations are not simply repeated at the beginning of Parshat Kedoshim but are, instead, reformulated and ordered from a didactic perspective.

— C —

A review of the texts reveals another purpose to the restatement of the Ten Declarations in Parshat Kedoshim. This crucial repetition enables the Torah to expand on a number of the original Sinaitic laws and translate them into practical terms.

To cite two examples:

1. A reasonable claim could be made that the Sinaitic commandment "You shall not bear false witness against your fellow" refers solely to testimony offered in a formal courtroom proceeding. As seen through the prism of Parshat Kedoshim, however, the prohibition expands to include cases of spreading damaging information about other individuals in any setting.

---

26. Rabbi David Tzvi Hoffman, Vayikra 19:3.
27. Leibowitz, *Iyunim Chadashim B'sefer Vayikra*, p. 223.

2. The "Do not murder" of Sinai would be of only theoretical concern for most readers. How many of us, after all, will ever find ourselves in a situation of potential homicide? The "You shall not stand idly by the blood of your neighbor" of Parshat Kedoshim, however, translates this admonition into eminently practical terms. One can be conceptually guilty of the crime of "murder" not only by doing something horribly wrong but by failing to do something right. The sin of uninvolvement, of failing to aid others in desperate need, is certainly a transgression within the realm of our experience.

Perhaps, however, the most dramatic expansion in the move from Sinai to Kedoshim is found in the laws concerning the parent-child relationship. In this case, the legal formulation in Parshat Kedoshim is not simply an extension of the vision of the original Sinaitic law. Instead, a whole new set of regulations are added to the mix with the admonition "You shall fear, every man, his mother and his father…"

The Talmud quantifies the biblical requirements as follows:

> What is "fear" [i.e., what practical regulations are contained in the Torah's mandate to fear one's parents] and what is "honor" [what practical regulations are contained in the Torah's mandate to honor one's parents]?
>
> "Fear" means that a child should not stand in his parent's designated spot; sit in his parent's designated seat; [publicly] contradict his parent's words; weigh in during a debate between his parent and another individual [even to take his parent's side; such involvement would indicate that the parent requires the child's support].
>
> "Honor" obligates a child to provide his parents with food and drink; to dress and cover them and to bring them in and take them out [provide them with mobility]."[28]

In typical fashion, the Oral Law translates the overarching biblical requirements into measurable behavior. From the Talmudic perspective, two clear sets of practical regulations govern a child's relationship to his parents. The Sinaitic commandment "Honor your father and your mother" demands that a child provide for his parents when they are in need of his care. The

---

28. Talmud Bavli Kiddushin 31b.

commandment "You shall fear, every man, his mother and his father" of Parshat Kedoshim, on the other hand, conveys requirements of respect and reverence. Both commandments are eminently practical, creating clearly delineated responsibilities.

Building upon these regulations, later halachists further define the concrete expectations upon a child vis-à-vis his parents. The first question, for example, raised in the Talmud immediately after the delineation of the requirements of parental honor is: Whose money should be used when a child cares for his parents? Must the child make use of his own funds or can he apply his parents' savings to the task? The scholars conclude, in a decision with far-reaching ramifications that reverberate to this day, that the child may use his parents' funds in the course of their care. If no parental funds are available, however, the child must still provide for his parents through the expenditure of his own funds.[29]

The laws governing the parent-child relationship thus provide a perfect example of the essential intertwining of Written and Oral Law (see *Shmot*: Yitro 5). The Torah lays out the lofty goals of parental honor and respect. From the text alone, however, we would not know what is required of us. It remains for the scholars of the Oral Law to clearly define and quantify the mandates of the Torah in measurable terms which can be fully understood and met. Through their analysis, the biblical commandments of parental honor and respect form a blueprint for one of the most complex and critical relationships in human experience.

Points to Ponder

Sometimes we "don't see the forest for the trees."

Our study has shown that the specific laws derived from the biblical commandments of parental honor and fear are of critical importance. Arguably of even greater significance, however, is the overall dialectic fashioned by these twin commandments. Seen through the prism of Torah law, the parent-child relationship is marked by a delicate balance between honor and fear; between personal closeness and distance.

On one hand, the commandment "Honor your father and your mother" demands that a child personally nurture his parents when they become dependent upon him. While the child's responsibilities towards his parents

---

29. Ibid., 31b–32a.

are clearly meant to mirror the sustenance the child himself should have received during the years of his own dependency, the obligations are unconditional. Regardless of the child's personal relationship with his parents, when the need arises he is obligated to draw close to them, to personally care and provide for their basic needs.

On the other hand, the commandment "You shall fear, every man, his mother and his father" mandates distance between parent and child. From a halachic perspective, *the parent-child relationship is not a relationship of equals*. Instead, the Torah demands that appropriate boundaries between the participants be strictly maintained. Jewish law recognizes a simple truth: *for a parent to be effective as a teacher and role model, he must be his child's parent and not his child's friend*.

I and many of my rabbinic colleagues have noted what we believe to be a pervasive, troubling phenomenon within our respective communities. While our observations are subjective and, for that matter, judgmental, they are worth noting.

Simply put, we find ourselves encountering more and more parents who seem "afraid" to parent their children.

Desirous of their children's affection and intent upon improving upon their own childhood experiences, these parents offer their children unqualified support, nonjudgmental acceptance, material bounty and great behavioral latitude. They often fail, however, to provide structure, clear limits and a sense of personal responsibility. The boundaries between parent and child become increasingly blurred. Consequently many children today grow into adulthood with a dangerously inflated sense of privilege and infallibility.

Centuries ago, the Torah clearly set the framework for a balanced, healthy parent-child relationship. Today that relationship is increasingly under stress.

Our children desperately need parents; they have enough friends.

3 Will the Real Owner Please Stand Up?

Context

The Torah obligates a landowner to a series of five mandatory *matanot la'evyonim*, "gifts to the poor." Four of these obligations are recorded in Parshat Kedoshim:

1. *Leket*: Stalks of grain that fall to the ground during the harvest must be left for collection by the poor.

2. *Peah*: A portion (preferably a corner) of the field must be left unharvested for harvest by the poor.

3. *Olelot*: Small, unformed clusters of grapes must be left on the vine for harvest by the poor.

4. *Peret*: Solitary grapes that fall to the ground during the grape harvest must be left for collection by the poor.[1]

One additional gift is not enumerated in Parshat Kedoshim, but is recorded elsewhere in the text:

5. *Shikcha*: "Forgotten" bushels that remain in the field after the ingathering has been completed must be left for collection by the poor.[2]

These obligations do not apply in our day due to the rabbinic concern, which developed over time, that these gifts would be taken by Gentiles and not left for the poor.[3]

Questions

Why does the Torah obligate a landowner to these specific "gifts" to the poor? In what ways, if any, do *matanot la'evyonim* differ from the general

---

1. Vayikra 19:9–10.
2. Devarim 24:19.
3. Arba Turim, Yoreh Deah 332; Rema, Yoreh De'ah 332:1. The Beit Yosef further explains that, because of these concerns, the poor have long given up hope of receiving these gifts and have thus relinquished all rights to them.

halachic requirement of *tzedaka,* charity, that remains incumbent upon the landowner, as well?[4]

Given that these laws are no longer observed in our day, what, if any, lessons can be learned from their study?

Approaches

—— **A** ——————————————————————————————————

Great attention is paid in the Oral Law, recorded in the Mishna, to the laws of *matanot la'evyonim.* From the rabbinic discussion, a striking distinction emerges between these gifts to the poor and the general obligation of *tzedaka.*

When we enter the world of *matanot la'evyonim,* we enter a world of conflicting potential ownership. Unlike *tzedaka,* which is given by an individual to those in need, these gifts are not "given" by the landowner to the poor. Once specific items attain the status of *matanot la'evyonim* they no longer belong to the landowner but are removed from his possession and placed into a unique ownership category known as *hefker ani'im* (ownerless objects over which only the poor can gain possession). In short, *matanot la'evyonim* are "gifts" legally granted *by God* to the poor.

A fundamental tension is consequently reflected in the extensive Mishnaic discussion on this topic. Exactly what, the rabbis ask, falls into the category of *matanot la'evyonim* and what does not? Where does the landowner's ownership end and the ownership of the poor begin? The scholars recognize that strict guidelines must be drawn to address potentially conflicting claims of ownership between the landowner and the poor.

The Mishna explains, for example, that *leket* includes only "expected loss" and is therefore limited to one or two stalks of grain falling from the farmer's hand at one time. If, for some reason, more than that amount falls at once, the grain remains in the possession of the landowner.[5] Even further, one or two stalks that fall due to unexpected circumstances (e.g.,

---

4. Note: The term *tzedaka* is usually translated as "charity." This translation, however, does not convey the full import of the Torah concept. The root of the word is "justice." That which we generally give to the poor is not "charity" but an obligation arising out of our general responsibility to partner with God in the creation of a just world.
5. Mishna Peah 6:5.

the farmer is stuck by a thorn, causing him to drop the grain in his hand) does not become *leket*.[6]

In the case of *shikcha*, only one or two "forgotten" bundles left behind in one location at the time of ingathering belong to the poor. If a greater number are forgotten they remain in the possession of the landowner.[7]

A landowner does not have the right to designate these "gifts" to specific individuals, even if those individuals are impoverished.[8] God grants equal access to all who are in need to enter the field and collect the material that is now legally theirs. The amount collected by any one individual will depend upon his industriousness.

On another front, the definition of who is "poor" is also discussed in the Mishna, with the rabbis limiting the designation of "poverty" to individuals who lack the funds necessary to provide for a year's worth of food and clothing.[9] Even an otherwise wealthy individual who finds himself temporarily in such a position (e.g., a traveler who is far from his home and has no access to his possessions) is considered "poor" and is entitled to benefit from the *matanot la'evyonim* in the locality in which he finds himself.[10]

These and a myriad of other detailed rulings reflect the unique nature of *matanot la'evyonim* as items that automatically move from the possession of one individual to the possession of another, without direct interaction between the participants. Great care is exhibited by the rabbis to clearly define the boundaries of ownership of these items, in order to protect the rights of both the landowner and the poor.

— **B** —

The fundamental question, however, still remains. Why does the Torah bequeath these specific gifts to the poor? Why not simply obligate the landowner to hand over a designated amount of *tzedaka* to those in need?

---

6. Ibid., 4:10.
7. Ibid., 6:5.
8. Ibid., 5:6.
9. Ibid., 8:8 as explained by Rabbi Shimon of Shantz.
10. Ibid., 5:4.

——C——

The answer lies in recognizing the significant place that *matanot la'evyonim* occupy in the majestic societal vision of Torah law.

Focusing on the phenomenon of land ownership, *the one specific criterion that has, throughout human history, distinguished the "haves" from the "have-nots,"* the law conveys critical lessons for both the landowner and the poor.

Lessons for the Landowner	Lessons for the Poor
1. The land is not truly yours. Your stewardship is contingent upon the divine beneficence of the "true owner of all." The limits of your possession will be marked by the rights of the poor who are granted free entry to the fields to harvest/collect that which is theirs.	1. You are not totally land poor. You have rights to the land and to its produce. You are granted free access to the fields to harvest/collect that which is yours.
2. You do not really need to "have it all." Your life will not be changed by that stalk or bundle that you leave behind. Move on with a full, peaceful heart and allow for collection by those in greater need.	2. "Workfare" and not "welfare" is the order of the day. You should not subsist on handouts from others. Enter "your" field, harvest and collect "your" produce with dignity and self-respect. No one will hand these gifts to you and the amount you acquire will directly depend upon your own industry and diligence.

With sensitivity and balance, the Torah moves to limit the hubris of the landowner and to magnify the dignity and self-reliance of the poor. Properly understood and observed, the visionary laws of *matanot la'evyonim* are designed to lessen the psychic gap between the landed and the landless, thus contributing towards the establishment of a truly just society.

Points to Ponder

While each of the lessons derived from the mitzvot of *matanot la'evyonim* are relevant for our times, one point resonates with particular power.

As indicated in our study, the Torah's demand that the landowner relinquish ownership over portions of his produce is designed to benefit not only the poor but the landowner himself. By forcing the farmer to "let go," the Torah reminds him that he does not really need to "have it all"; happiness will not be found in that last piece of grain, that fallen stalk of wheat.

This paradigm should move us to ask ourselves: *do we really need to "have it all"*? Will the next acquisition, the next addition to the house, the next technological gadget, make the difference that we look for in our lives?

A study performed in the University of Rochester and published in the June 2009 *Journal of Research in Personality* yielded surprising results concerning the relationship between happiness and wealth. Dividing goals into two categories, *extrinsic* (e.g., wealth, fame and personal image) and *intrinsic* (e.g., meaningful relationships, health and personal growth), the study surveyed 147 recent graduates concerning their central life objectives. The researchers discovered that those subjects who focused on and achieved intrinsic goals attained higher levels of self-esteem and a greater sense of well-being. *Those who focused on and attained the extrinsic goals of wealth and fame, on the other hand, experienced higher levels of anxiety and unhappiness.*[11]

In a similar vein, highly acclaimed University of Illinois psychologist Ed Diener, who has been doing research on happiness for more than two decades, maintains: "Materialism is toxic to happiness."[12] Even rich materialists, he concludes, are not as happy as those who care less about getting and spending.[13]

---

11. Christopher P. Niemiec, Richard M. Ryan and Edward L. Deci, "The Path Taken: Consequences of Attaining Intrinsic and Extrinsic Aspirations in Post-College Life," *Journal of Research in Personality* 43 (June 2009): 291–306.
12. Quoted in Marilyn Elias, "Psychologists Now Know What Makes People Happy," *USA Today*, December 8, 2002.
13. Ibid.

Judaism embraces the notion of material success and achievement. The physical world is a gift from God, meant to be appreciated and enjoyed. When, however, material success becomes our central life goal, we doom ourselves to continued frustration. Nothing we have will ever be enough; nothing we attain will satisfy us.

Like the long-ago farmer in that forgotten field, we must come to recognize that true happiness can only be achieved when we learn to "let go."

4 My Brother's Keeper

At the core of Parshat Kedoshim lies a series of interpersonal edicts that serve as the foundation of the Torah's moral code. Each of these laws is powerful in scope and sets off halachic conversations that stretch across the generations.

This study, in which one of these laws will be covered in depth, is meant to serve as a paradigm, demonstrating the continuing ability of Torah and rabbinic law to speak to our ever-changing world.

Context

A dramatic directive with far-reaching ramifications, popularly known as the prohibition of *lifnei iveir* (literally "before the blind"), is one of the many laws presented in Parshat Kedoshim. This mitzva opens a door into the Torah's vast world of interpersonal responsibility.

V'lifnei iveir lo titein michshol, v'yareita mei'Elokecha ani Hashem, "And before the blind you shall not place [literally give] a stumbling block, and you shall fear your God; I am the Lord."[1]

A review of rabbinic literature reveals a three-tiered elaboration of this prohibition.

Level 1. *Do not mislead.* Rashi, quoting a halachic Midrash, immediately expands the mitzva beyond its literal sense, setting the tone for all rabbinic commentary that follows: "[The text also speaks of] someone who is [figuratively] blind to an issue. Do not give someone inappropriate advice."[2]

---

1. Vayikra 19:14.
2. Rashi, Vayikra 19:14; Torat Kohanim, Kedoshim 19:14.

Level 2. *Do not aid someone even in the conscious commission of a sin.* Moving a step further, the Talmud shifts this edict into yet another realm.

> Rabbi Natan stated: From where do we know that one may not extend a cup of wine to a Nazir or the limb of a living animal to a Noachide [each of these individuals is prohibited from consuming the foodstuff in question]? The source is from the verse: "And before the blind you shall not place a stumbling block."[3]

Rabbi Natan fails to distinguish between an intentional and unintentional sinner, thus indicating that *the Torah forbids aiding a sinner even when he is cognizant of his actions.*

Rabbi Natan expands the parameters of the biblical prohibition in other ways as well. By citing the example of a Nazir, he demonstrates that one can even be held guilty under Torah law for aiding in a transgression that does not apply to the abettor himself. After all, while wine is prohibited to the Nazir, it is fully permitted to another Jew. In addition, by choosing the case of a Noachide, Rabbi Natan indicates that the Torah prohibits "placing a stumbling block" before Gentiles as well as Jews.[4]

The full extent of the Torah's ban on actively aiding a sinner is reflected in a Talmudic passage concerning the prohibition of lending or borrowing money on interest. There, the rabbis find both the lender and the borrower guilty not only for the loan itself but also for the crime of *lifnei iveir*. Each participant in the loan is responsible for the role he plays in enabling the other participant to sin through participation in a prohibited transaction.[5]

Level 3. *Do not create an environment that would encourage or lead another to sin.* So great is our interpersonal responsibility, the rabbis maintain, that the Torah forbids not only concrete assistance in another's sin but even any act that potentially promotes another's sin.

---

3. Talmud Bavli Pesachim 22b.
4. Ran, Avoda Zara 6b.
5. Talmud Bavli, Bava Metzia 75b.

The Talmud thus prohibits a parent from striking a grown child because the child might be moved to sin through physical retaliation. The parent transgresses *lifnei iveir* by potentially precipitating a sin on the part of his child.[6]

Another Talmudic passage concerning loans reflects an even more striking iteration of this level of *lifnei iveir*: "Rabbi Yehuda said in the name of Rav: Any individual who possesses money and lends it to another without witnesses is guilty of the crime of 'placing a stumbling block before the blind.'" [The lender's "trusting" actions tempt the borrower to lie and deny the loan.][7]

Questions

What motivates the Midrash, Talmud, Rashi and all subsequent scholars to expand the biblical prohibition of *lifnei iveir* beyond its literal meaning?

Even if we accept the expansion of the prohibition of *lifnei iveir* to the realm of figurative blindness (blindness to an issue; see above *Context*, Level 1), what justifies the Talmudic leap to cases of aiding or even encouraging an intentional sinner? How can someone who is fully cognizant of his actions be considered "blind"?

Generally, Torah prohibitions are directly stated, not couched in poetic or figurative terms. If the Torah wants to state "Do not give inappropriate advice," or "Do not aid a sinner," why not state these prohibitions clearly?

As the rabbis continue to push the boundaries of the prohibition of *lifnei iveir*, the question of limits arises. How responsible must I truly be for the actions of others? At what point, if any, does that responsibility end? What are the full parameters and limits of this seemingly overwhelming biblical edict?

Approaches

—A—

Two textual clues are cited by the commentaries to justify the extension of *lifnei iveir* to cases of figurative blindness.

---

6. Ibid., Moed Katan 17a.
7. Ibid., Bava Metzia 75b.

1. The Torah literally states, *Lo titein michshol*, "Do not *give* a stumbling block [before the blind]" and not, as one would expect, *Lo tasim michshol*, "Do not *place* a stumbling block [before the blind]." The unusual application of the verb *latet* (to give) in this context extends the prohibition beyond the physical realm.[8]

2. The commandment of *lifnei iveir* closes with the seemingly superfluous phrase "And you shall fear your God; I am the Lord."

This admonition appears in the Torah, the rabbis note, only in connection with sins that are not public and concerning which the perpetrator can feel secure in his own perceived anonymity. The Torah therefore warns, "And you shall fear your God; I am the Lord." Rashi elucidates: "*Nothing is hidden from God.*"[9]

The appearance of this warning in connection with the mitzva of *lifnei iveir* is a clear indication that the prohibition extends beyond the physical realm. Only crimes such as misleading another, where guilt depends upon intent known only to the perpetrator and to God, would require this specific admonition.[10]

— B —

The Talmudic leap to cases of aiding even an intentional sinner is addressed by the Rambam in *Sefer Hamitzvot*. "And this prohibition [*lifnei iveir*] also includes someone who aids in or enables the sin of another; for he [the abettor] approaches a person *whose 'sight' has been 'blinded' by desire* and assists him in his transgression."[11]

From the halachic perspective, even an intentional sinner is "blind." Were he fully aware of the consequences of his actions, he would never sin.

— C —

While all elements of *lifnei iveir* are discussed in halachic literature, the greatest volume of rabbinic discussion centers on the issue of aiding or promoting another's sin.

---

8. Torah Temima Vayikra 19:14.
9. Rashi, Vayikra 19:14.
10. Siftei Chachamim, Vayikra 19:14.
11. Rambam, *Sefer Hamitzvot*, negative prohibition 299.

Clearly the guilt of the abettor under the law of *lifnei iveir* does not in any way mitigate the guilt of the sinner. If one, for example, sells a gun to an individual who clearly intends to and subsequently does commit a murder, the murderer remains fully guilty of his crime. The abettor's assistance does not diminish the perpetrator's responsibility. Halacha instead postulates the existence of a separate sin for which the abettor is guilty: the sin of assisting another human being in precipitating his own downfall.

What exactly, however, are the parameters of this prohibition? Under what circumstances should an individual be held culpable for enabling or encouraging the negative acts of another, even when those acts are performed with full cognizance and intent?

A critical, unspoken issue emerges as central to the rabbinic discussion: Is *lifnei iveir* an "*other-directed*" or "*self-directed*" prohibition? Am I enjoined from aiding another in his violation of the law in order to prevent *him* from sinning or because even indirect participation in a sinful act is *detrimental to me*?

The potential ramifications of this question play out in a very practical way. *What is the law*, the rabbis ask, *if the individual can act without my assistance? What if others will help him upon my refusal?* If the mitzva's purpose is to prevent the "other" from sinning, the prohibition against rendering assistance should not apply. This individual will sin whether or not I aid him. If, however, *lifnei iveir* is self-directed, I should be prohibited from rendering assistance even if the sin will occur without my help.

The Talmud weighs in on this issue, indicating that one is only guilty of *lifnei iveir* if the assistance offered is essential to the performance of the act.[12] Not all authorities accept this ruling as definitive, however, and three positions are staked out by the early halachists.

1. A number of authorities maintain that that the biblical prohibition of *lifnei iveir* remains in force under all circumstances, even if the sin can (and conceivably would) be accomplished without my help.

This position is attributed by some commentaries[13] to the Rambam, who, in his halachic works, makes no distinction between situations where

---

12. Talmud Bavli Avoda Zara 6b.
13. Minchat Chinuch, negative commandment 232:3; Melamed L'ho'il 1:34.

the abettor's assistance is crucial to the performance of the crime and situations where it is not.[14]

In his halachic code, the *Shulchan Aruch*, Rabbi Yosef Caro appears to adopt this position as law.[15]

2. Other scholars, including the Ran[16] and one opinion cited in Tosafot,[17] argue that while the biblical prohibition of *lifnei iveir* is limited to situations where the abettor's assistance is necessary for the performance of the forbidden act, *rabbinic law enacts a prohibition even when that assistance is not essential.*

From the perspective of these rabbis, the very act of assisting in the performance of a forbidden act should itself be prohibited, regardless of whether or not the act could be performed without the abettor's assistance. One who aids a sinner under these circumstances, they maintain, transgresses a rabbinic (rather than a biblical) law. This rabbinic prohibition is often referred to by the title *mesayeia yedei ovrei aveira,* "aiding the hands of those who sin."

3. Finally, a third position, elucidated by another opinion in Tosafot,[18] maintains that if the sinner can perform his act unassisted or if there are others available to assist him, neither a biblical nor a rabbinic prohibition of *lifnei iveir* applies.

In his gloss to the *Shulchan Aruch*, Rabbi Moshe Isserles codifies this position as law. He recommends, however, that "pious people" should act in accordance with the more stringent positions and avoid assisting the sin of another under any circumstance.[19]

With few exceptions, later scholars accept that the biblical prohibition of *lifnei iveir* only applies when the abettor's assistance is necessary. *When the sinner can act independently, at most the rabbinic prohibition of* mesayeia *(aiding the hands of those who sin; see above) applies.* This halachic approach reduces the stringency of the problem and allows for greater leniency in exceptional cases.

---

14. Rambam, *Sefer Hamitzvot*, negative commandment 299; *Mishneh Torah*, Hilchot Rotzeiach U'shmirat Nefesh 12:12–13.
15. Shulchan Aruch, Yoreh Deah, 151:1.
16. Ran, Talmud Bavli Avoda Zara 6b.
17. Tosafot, Talmud Bavli Shabbat 3:1.
18. Tosafot, Talmud Bavli Avoda Zara 6:2.
19. Hagot HaRema, Yoreh Deah 151:1; see Orach Chaim 163.

Some authorities add the caveat, however, that if the only other course available to the sinner is assistance from another Jew, the enabler cannot use the excuse that his assistance is unnecessary. Since, one way or the other, the sinner can only perform the act with the assistance of a Jew (upon whom the prohibition of *lifnei iveir* falls), any Jew who offers assistance is biblically liable.[20]

— **D** —————————————————————————————

As the laws of *lifnei iveir* and *mesayeia* are applied to practical circumstances in each generation, additional refinements are proposed and debated by the rabbis. These refinements focus on the variables present in each specific case, such as the biblical or rabbinic status of the event, the character of the sinner, the nature of the sin, the relationship between the assistance and the sin.

As always, these rabbinic discussions and decisions reflect the great care and thought given to every detail in the ongoing application of Jewish law.

Rabbi Shabtai ben Meir Hakohen (the Shach), for example, in his classical commentary on the *Shulchan Aruch*, maintains that the rabbinic extension of *mesayeia* (the rabbinic prohibition that applies in cases where the sinner can act independently) is variably applied, dependent on the character of the sinner.

If the sinner is another Jew, whom I am obligated to separate from sin, I may not aid him even if my assistance is superfluous. If, however, the sinner is a non-Jew or an apostate, I bear no active responsibility to prevent him from sinning and I may, therefore, lend assistance in a case where he can act independently. In such circumstances, even the rabbinic law of *mesayeia* does not apply. [21]

The Dagul Mei'rivava goes one step further, interpreting the Shach to mean that any person who knowingly violates a law is considered an "apostate" with regard to that law. *Under circumstances where the sinner can act independently I am therefore never forbidden from aiding him in an intentional sin.* One could, for example, according to the Dagul Mei'rivava, sell nonkosher meat to an otherwise religious Jew who knowingly intends to

———————————————
20. Mishneh L'melech, Hilchot Malveh V'loveh 4:2.
21. Shach, Yoreh Deah 151:6.

eat that meat, as long as the same type of meat is available elsewhere. Since the sinner performs the act intentionally, he is considered an apostate and the rabbinic law does not apply.[22] (If this type of meat is not available elsewhere, however, selling to the Jew would be prohibited under the stricter biblical law of *lifnei iveir*.)

At the opposite end of the spectrum, other classical commentaries on the *Shulchan Aruch*, including the Magen Avraham and the Vilna Gaon, disagree with the foundation of the Shach's position. *One is rabbinically prohibited, they insist, from aiding even an apostate or a non-Jew in the commission of a sin, even if the assistance is not critical to the act.*[23]

In a responsa concerning work given in advance to a print shop that employs Jewish workers and is open on Shabbat, Rabbi Yaakov Ettlinger first establishes that the existence of other customers places the issue within the rabbinic realm of *mesayeia*. The abettor's assistance, in this case, is not essential to the sin. If the shop workers do not work on this individual's order on Shabbat, they will work on someone else's. Rabbi Ettlinger then focuses upon the relationship between the "aid" and the "sin." Unlike the biblical prohibition of *lifnei iveir*, he maintains, the rabbinic law of *mesayeia yedei ovrei aveira* only applies when the aid is given directly at the time of the transgression or is specifically requested by the sinner for a later date. One is therefore allowed to patronize an establishment that hires Jews and is open on Shabbat as long as the work involved will not definitely be done by Jews on Shabbat.[24] Using similar logic, the Netziv allows a rabbi to officiate at the marriage of a couple who he knows will not observe the laws of family purity in the future.[25]

In a bold stroke, a number of authorities suggest that the rabbinic prohibition of *mesayeia* be set aside in situations where indirect participation in one sin actually reduces the overall scope of possible sins involved. Rabbi Moshe Feinstein, for example, rules that one may cater an event that will feature non-halachic socialization. Failure to do so, he says, will cause the consumers to select another caterer with less stringent kashrut standards.[26] Similarly, the Avnei Nezer permits the sale of improperly slaughtered

---

22. Dagul Mei'rivava commenting on Shach, Yoreh Deah 151:6.
23. Magen Avraham 347:4; Biur HaGra, Yoreh Deah 151:8.
24. Binyan Tzion 1:15.
25. Meishiv Davar 232.
26. Igrot Moshe, Yoreh Deah 1:72.

animals to a habitual sinner in order to avoid his transgressing the more numerous prohibitions entailed in eating meat of a nonkosher species.[27]

Leniency is suggested by the former Sephardic chief rabbi of Israel, Rabbi Ovadia Yosef, concerning cases of *lifnei iveir* where the "sin" in question originates from a relatively weak halachic source. Rabbi Yosef rules, for example, that meat may be sold to Jewish customers during the nine-day period prior to Tisha B'Av, when the consumption of meat is halachically contraindicated, even if the butcher suspects that these customers will eat the meat during the prohibited period. Since the status of the prohibition is only a *minhag* (an obligatory custom), as opposed to a biblically or rabbinically ordained law, the concern of *mesayeia* can be set aside in the face of the butcher's concerns over a potential loss of customers.[28]

Countless other discussions and decisions mark the ongoing halachic effort to define and apply the laws of *lifnei iveir* and *mesayeia* to everyday experience.

— **E** —————————————————————————

Some observers have suggested that, at a certain level, the entire Torah can be viewed as God's response to Kayin's challenge, thrust heavenward at the dawn of human history: "Am I my brother's keeper?"

Laws such as the edict of *lifnei iveir*, with their overarching message of interpersonal responsibility, loudly proclaim: *Yes, as a matter of fact, you are!*

Points to Ponder

The strength of Jewish law lies in its continuing ability to speak to changing times and circumstances (see *Shmot*: Yitro 5). The biblical prohibition of *lifnei iveir* and the rabbinic extension of *mesayeia* are perfect examples of this evolutionary vigor.

Two practical cases, chosen from a myriad of possibilities, demonstrate the relevance of these laws to modern concerns.

1. *Is one permitted to extend personal or public invitations that will potentially cause Jews to travel, in non-halachic fashion, on Shabbat or Jewish festivals?*

---

27. Avnei Nezer, Yoreh Deah 126.
28. Yechaveh Da'at 3:38.

For decades, this question has been raised by observant Jews seeking to invite less observant relatives or friends to a Pesach Seder, a bar/bat mitzvah or a simple Shabbat meal.

Today, however, this issue acquires greater urgency in light of the established Jewish community's efforts at outreach to the vast population of unaffiliated Jews. Recognizing that even a one-time Shabbat or festival experience can be of critical educational benefit, numerous organizations and synagogues have embarked on programs specifically designed to attract less observant Jews to their doors. In many cases, at least a portion of the target audience will drive to the event.

The question is thus raised: *does the potential benefit of participation in these events outweigh the encouragement of sin?*

In a series of responsa, the preeminent halachic arbiter of twentieth-century American Jewry, Rabbi Moshe Feinstein, takes a restrictive view. Postulating that public events that knowingly encourage the desecration of Shabbat enter the realm of active religious subversion, Rav Moshe explicitly prohibits the issuance of invitations to such events.[29]

The equally respected twentieth–twenty-first-century Israeli halachist Rabbi Shlomo Zalman Auerbach, on the other hand, suggests a potential leniency. If the "host" sincerely offers Shabbat or festival lodging as part of the invitation, even with the full expectation that the offer will be declined, the problems are mitigated. The offer of housing places the onus directly on the invitee and removes the concern for *lifnei iveir*. If the individual chooses to drive under these circumstances, the choice is his own and the abettor is no longer involved.[30]

While some authorities accept Rabbi Auerbach's leniency only in personal cases, others make use of it for communal events, as well.

In yet another responsa concerning Shabbat invitations, Rabbi Moshe Sternbuch suggests a revolutionary approach to the entire prohibition of *lifnei iveir*. Responding to a query from an individual concerning the permissibility of inviting non-observant parents to a Shabbat meal in the hope of their eventual increased observance, Sternbuch melds the tiers of the biblical prohibition. Fundamentally, he maintains, the mandate of *lifnei*

---

29. Igrot Moshe, Orach Chaim 1:98–99.
30. In a letter written to the administration of Yeshivat Ohr Somayach in Yerushalayim recorded in J. David Bleich, *Contemporary Halakhic Problems*, vol. 4 (New York: Ktav Publishing House, 1995), p. 103.

iveir, in all of its facets, is *do no conscious harm*. Just as one transgresses the ban on giving false advice only if the deceit is deliberate, similarly, an abettor is only culpable for assisting in a sin when his ultimate intent is to hurt the sinner. In a situation, however, where the abettor's true goal is to benefit the sinner, no prohibition applies. One would, therefore, be allowed to issue Shabbat and festival invitations, as long as the intended purpose was to eventually benefit the invitee.[31]

Rabbi J. David Bleich, rosh yeshiva at Yeshiva University and professor of law at Cardozo School of Law, maintains that Sternbuch's position is "not supported by the sources that serve to define the prohibition." Bleich does acknowledge the relationship between Sternbuch's ideas and the earlier mentioned suggestions of leniency when indirect participation in one sin reduces the possibility of future sins (see *Approaches* C). He expresses doubt, however, as to whether this reasoning applies in cases of deeply uncertain potential benefit, such as the tentative possibility of increased religious observance on the part of the recipient of a Shabbat invitation.[32]

Two responsa printed through Eretz Chemda, a renowned Israeli rabbinic academy, go one step further. The authors of these responsa suggest that, in the face of the grave dangers posed to Jewish survival by the specter of assimilation, the Jewish community should, perhaps, "turn a blind eye" and not discourage the attendance of those who will drive to services and events on Shabbat. This is particularly true, these scholars maintain, when the alternative for this population would be to travel to other, less meaningful, destinations on the festivals and Shabbat. The authors do counsel, however, that such decisions carry weighty public ramifications and should be considered and applied with great caution.[33]

We can fully expect this debate to continue as outreach to the unaffiliated becomes even more critical in the years to come.

2. The advent of the "information age" has created lines of interpersonal connectivity that scarcely could have been imagined in years past. The application of laws such as *lifnei iveir* becomes infinitely more complex in a world where one's actions can have an immediate and powerful bearing on countless anonymous "others" across the globe. One of the many possible

---

31. Tshuvot V'hanhagot 1:358.
32. Bleich, *Contemporary Halakhic Problems*, vol. 4, p. 98.
33. She'eilot U'tshuvot Bamareh Habazak 1:31; 3:37.

scenarios created by this new reality gives rise to the following question: *is one permitted to operate an on-line business that will potentially be accessed by Jews on Shabbat or the festivals?*

The authors of yet another responsa printed through Eretz Chemda postulate a distinction between Internet sites offering a unique product and sites whose focus is more generic. If customers can access the same product from other (particularly non-Jewish) sites, the abettor's involvement is not essential and the biblical prohibition of *lifnei iveir* does not apply. Once the concern is reduced to the rabbinic level of *mesayeia*, leniency can be suggested, based upon the conscious nature of the customer's act, the lack of temporal linkage between the aid and the sin, the lack of certainty that Jews will indeed access the site on Shabbat, the passive character of the abettor's involvement at the time of the sin, etc.

The authors conclude, however, that before ruling on the permissibility of operating an on-line business on Shabbat or the festivals, other halachic concerns beyond *lifnei iveir* and *mesayeia* must be considered, as well. These include the prohibition of conducting a business on Shabbat and/or benefiting from such a business.[34]

From Sinai to cyberspace, Torah law guides our efforts to define the boundaries of interpersonal responsibility in a world of ever-increasing interpersonal connection.

---

34. Ibid., 3:37.

4b When Prohibitions Collide

Two sentences after the Torah's mandate of *Lifnei iveir lo titein michshol* (which includes the prohibition of misleading another, even through the passive withholding of vital information;[1] see previous study), the text delineates an equally powerful, far-reaching directive: *Lo telech rachil b'amecha*, "Do not travel as a gossipmonger among your people."

From this commandment and other sources in the Torah the rabbis identify three levels of prohibited interpersonal speech as falling under the general prohibition of *rechilut* (gossip).

1. *Motzi shem ra*, slander: The most severe form of prohibited interpersonal speech: the intentional spreading of damaging untruths about another individual.

2. *Lashon hara*, evil speech: The spreading of damaging information about another individual, even if the information is true.

3. *Rechilut*, gossip: The sharing of any personal information about another individual outside of that individual's presence, if there is the slightest chance that the information shared will result in the creation of ill will.

Rabbinic literature is replete with references concerning the tragic effects of unfettered speech (see Tazria-Metzora 3, *Approaches* D, E). The prevalence of this phenomenon (we are almost all guilty of the transgressions of prohibited speech) combines with the terrible damage that can be wrought upon the lives of others to make the ongoing effect of these sins particularly devastating.

What should our posture be, however, when the prohibition against *rechilut* conflicts with the prohibition of *lifnei iveir*; when information is

---

1. Talmud Bavli Moed Katan 5a.

requested of us, the sharing of which might be damaging to one individual while the withholding of which might be damaging to another?

What if, for example, I am requested to give a job reference concerning an acquaintance and the information to which I am privy will be harmful to the candidate? What if I am asked by a friend concerning a budding romantic relationship and, again, the information that I would share would be less than flattering?

The responses of halacha to these commonly occurring dilemmas are complex and vary on a case–by-case basis, as the law struggles to reconcile the conflicting demands of these two significant mitzvot.

Four commonsense rules, however, can be helpful as a guide in all cases.

1. *Explore the motivations*: What is the impetus behind our intent to share this information? Are we motivated in any way by jealousy or personal animus? Are we fully aware of the underlying forces that drive us to speak?

2. *Study the facts*: Are we certain of the veracity of information that we intend to share? What is the nature of our sources? Too often, damaging hearsay is repeated as fact, with devastating consequences.

3. *Examine the relevance*: Is the information we plan to share relevant to the situation at hand? Are we limiting our response to the necessary information or are we adding and embellishing beyond the essential facts?

4. *Seek halachic counsel*: Many of us tend to request halachic guidance only in areas of ritual concern such as kashrut and Shabbat. Jewish law, however, is meant to serve as a guide in all arenas of life, particularly when it comes to our ethical and moral behavior.

Seeking appropriate halachic counsel before we speak about others is a sensible, often necessary step. Words, once spoken, can never be fully retracted. On the other hand, the failure to share warranted information can cause irreparable damage to the unsuspecting. The burden of our intended action or inaction should, therefore, weigh heavily upon us. Decisions should not be made in haste, but only after due deliberation. Consultation with the proper halachic advisor can help grant perspective, allowing the wide-ranging experience of Jewish law to inform those decisions.

Great caution must be exercised when the prohibitions of *lifnei iver* and *rechilut* collide. The welfare of others hangs in the balance.

5 An Impossible Directive?

Context

Roughly midpoint in the text of the Torah, at the culmination of the series of vital interpersonal laws of Parshat Kedoshim, lies a three-word mandate considered by sages such as Hillel[1] and Rabbi Akiva[2] to be the foundation of all Torah law: *V'ahavta l'reiacha kamocha*, "And you shall love your fellow as yourself."[3]

Questions

How can the Torah demand the impossible? How can God insist that I should love everyone – even a passing acquaintance or, for that matter, even a stranger – as I love myself? Such a requirement seems well beyond our reach.

To go a step further, as many sages note, this demand is not only antithetical to human nature but *contrary to practical halachic dictate.* The Ramban[4] points out that the very same Rabbi Akiva, who considers this commandment to be "the fundamental rule of the Torah,"[5] elsewhere maintains: "*Your life takes precedence over the life of your friend.*"[6]

Practical application of this latter mandate, the Talmud explains, indicates that if two individuals are traveling in the desert and one of them carries a flask that holds enough water for only one to survive and reach civilization, the individual who possesses the water should not share with

---

1. Talmud Bavli Shabbat 31a.
2. Talmud Yerushalmi Nedarim 9:4.
3. Vayikra 19:18.
4. Ramban, Vayikra 19:18.
5. Talmud Yerushalmi Nedarim 9:4.
6. Talmud Bavli Bava Metzia 62a.

his co-traveler. His own need to survive takes precedence over any responsibility he might have towards his fellow.[7]

We are thus faced, the Ramban argues, with a clear halachic contradiction…

If the Torah's commandment of V'ahavta literally means that I must "love my fellow as [I love] myself," I should have no right to withhold lifesaving sustenance from another, even at the cost of my own survival. I should be required to consider his immediate welfare as precious to me as my own![8]

Approaches

— A ——

Rabbinic recognition of the difficulties inherent in the commandment V'ahavta l'reiacha kamocha is evidenced in a number of sources.

When, for example, a potential convert demands to be taught the entire Torah "while standing on one foot," Hillel chooses this commandment as the foundation all of Jewish law. He does not, however, quote the text directly. Instead, he transposes the directive into the more palatable (and limited) negative: "What is hateful to you do not do to your fellow."[9]

Elsewhere, the rabbis find concrete application for the edict of V'ahavta in disparate areas ranging from marriage to capital punishment.[10] Their search appears to mirror a desire to find distinct, limited spheres of law where the text's formulation can be applied without contradicting other halachic precepts.

— B ——

Can, however, the sweeping majesty of this edict, described by Rabbi Akiva as *the* fundamental precept of the Torah, be preserved?

Can the text be understood as written, without editorial change and without limiting its application to narrow areas of the law?

---

7. Ibid.
8. Ramban, Vayikra 19:18.
9. Talmud Bavli Shabbat 31a.
10. Talmud Bavli Kiddushin 41a; Nidda 17a; Ketubot 37b; Sanhedrin 45a.

— **C** —————————————————————————————

Some scholars maintain that the problems associated with the text should be addressed through a simple change of focus. The term *kamocha*, "as yourself," they claim, is not an adverb defining the boundaries of commanded love (as in: love your fellow "as you love yourself"). It is, instead, an adjective delineating the basis of fellowship (as in: love your fellow "who is as yourself"). Since all men are created in the image of God,[11] the Torah maintains, all are *kamocha*, "similar to you," and all are, therefore, deserving of your love.[12]

This approach avoids the issues raised above. The text is not commanding us to love others as we love ourselves, a commandment problematic in both behavioral and halachic terms. The Torah is instead informing us why we should love others in the first place: *"Love your fellow," who is, after all, "as yourself" – created, like you, in God's image and, therefore, worthy of your love.*

Nehama Leibowitz finds support for this approach in a similar biblical passage: "The stranger [convert] who dwells with you shall be like the native-born among you; and you shall love him *kamocha*, as yourself, for you were strangers in the land of Egypt."[13]

In this case, Leibowitz maintains, the last phrase of the commandment clearly reflects back on the meaning of the term *kamocha*. Effectively, the text states: *You should love the stranger, for he is like you. After all, you were once strangers in the land of Egypt.*[14]

— **D** —————————————————————————————

Other authorities, including the Ramban and the Chizkuni, choose another, bolder, path.

They maintain that the commonly accepted translation of the phrase "*V'ahavta l'reiacha kamocha*" is incorrect. Had the Torah meant to say, "Love your fellow, as yourself," the text should have read: *V'ahavta <u>et</u> reiacha kamocha.*"

---

11. Bereishit 5:1.
12. Naphtali Herz Wessely, *Biur*, Vayikra 19:18.
13. Vayikra 19:34.
14. Nehama Leibowitz, *Iyunim Chadashim B'sefer Vayikra*, p. 301.

Literally, as written, the text before us translates as "Love *for* your fellow, as *for* yourself."[15]

An overwhelmingly powerful lesson is thus transmitted by this passage, as explained by the Ramban:

> Sometimes an individual may wish well for his fellow only in specific areas. He may wish him wealth but not wisdom and the like; and, even if he wishes him well in all areas – desiring that his beloved fellow attain wealth, honor, learning and wisdom – *he will still not want him to achieve the same level that he, himself, achieves. He will still desire to be superior to his fellow* [my italics].
>
> The Torah, therefore, commands that the individual eradicate such selfish jealousy from his heart; that he should love [desire] well for his friend – as he would want for himself – without limits or reservations.[16]

Through the eyes of these scholars, the Torah is not demanding the impossible – only the overwhelmingly difficult. Capping the list of interpersonal laws of Parshat Kedoshim is the one commandment that sums them all up: *Truly desire for others what you desire for yourself.*

If you can achieve that level of love, all the other obligations between you and those around you will be easily met.

Points to Ponder

Sometimes limiting the scope can increase the burden...

By placing the commandment of *V'ahavta l'reiacha kamocha* within our reach, scholars such as the Ramban and the Chizkuni actually make the Torah's demands upon us more difficult. As long as the commandment remained impossible to attain, we were "safe." We could be proud to be part of a people whose tradition included this wonderful idea of *V'ahavta l'reiacha kamocha*, yet avoid its practical implications. We could repeat the words as a litany, admire their poetic majesty; but remain beyond their claim on our behavior. Who, after all, could possibly be expected to love someone as himself? Clearly, the Torah could not be talking to us.

---

15. Ramban, Vayikra 19:18, Chizkuni, Vayikra 19:18.
16. Ramban, ibid.

Our escape is thwarted, however by the rereading of the text.

Truly desire for others what you desire for yourself.

This commandment is attainable, albeit with great difficulty. Conformance requires the cultivation of the purest of hearts; a soul that can truly rejoice in the success and happiness of others without the taint of jealousy. It means that a student rejected for medical school must be as happy over the admission of his friend as if he, himself, had made the grade; that a young single man or woman, actively seeking a *shidduch* (marital match), must rejoice wholeheartedly at the wedding of his/her friend; that an individual denied a promotion must feel gratitude for the promotion of his colleagues to that very same spot.

The challenge is far from easily met, but the potential rewards are great. If each of us cultivates a heart that truly desires for others what we desire for ourselves – without jealousy, bitterness and rancor – we will each learn to rest easy with our own life accomplishments, as well.

5b A Strange Segue

Arguably the strangest textual transition within the Torah is found immediately after the towering commandment of *V'ahavta l'reiacha kamocha*. No sooner does the Torah state this mandate, capping off a series of foundational interpersonal laws, when the text continues: *Et chukotai tishmoru*, "Observe my statutes; you shall not breed your animal in a mixture of species, you shall not plant your field with mixed seed, and a garment that is *shaatnez*, a mixture of combined fibers, shall not come upon you."[1]

With these commandments the Torah not only shifts gears but abruptly moves us to a different world. From one sentence to the next, we are thrust from the sensible, logical realm of *mishpatim* (mitzvot that are easily understandable) into the sphere of *chukim* (mitzvot for which no reason is given in the text and which seem to defy logical explanation; see *Shmot*: Teruma 3).

Why does the Torah move so abruptly from the most overarching ethical law of the text, the law which Rabbi Akiva refers to as "the fundamental rule of the Torah,"[2] to some of Jewish law's most mysterious ritual edicts, the regulations of forbidden mixtures? These themes have no apparent philosophical connection. Why, then, does the Torah forcibly connect them in the text?

Perhaps the simplest answer is that the Torah is consciously contradicting the basic premise of our question, informing us that the question is not really a question at all.

---

1. Vayikra 19:19.
2. Talmud Yerushalmi Nedarim 9:4.

181

The Torah orchestrates the seemingly abrupt journey from mishpatim *to* chukim *to demonstrate that the journey is not abrupt, that there is no gap between these two sets of laws in the first place.* All mitzvot, from the ethical to the ritual, are to be observed because they are divinely commanded decrees. All emerge from the same source at Sinai and all, from the majestic commandment of *V'ahavta* to the mysterious commandment of *shaatnez,* are essential components in the tapestry of our tradition.

Emor

אמור

CHAPTER 21:1–24:23

פרק כא:א-כד:כג

Parsha Summary

Sanctified persons, sanctified times...

Once again, the text takes an abrupt turn as Parshat Emor opens.

God commands Moshe to instruct the Kohanim concerning a number of obligations specific to their priestly role. Included are the prohibition of involvement with death and burial (except in cases of the death of immediate relatives); the prohibition of marrying a divorcee; laws concerning blemishes that disqualify a Kohen from active service in the Sanctuary and specific laws of tuma *and* tahara *(ritual impurity and purity). Outlined, as well, are the even more severe restrictions applying to the Kohen Gadol.*

The text then outlines specific laws of korbanot, *including a list of blemishes disqualifying animals from serving as sacrifices and the prohibition of slaughtering an animal and its offspring on the same day.*

An abrupt textual transition takes place yet again as the Torah turns its attention to the yearly calendar cycle. The biblical holy occasions – Shabbat, Pesach, the counting of the Omer, Shavuot, Rosh Hashana, Yom Kippur, Succot and Shmini Atzeret – are all mentioned and discussed (with the exception of Shmini Atzeret, which is only noted in passing).

The parsha continues with laws concerning the Menora and the Showbread in the Sanctuary.

Finally, Parshat Emor describes a tragic episode of public blasphemy and its aftermath.

1 A Decades-Old Bar Mitzva Challenge

Context and Questions

A personal reflection...

Parshat Emor is my bar mitzva parsha. Over the years it has served me well. Since sections of this parsha are read during the yearly festival cycle, I quickly realized that I, a youngster who enjoyed the spotlight but was not particularly industrious, could be a "star" without much effort. I was able to volunteer for those public holiday readings in the synagogue without extra preparation.

At the same time, however, another section of Emor's text disturbed me greatly the first time I read it. In this parsha, the Torah lists, at length, a series of personal blemishes and injuries that disqualify a Kohen from the active priesthood.[1]

How could Jewish law, I wondered as a bar mitzva, be so painfully (to use current vernacular) politically incorrect? Why should a Kohen be barred from serving in the Temple through no fault of his own, simply because he is not physically perfect?

My questions, latent over the years, came to a head with the preparation of this volume. In previous volumes, I had deliberately tackled the tough issues, choosing sections of the text that I felt could not be ignored. How could I now ignore a segment in my own bar mitzvah parsha that called out for explanation?

The time had come to confront the challenge of Parshat Emor...

Approaches

— A —

Initially, my foray into the world of commentary concerning the blemished Kohanim met with general silence. Few, if any, of the classical commentaries seemed to be bothered by my questions at all.

---

1. Vayikra 21:16–24.

Faced with their silence, I began to wonder what I might be missing. What was problematic to me was clearly not problematic to Rashi, the Ramban, the Ibn Ezra and to so many others.

Perhaps, as Rabbi Eliyahu Mizrachi seems to suggest, the classical commentaries view the rules concerning the Kohanim simply as an extension of the regulations that govern the sacrifices that they offer. Just as the *korbanot* brought to the Sanctuary must be whole and unblemished,[2] so, too, those performing the sacrificial rites must be physically flawless, as well.[3] The connection between these two sets of regulations is, after all, underscored by the fact that they are both recorded in Parshat Emor.

Or, perhaps, an answer lies in the terse observation that is offered by Rashi on the second sentence of this passage. Commenting on the sentence *Ki kol ish...*, "For any man, in whom there is a blemish shall not approach...," Rashi simply explains: "It is not proper that he [the blemished Kohen] should approach..."[4]

Numerous commentaries explain that Rashi views this sentence as offering a rationale, of sorts, for the laws concerning the blemished Kohanim.[5] Perhaps, as later scholars suggest, the Torah simply demands that we show God the same respect that we would show for an earthly king. Just as a monarch of flesh and blood would not be waited upon by servants with obvious physical afflictions, so too, the divine King of Kings should be served by those who are physically unblemished.[6]

Such approaches require, of course, that we set our modern sensibilities aside. At issue here are neither the rights nor the feelings of the blemished priests. The privilege of serving in the Sanctuary is a divinely determined opportunity granted only to a select few. Just as the vast majority of the Jewish nation is denied that right – for no reason other than they are not Kohanim – so, too, the blemished Kohanim are now excluded, as well.

The classical commentaries clearly understood a truth that I was having trouble accepting since my bar mitzvah. *God's choices need not, and will not, always comply with human logic and sensibility.*

---

2. Ibid., 22:20–25.
3. Mizrachi, Vayikra 21:18.
4. Rashi, Vayikra 21:18.
5. Siftei Chachamim, Vayikra 21:18; Mizrachi, Vayikra 21:18.
6. Torat Moshe, Vayikra 21:18.

Underscoring this point, a later scholar, Rabbi Baruch Halevi Epstein, offers an explanation for the strange textual flow with which this section opens:

> And the Lord spoke to Moshe saying: "Speak to Aharon saying: Any man of your offspring throughout the generations in whom there would be a blemish shall not come near to offer the bread of his God. For any man [*Ki kol ish*] in whom there is a blemish shall not approach…"[7]

As a rule, notes Epstein, biblical phrases beginning with the word *ki* ("for" or "because"), in contexts such as this, are designed to offer explanations, to suggest reasons. Rashi, as indicated above, does, in fact, interpret this verse as suggesting a rationale (albeit an arbitrary one) for these laws. Epstein, however, sees in this sentence a reiteration of the law rather than an explanation. Why, he asks, is such reiteration necessary? Even further, why does the text indicate that it is about to give a rationale for these edicts, yet ultimately offers no real rationale at all?

Perhaps, reasons Epstein, the text, through omission, makes an emphatic point: *Concerning the laws of the blemished Kohanim, no rationale is available to man. Any attempt at understanding, in fact, will not only prove futile, but will jeopardize the very performance of the mitzva itself.* The Torah therefore deliberately introduces the arena of logic and reason, but fails to provide any answers. There are times when we should make no attempt to understand that which lies beyond our ken.[8]

Strangely enough, my discovery of Epstein's comments reassured me. A warning in the Torah against the search for a rationale concerning specific laws, is, after all, a clear indication that those very laws might be troubling to the mind of the reader. Clearly, I was not alone in my questioning.

—— **B** ——————————————————————————

I determined to search further, to discover whether any other commentaries had additional views on these issues.

My search revealed a few isolated suggestions.

---

7. Vayikra 21:16–18.
8. Tosefet Bracha, Vayikra 21:17–18.

Rabbi Avraham Shmuel Binyamin Sofer, for example, the nineteenth-century scholar known as the Ktav Sofer (after his work of that name), is among a group of scholars who are unwilling to accept that a merciful God would exclude Kohanim from serving within the Temple simply because they are physically blemished. Instead, this scholar maintains, the afflictions listed in the Torah invariably reflect the presence of deeper spiritual shortcomings on the part of the affected Kohanim. These internal failings are the true cause of their exclusion from the Temple service.[9]

Centuries earlier, the Kli Yakar makes an even more daring assertion. He notes that the passage concerning blemishes actually opens in the future tense: "Any man of your [Aaron's] offspring throughout the generations in whom *there will be* a blemish..."

The sages of the Temple period, claims the Kli Yakar, possessed the unique ability to predict the development of specific physical maladies on the basis of existing spiritual shortcomings. The Torah, therefore, prohibits the participation of even those Kohanim in whom *there will be* a blemish. Priests who are identified by the sages as spiritually incomplete and destined to become blemished are thus to be excluded even before the physical affliction appears. Unlike the Ktav Sofer, however, the Kli Yakar recognizes the existence of some physical blemishes, independent of spiritual shortcomings.[10]

The contemporary scholar Harav Shlomo Aviner perceives in the exclusion of Kohanim with physical blemishes a critical lesson concerning the relationship between physical and spiritual well-being. True holiness is founded, says Aviner, upon completeness in all aspects of life. Thus the Talmud maintains: "The Holy One Blessed Be He only [fully] rests his presence upon [an individual who is, at once] wise, strong, wealthy and humble."[11]

In the search for a sanctified life, one must strive for wisdom, health, material self-sufficiency and moral purity. Representing this search in the Temple, therefore, will be only those Kohanim who are visibly "complete."[12]

---

9. Ktav Sofer, Vayikra, Emor.
10. Kli Yakar, Vayikra 21:17.
11. Talmud Bavli Nedarim 38a.
12. Shlomo Chaim Hakohen Aviner, *Tal Chermon*, translated by Bracha Slae (Jerusalem: privately printed, 1985).

— **C** ———————————————————————————

Perhaps the most refreshing answers to my bar mitzva questions, however, actually came from a source much closer to home.

When I shared my decades-old quandary concerning Parshat Emor with my wife, Barbara, she suggested that we look at the text from a totally different perspective. Perhaps, she said, the Torah is not focusing on the needs of the Kohanim but on those of the rest of the nation. With this shift of focus, the Torah actually ends up protecting the rights of the Kohanim, as well.

If a blemished Kohen had been allowed a public role within the Temple:

1. The attention of the Israelites witnessing the Temple service would have been inexorably drawn to the Kohen, rather than to the rituals he was performing. This loss of appropriate focus would have undermined the Temple proceedings which were designed, through intricate rite and ritual, to draw those in attendance into a closer relationship with their Creator.

2. Public focus on the visible physical flaw of a priest would have also quickly caused that flaw to become the subject of prurient curiosity and rampant discussion among the onlookers. The sanctity of the Temple service would have been marred by the sin of harmful speech on the part of the Israelites and by the resultant psychic pain caused to the Kohen.

Many blemished priests, under these circumstances, might have understandably opted not to serve.

I have observed, however, that the Torah does not generally distinguish between *opportunity* and *obligation*. If a Kohen is halachically allowed to serve, he is automatically obligated to serve. By releasing the blemished Kohanim from their priestly obligations, the Torah actually preserves the personal dignity and privacy of those priests.

From this perspective, what originally seemed to be an insensitive set of edicts within the Torah text actually emerges as a set of laws fashioned to protect the integrity of the Temple service and the dignity of all involved.

Following my discussions with Barbara, I noted two sources that support her basic premise. The Abravanel, in his discussion of this passage, maintains that blemished Kohanim are excluded from the Temple service because of the unsettling effect that their involvement would have upon those present.[13]

Rav Moshe Feinstein goes a step further. In his comments on this passage, he notes Rashi's opinion that the Torah does provide a rationale for the laws concerning the blemished Kohanim (see above, *Approaches* A). According to Rashi, asks Rav Moshe, why does the text feel compelled to offer an explanation for these regulations when so many edicts in the Torah are presented with no recorded rationale?

Rav Moshe answers his own question in typically brilliant fashion. A reason must be proffered in this case because these edicts seem to contradict the very behavior we have come to expect from God. God's presence is expressly found, according to Jewish tradition, among the downtrodden and the weak, among those most in need of His divine support and sustenance. One would, therefore, specifically expect the inclusion of afflicted Kohanim in the service of God. The text, therefore, informs us that the exclusion of these Kohanim is not for God's sake but for man's. The Temple service must be honored, in all ways, in the eyes of the beholders.

--- **D** ---

Obviously, I've come a long way since my bar mitzva. Nonetheless, I find that the questions that I raised then, as a naïve thirteen-year-old, still carry weight these many years later. While the approaches outlined above certainly have much to recommend in them, I have a feeling that my relationship with this passage of Parshat Emor will continue to evolve.

Isn't that the way it should be with every passage of Torah text, throughout our lives?

---

13. Abravanel, Vayikra 21:17.

2 The Bottom Line

Context

As the first half of Parshat Emor draws to a close, with its detailed laws concerning the priesthood and aspects of the sacrificial rite, God delivers the following general proclamation: "And you shall observe My commandments and perform them; I am the Lord. And you shall not profane My holy name, and I will be sanctified in the midst of the children of Israel; I am the Lord Who sanctifies you."[1]

Questions

What specific imperative is contained in the broad mandate "And you shall not profane My holy name, and I will be sanctified in the midst of the children of Israel"?

Why is this mandate specifically placed at this point in the Torah text?

Approaches

—A—

Some commentaries, including the Ibn Ezra, interpret the dual mandate concerning the sanctification and non-profanation of God's name as a concluding directive to the Kohanim.

By publicly following God's commandments to the letter, these scholars maintain, the Kohanim will actively sanctify God's name in "the midst of the children of Israel."

—B—

The vast majority of authorities, however, choose to understand these verses much more broadly, *as an overarching imperative directed to the entire nation.*

---

1. Vayikra 22:31–32.

At this point, God brings to a close not only the first half of Parshat Emor, but a much larger section of text which opened with the global directive at the beginning of Parshat Kedoshim: "Holy shall you be."[2] Now, a parsha and a half later, after outlining a wide range of precepts designed to guide man towards the goal of holiness, God caps this section with a second, overriding global imperative:[3]

> And you shall observe My commandments and perform them; I am the Lord. And you shall not profane My holy name, and I will be sanctified in the midst of the children of Israel; I am the Lord Who sanctifies you.[4]

Through the eyes of these scholars, the verses before us emerge as the source of two towering commandments: the positive mitzva of *kiddush Hashem* (the sanctification of God's name) and the prohibition of *chillul Hashem* (the desecration of God's name). No commandments in the Torah speak more clearly to the depth and breadth of our obligations as Jews.

─ C ─

The Rambam, for example, based on a Talmudic discussion in the tractate of Sanhedrin,[5] opens his discussion of these mitzvot by citing them as the source of the most extreme obligation in Jewish experience, the imperative of martyrdom, when necessary, for the sanctification of God's name:

> The whole house of Israel is commanded concerning the sanctification of His Great Name, as it states: "And I will be sanctified in the midst of the children of Israel." And they are warned not to desecrate it, as it states: "And you shall not profane My holy name."[6]

The Rambam goes on to explain that, when confronted with a heartrending situation of forced transgression, these two precepts are to be fulfilled according to the following guidelines:

---

2. Vayikra 19:2.
3. Nehama Leibowitz, *Iyunim Chadashim B'sefer Vayikra*, pp. 322–323.
4. Vayikra 22:31–32.
5. Talmud Bavli Sanhedrin 74a.
6. Rambam, *Mishneh Torah*, Hilchot Yesodei HaTorah 5:1–3.

1. A Jew must be willing to martyr himself rather than allow himself to be coerced to commit the sins of idolatry, sexual immorality or murder under any circumstance.

2. A Jew must be willing to martyr himself rather than allow himself to be coerced to commit any sin in public (as defined by the presence of ten other Jews; see *Approaches* H).

3. If the attempt at personal coercion takes place against the backdrop of a systematic effort to eradicate Jewish tradition on a national level, a Jew must be willing to martyr himself rather than allow himself to be coerced to commit any sin, even in private.[7]

An individual Jew's ultimate sacrifice, under circumstances too often experienced in our tragic history, thus becomes the definitive example of an act performed *al kiddush Hashem*, for the sanctification of God's name.

— **D** —————————————————————————

The fulfillment of the mandates found in Parshat Emor, however, is not relegated only to the most extreme of circumstances.

As many scholars, including the Rambam himself,[8] note, opportunities for the sanctification of God's name can be found throughout our lives. *Such sanctification is, in fact, arguably the "bottom line," the ultimate goal of Jewish life.* Our personal and national role is to partner with God in the sanctification of His world; to be *mekadesh Shem Shamayim*, to sanctify God's name and make His presence felt through the things we do and the people we become.

— **E** —————————————————————————

This Divine-human partnership emerges from the very beginning of Jewish history.

A fascinating Midrash, concerning the end of Avraham's career, clearly makes this point as it reflects back upon the patriarch's life work. The rabbis note a striking discrepancy between two distinct ways in which Avraham refers to God as he instructs his trusted servant, Eliezer, to search for a wife for Yitzchak.

---

7. Ibid.
8. Ibid., 5:11.

When Avraham describes the God Who commanded him to leave his home and begin his historic journey, he refers to *"the Lord, God of heaven,* Who took me from the house of my father and from the land of my birth…"[9]

When, however, Avraham refers to the God with Whom he now relates, towards the end of his life, he tells Eliezer: "And I will have you swear by *the Lord, God of heaven and God of earth…"*[10]

Why the shift?

The Midrash explains that Avraham's words quietly capture the towering quality of his own life journey:

> Until Avraham entered the world, the Lord, as it were, was only God of heaven [for the Lord was not truly known to man]. The patriarch therefore states: "The Lord, *God of heaven,* Who took me from the house of my father and from the land of my birth…" When Avraham entered the world, however, he [spread an awareness of God's existence and effectively] crowned God king over both heaven and earth. The patriarch can therefore now confidently state, looking back on his career: "And I will have you swear by *the Lord, God of heaven and God of earth…*[11]

Avraham crowns God king… One can scarcely imagine a clearer iteration of man's necessary role in the partnership that God Himself creates.

—— **F** ————————————————————————————

Avraham's journey, which begins with the mandate "and all the nations of the earth shall be blessed through you…,"[12] foreshadows the continuing contribution of his progeny for generations to come. As their story unfolds, therefore, several foundational events further entrench the mission of *kiddush Hashem* within the character of the developing Jewish nation.

Centuries after Avraham, Moshe is called to leadership at the burning bush with the challenge "The place upon which you stand is holy ground."[13]

---

9. Bereishit 24:7.
10. Ibid., 24:3.
11. Sifrei, Devarim 32:10.
12. Bereishit 12:3.
13. Shmot 3:5.

Sanctity, God says to Moshe, *is potentially to be found wherever you stand, wherever you are. As your journey towards leadership begins, recognize that you and your people are about to become partners with Me in the creation of holiness in this world* (see *Shmot*: Shmot 3, *Approaches* E).

A short time later, on this very spot, the people who are to become "a kingdom of priests, and a holy nation,"[14] stand at the foot of Mount Sinai, receiving God's commandments. Sanctity, the Israelites learn, is not to be found in the mists of the summit of the mountain, but rooted to the ground, within their own life experience. By partnering with God through the performance of His law, this newborn nation will bring God into their world (see Yitro 2, *Approaches* C).

With the nation still encamped at the foot of Mount Sinai, God further commands: "And they [the Israelites] shall make for me *a holy place* and I will dwell within them."[15] The holiness of the Sanctuary, the precursor of the Holy Temple in Jerusalem, precedes the investiture of God's presence. By referring to the Sanctuary immediately as a mikdash, a holy place, the Torah clearly conveys man's role in the creation of sanctity. The Temple is holy from the moment that the Israelites create it – even before God fulfills His commitment to "dwell" within the nation.[16]

Once again, the Torah confirms the fundamental truth repeated over and over again, in different ways, during the critical period of our nation's birth: holiness is created in this world when man acts in accordance with God's will (see *Shmot*: Teruma 2, *Approaches* C).

—— **G** ————————————————————————

How, however, can we fulfill this mitzvah of *kiddush Hashem* today? What are the practical implications of this commandment within our daily lives?

Perhaps the clearest iteration of the ongoing imperative to sanctify God's name each day is found in the rabbinic interpretation of one of the most familiar passages of the Torah, a passage recited by observant Jews at least two times daily.

---

14. Ibid., 19:6.
15. Ibid., 25:8.
16. Ohr Hachaim, Shmot 25:8.

Confronted with the opening commandment of the first paragraph of the Shma, *V'ahavta et Hashem Elokecha*, "And you shall love the Lord, your God…," the rabbis ask: *How does one "love God"?*

Their answer is telling:

> *The name of Heaven should become beloved through you…*
>
> A man should study the Written and Oral Law, minister to Torah scholars, speak gently to his fellow man and be honest and honorable in his business and other dealings. Of such a man, what do people say? [They say:] "This individual who studied Torah – fortunate is the father who taught him Torah! Fortunate is the teacher who taught him Torah! Woe to them who have not studied Torah! Have you seen this individual who studied Torah? How pleasant is his manner, how upright his deeds…"
>
> But when a man who studies Written and Oral Law and ministers to Torah scholars does not speak gently to his fellow man and does not deal honestly in the marketplace and elsewhere…of such a man, what do people say? [They say:] "Woe to this individual who studied Torah! Woe to his father who taught him Torah! Woe to his teacher who taught him Torah! Fortunate are those individuals who have not studied Torah! Have you seen this individual who studied Torah? How objectionable are his deeds, how corrupt his ways…"[17]

Based on this and other sources, the Rambam, after detailing the extreme case of martyrdom (see above, *Approaches* C), summarizes the continuing responsibility to sanctify God's name through our actions as follows:

> And if the wise man is scrupulous with himself; and speaks gently to his fellow man; and is sociable, amiable and welcomes all he meets with a favorable countenance; if he takes insult but does not give it; respects all, even those who make light of him; if he is honest in all his dealings…and acts in all ways beyond the letter of the law…so that all praise him, love him and are desirous of emulating his deeds… .
>
> Behold, this individual has sanctified the Lord.[18]

---

17. Talmud Bavli Yoma 86a.
18. Rambam, *Mishneh Torah*, Hilchot Yesodei HaTorah 5:11.

In short, we are God's representatives to the world. How we act, what we do, who we are – each and every day – reflects not only upon us, but upon our tradition and, ultimately, upon its divine source.

———**H**———————————————————————————

One last technical point emerges from the passages concerning *kiddush Hashem* in Parshat Emor. Commenting on the statement "And I [God] will be sanctified *in the midst* of the children of Israel," and using set principles of derivation to quantify the definition of a quorum, the rabbis rule that prayers of particular sanctity can only be stated in the presence ("in the midst") of a minyan (ten adult males).

Even this technical rule, however, carries great moral imperative. Our search for sanctity should not be isolating. We are meant to find paths of holiness not through separation from but through involvement with those around us. In this way, we emulate the sanctity of God, which is found "*in the midst* of the children of Israel."

Points to Ponder

How are we doing?

No enterprise can thrive without regular assessment of ongoing success or failure. Periodic audits and reviews are, of course, standard fare throughout the secular world.

And yet, when it comes to one of the most pivotal areas of our performance as Jews – the education of our children towards their obligations of *kiddush Hashem* – we rarely pause for such formal reckonings. Our schools consistently review attendance, test performance and the like. Our synagogues provide ongoing youth programs and services. Within the family setting, we ensure that our children toe the line, succeed in their studies and prepare for their life careers. But concerning the moral and ethical product we produce, we are often too busy to stop and gauge "success."

The yardstick is simply defined: *bottom line, are we raising children who will sanctify the name of heaven during their lifetimes*? The answer to this question cannot be measured on the basis of information accrued or knowledge gained. More to the point are our children's personal attributes, their character traits and their approach to the world around them.

The task handed to us by the "system" is a particularly difficult one. After all, how do you train children to feel special without feeling superior;

to take pride in their own traditions without denigrating the traditions of others? And yet, that delicate balance is critical to the creation of young men and women capable of bringing God into the world. Without pride in what is theirs, our children will easily fall prey to the temptations of secular society. If that pride, however, turns into hubris, and our children lose sight of the inherent value of others, their ability to sanctify God's name is sorely compromised.

The litmus tests are potentially numerous: How do our children speak to and relate to their peers? How do they interact with adults? How do they relate to those outside their personal circle: the custodian in the synagogue, the waiter in the restaurant, those standing in line with them at the supermarket, the stranger on the street? Do they show fineness of character, true sensitivity towards others in their everyday dealings?

Who our children are, rather than what they know, will determine their success as mekadshei Shem Shamayim, *God's representatives to the world.*

3 Why Do We Count?

Context

In the midst of the Torah's discussion concerning the festival cycle, immediately after the commandment concerning the Omer offering (a barley offering in the Temple which marks the beginning of the harvest and allows the use of that season's grain), the following mandate is found:

> And you shall count for yourselves – from the day after the Sabbath, from the day you bring the waved offering of the Omer – seven weeks; complete shall they be. Until the day after the seventh Sabbath, shall you count fifty days; and you will offer a new meal offering to the Lord.[1]

This commandment is reiterated in the book of Devarim: "Seven weeks shall you count for yourselves; from the time the sickle is first put to the standing crop, you shall begin to count seven weeks."[2]

As codified by the rabbis, this mitzva, known as the mitzva of Sfirat Ha'omer, the Counting of the Omer, obligates each Jew to verbally count the days and weeks from the second day of the holiday of Pesach until the first day of the holiday of Shavuot.[3]

Questions

What possible purpose can there be in verbally counting the days and weeks between Pesach and Shavuot?

The Torah offers no explanation for this mitzva.

---

1. Vayikra 23:15–16.
2. Devarim 16:9.
3. Shulchan Aruch, Ohr Hachaim 489:1.

Approaches

Responding to the Torah's silence concerning the purpose of Sfirat Ha'omer, classical and contemporary scholars suggest a wide variety of approaches.

— A —

Most obviously, the Counting of the Omer is perceived by many scholars as an act of linkage between the two holidays that border the mitzva, Pesach and Shavuot. Through the act of counting we testify that the Revelation at Sinai (commemorated on Shavuot) was the goal and purpose of the Exodus from Egypt (commemorated on Pesach).[4] This relationship is established at the outset when God informs Moshe at the burning bush: "And this is your sign that I have sent you: when you take the people out of Egypt, you shall serve God on this mountain."[5]

On a deeper level, our counting consequently affirms that the physical freedom of the Exodus is incomplete without the spiritual freedom granted by God's law; a truth mirrored in the famous rabbinic dictum: "*No one is truly free other than he who is involved in the study of Torah.*"[6]

By counting the days between Pesach and Shavuot, many scholars continue, we also are meant to re-experience the sense of excitement and anticipation that marked this period for the Israelites, newly redeemed from Egypt.[7] Just as we would "count the remaining days" towards an extraordinary event in our personal lives, so too we should feel a real sense of anticipation each year as we again approach the holiday that marks the Revelation at Sinai.

— B —

Other authorities choose to view these days primarily as a period of "purification from" rather than "anticipation towards."

By the time of the Exodus, the Israelites have been defiled from centuries of immersion in Egyptian society and culture. Numerous sources, in fact, maintain that they have descended to the forty-ninth of fifty possible stages of defilement and are on the verge of becoming irredeemable.[8]

---

4. Sefer Hachinuch, mitzva 273.
5. Shmot 3:12.
6. Pirkei Avot 6:2.
7. Sefer Hachinuch, mitzva 273.
8. Shla Hakadosh, commentary on the Haggada: "Matza Zu."

With haste,[9] at the last moment, God pulls the nation back from the brink. The newly freed slaves, however, must now undergo a process of purification before they can encounter God and receive the Torah at Sinai. Forty-nine days – to counter each level of defilement experienced – must elapse before Revelation can take place.

By counting the days between Pesach and Shavuot each year, we remember and mark this refining journey. Just as a married woman monthly counts the days leading to her immersion in a mikva we must count and spiritually prepare ourselves for our reunion with God at Sinai.

Based on this approach, the Ohr Hachaim explains why Sfirat Ha'omer begins each year on the *second* day of Pesach, rather than on the *first*. The Exodus, he observes, occurs on the first day of the festival. For a portion of that day, therefore, the Israelites yet remain in Egypt and the journey of purification cannot yet begin.[10]

— C —

In stark contrast to the opinions cited above, a number of scholars emphasize the agricultural, rather than the historical, dimension of the Omer period. Opening the yearly harvest season, these days stretch from the beginning of the barley harvest (marked on the holiday of Pesach) to the beginning of the wheat harvest (marked on the holiday of Shavuot).[11]

As the weather conditions over this period are critical determinants of the success or failure of the entire harvest, the Sforno perceives the associated rituals to be expressions of thanksgiving and prayer. The Omer offering itself, he says, was brought in thanks for the barley harvest. An accompanying *korban*[12] served as a prayer for future success. The Counting of the Omer represents the daily prayers during this period, while the holiday of Shavuot is celebrated, in part, as an expression of thanks for the grain harvest.[13]

Choosing an eminently practical path, the Abudarham maintains that the Counting of the Omer was meant to counteract a farmer's inevitable preoccupation with his harvest. Counting the days towards Shavuot would

---

9. Shmot 12:12.
10. Ohr Hachaim, Vayikra 23:15.
11. Ramban, Vayikra 23:15.
12. Vayikra 23:12.
13. Sforno, Vayikra 23:10.

ensure that he would not forget his obligation to travel to Jerusalem for the celebration of the holiday.[14]

Finally, the Maharal finds reference to the global connection between the physical and spiritual dimensions of our lives within the ritual of the Counting of the Omer. We are enjoined to number the days towards Revelation specifically as the harvest season begins, in order to underscore the well-known rabbinic maxim "Where there is no flour, there is no Torah."[15] Proper Torah study can only take place against the backdrop of a healthy, well-nourished lifestyle.[16]

— **D** —

Rabbi Joseph Soloveitchik perceives yet another lesson embedded in the act of Sfirat Ha'omer. The Rav suggests that, in Jewish experience, an individual can perform the act of counting within two realms: the realm of Sfira and the realm of minyan (the root of each of these terms means "to count").

When you count in the realm of minyan, the Rav explains, all that matters is the attainment of the ultimate goal, the endpoint of your counting. Nine upstanding, righteous men can assemble for a prayer service but, without a tenth, there is no minyan.

When you count in the realm of Sfira, however, things are different. Although you still count towards a goal, each individual unit in the calculation becomes a goal, as well. While someone counting precious diamonds, for example, is certainly interested in the total number of diamonds he has, he also pauses and holds each gem up to the rays of the sun, admiring its unique facets, color and shape.

The act of Sfirat Ha'omer teaches us to "count our days in the realm of Sfira" – to see each day as a goal unto itself.

Too often, we live exclusively goal-oriented lives; moving from accomplishment to accomplishment, from milestone to milestone, rarely stopping to appreciate the significance of each passing day. And yet, when all is said and done, the quality of the journey, in large measure, defines our lives – and the ordinary moments spent with family and friends are as significant, if not more significant, than the milestones themselves.

---

14. *Sefer Abudarham*: Sfirat Ha'omer.
15. Pirkei Avot 3:21.
16. *Sefer Drashot Maharal Mi'Prague*: Drush al HaTorah.

The Rav's observation may also be mirrored in two versions of the verbal formula for Sfirat Ha'omer which have developed over the years. Some communities recite, "Today is the ----day *la'Omer* (literally "to the Omer")" while others count "*ba'Omer* (literally "in the midst of the Omer")." Taken together, these two versions form the balance that should mark our approach to life. On the one hand, without goals our lives are aimless. We therefore count *la'Omer*, towards the endpoint of the Omer count. On the other hand, never losing sight of the journey's value, we also count *ba'Omer*, in the midst of the Omer.

— **E** —————————————————————————

A historical overlay, emerging from the first-second century CE, dramatically transforms the days of the Omer from a time of anticipation and celebration to a period of sorrow and mourning. The Talmud relates: "Rabbi Akiva had twelve thousand pairs of students…and all of them died in one period because they failed to treat each other with respect…. They all died during the period between Pesach and Shavuot."[17]

In commemoration of this tragedy, the rabbis ordained that a portion of the Omer period be circumscribed by laws of mourning. Marriages, other festive celebrations and haircuts are prohibited during the restricted period, the exact computation of which varies according to custom, from community to community.[18]

At first glance, the powerful reaction of Jewish law to the death of Rabbi Akiva's students seems strange. Jewish history is, unfortunately, marked by a myriad of overwhelming tragedies that do not result in similar halachic commemorations. What makes this event different?

The Talmud explains that the death of these sages, tragic as it was in and of itself, actually resulted in a greater calamity. At a critical juncture of Jewish history, during the vulnerable period following the destruction of the Second Temple, the loss of Rabbi Akiva's students left the world "desolate" through loss of Torah study.[19] Their death represented a break in the chain of oral tradition at a time when such a rupture threatened the very survival of the Jewish nation. Only Rabbi Akiva's success in finding

17. Talmud Bavli Yevamot 62b.
18. Shulchan Aruch, Orach Chaim 493; Mishna Berura, ibid.
19. Talmud Bavli Yevamot 62b; Rashi, ibid.

and teaching new students "in the south" mitigated the calamitous effects of this tragedy.[20]

This historical overlay placed upon the days of the Omer is clearly neither arbitrary nor coincidental. Both the potential effects of the death of Rabbi Akiva's students and the fundamental cause of their demise connect directly to the period leading to Sinai.

Revelation marks not only the communication of the Written Law, but the launching of the Oral Law, as well (see *Shmot*: Yitro 5). The rupture in the transmission of that oral tradition, caused by the loss of Rabbi Akiva's students, threatens the very legacy of Sinai.

Concerning the relationship between the cause of the tragedy and the Omer period, one need look no further than at the teachings of Rabbi Akiva himself. As we have noted, Rabbi Akiva considers "*V'ahavta l'reiacha kamocha*, Love your fellow as yourself," to be the most important principle of the Torah (see Kedoshim 5).[21] By negating that very principle through their behavior, the students of this great sage contradict the very Torah to which they have otherwise dedicated their lives.

Points to Ponder

A powerfully perplexing mystery arises from the Omer period.

As noted above, Rabbi Akiva emphatically identifies "Love your fellow as yourself" as the most important principle of the Torah. Yet, his students perish because they "fail to treat each other with respect."

Can it be that one of our sages fails to impart his core belief to his students? The problem would be less glaring had Rabbi Akiva's students perished as a result of any other sin. But to transgress the very precept that serves as the core of their mentor's beliefs and practices... How can it be?

Perhaps the issue is one of chronology. We do not know when Rabbi Akiva determines the centrality of the mitzva of *V'ahavta*. Perhaps he reaches this realization only in sorrowful retrospect, as a result of the tragic loss of his students. Perhaps it is precisely their death which leads their mentor to recognize the emptiness of Torah observance absent a foundation of interpersonal respect.

---

20. Talmud Bavli, ibid.
21. Talmud Yerushalmi Nedarim 9:4.

Or, perhaps, our tradition is referencing an entirely different life lesson through this tragedy – a lesson of overarching significance for us all. The stark inconsistency between Rabbi Akiva's core belief and the actions of his students may reflect the universal challenge of intergenerational transmission.

I feel that we often make the mistake of assuming that just because something is vital to us, it will automatically be of importance to our children; that the ideas and beliefs that lie at the heart of our worldview are so obvious, they need not be openly stated and taught.

Nothing could be further from the truth…

Our children grow up in worlds different from our own, and within those worlds they form their own personal convictions. The basic foundations that we consider central to our lives are not automatically "givens" within theirs. The deep connection, for example, that we feel towards the State of Israel – in large measure a product of our own life experiences and the experiences of our parents – will not automatically develop in the hearts of our progeny, who are more temporally and emotionally removed than us from the creation of the state.

As we strive to convey critical ideas and principles to future generations, we can make no assumptions of prior knowledge and conviction. We must consciously and actively teach each and every one of the ideas and principles we feel important, through open discussion and deed.

Perhaps Rabbi Akiva fails to teach his students the central value of his worldview precisely because he considers that value to be self-evident. And just perhaps, across the centuries, he teaches us not to make the same mistake.

4 Mysterious Majesty

Context

As Parshat Emor continues with its description of the festival cycle, we encounter a holiday shrouded in mystery.

A series of enigmas surround both the festival of Shavuot, introduced for the first time in this parsha, and Revelation, the historical event with which Shavuot is associated.

1. Although the rabbis identify Shavuot as *Zman Matan Torateinu*, the anniversary of the giving of our Torah, *no actual connection between the holiday and Revelation is made in the text*. Shavuot, in fact, emerges as the only one of the three pilgrimage festivals (Pesach, Shavuot and Succot) for which no historical foundation is recorded in the Torah.

2. At no point does the Torah mention an independent calendar date for the festival of Shavuot. Most often, this holiday is identified as the endpoint of the Omer count (see previous study). The festival's very title, Shavuot (literally "Weeks") derives from the celebration's position as the culmination of the seven-week Omer period.

On one occasion, in a series of passages clearly identifying the holidays by their calendar dates, Shavuot is again the glaring exception, with even the festival's relationship to the Omer period omitted. In that case, Shavuot is mentioned without any calendar reference at all.[1]

3. The Torah also fails to pinpoint the specific date of the onset of Revelation at Sinai. The text, in fact, seems to deliberately go out of its way to avoid any clear dating of this event.

---

1. Bamidbar 28:16–39.

The arrival of the Israelites at the site of Revelation is, for example, described in the Torah as follows: "In the third month from the Exodus of the children of Israel from the Land of Egypt, *on this day*, they came to the Wilderness of Sinai."[2]

Failing to identify "this day," the Torah leaves it to the rabbis to compute the chronology and explain that the Israelites arrive at Sinai on the *first day* of the third month, Sivan.

To make matters even more confusing, uncertainty emerges concerning the timetable of events immediately prior to Revelation. Based on ambiguity in the text, the rabbis debate whether or not Moshe, divinely commanded to set aside three days preparatory to Revelation, "adds an additional preparatory day of his own."[3] This disagreement over Moshe's actions, in turn, leads to an even more significant divergence of opinion concerning the exact date of Revelation.[4]

The majority of the rabbis, maintaining that Moshe followed God's instructions to the letter, correlate the onset of Revelation to the sixth day of Sivan, the date of the Shavuot festival. Rabbi Yossi, however, the author of the position that Moshe added an additional preparatory day, insists that Revelation does not begin until the seventh day of Sivan – the day after Shavuot.[5]

According to Rabbi Yossi's calculations, we are thus faced with the startling conclusion that Revelation *does not occur* on the date of the festival identified by the rabbis as the anniversary of the event. (In the diaspora, Shavuot is observed on the seventh day of Sivan, as well as the sixth. This observance, however, does not relate to the above discussion but is the result of a general rabbinic decree concerning calendar uncertainty: *yom tov sheini shel galuyot*, the added second day of observance of all the festivals in the diaspora.)

4. Finally, in contrast to other festivals, no unique observance is associated in the text with the holiday of Shavuot (all-night learning sessions are a *minhag*, a custom, and not biblically or even rabbinically mandated). This festival is governed only by the generic laws common to all biblical holidays.

---

2. Shmot 19:1.
3. Talmud Bavli Shabbat 86b–87a.
4. Ibid.
5. Ibid.

Questions

Why does so much mystery surround the festival of Shavuot and the commemoration of Revelation?

Shouldn't the single most important formative event in Jewish history be clearly dated and uniquely celebrated?

Approaches

— A —

The Torah's identification of Shavuot as the culmination of the Omer count, as opposed to a holiday with a separate calendar date of its own, may well reflect and expand upon lessons learned from the Omer period itself (see previous study).

As discussed, many authorities see the mitzva of Sfirat Ha'omer, the counting of the Omer, as an act linking Pesach to Shavuot. In this light, Shavuot is best understood, not as a totally autonomous festival, but as something of a "hybrid" – a continuation of Pesach, yet also a commemoration with its own unique identity and message. Shavuot stands as Pesach's goal, a reminder that the physical freedom achieved with the Exodus is incomplete without the spiritual freedom granted at Sinai.

— B —

Unexpected precedent for this approach is found in the form of another two-tiered biblical festival, distant on the calendar from but in many ways similar to the festival of Shavuot.

Immediately after the holiday of Succot, the Torah mandates a one-day festival known as Shmini Atzeret. While this celebration is clearly connected to Succot, the rabbis are nonetheless emphatic in their contention that Shmini Atzeret is a "festival unto itself," with its own identity and message.[6] We are thus again confronted with a "hybrid holiday," a celebration which, like Shavuot, is at once a continuation of what comes before (even the title Shmini Atzeret, the Eighth Day of Assembly, references the connection to the seven days of Succot) and at the same time a separate occasion.

---

6. Talmud Bavli Succa 47b–48a.

Furthermore, while Shmini Atzeret and Shavuot stand at opposite ends of the calendar, rabbinic thought connects them closely. Shavuot is referred to within Talmudic literature simply as Atzeret, the Day of Assembly.[7] Rabbi Yehoshua ben Levi even maintains that Shmini Atzeret should rightfully be as distant from Succot as Shavuot is from Pesach. Mercifully, however, God places Shmini Atzeret immediately following Succot so that the people will not have to make an additional pilgrimage back to Jerusalem during the winter season.[8]

The implied equation is clear: *Shavuot is to Pesach as Shmini Atzeret is to Succot.*

The parallel between these two festivals, however, runs even deeper. Like Shavuot, Shmini Atzeret has no unique mitzva of its own. The silence of this festival, coming on the heels of the ritually richest time in the Jewish year (the month of Tishrei, containing Rosh Hashana, Yom Kippur and Succot), is, in fact, deafening. And yet, according to rabbinic tradition, Shmini Atzeret is the culmination of all that comes before: a day marking the intimate, personal relationship between God and his people.

Neither Shavuot nor Shmini Atzeret need be marked by a mitzva specific to the day because each of these festivals celebrates, in its own way and at the close of a holiday period, the *complete relationship* between God and His people.

Shmini Atzeret caps the personal passage through Rosh Hashana, Yom Kippur and Succot, culminating each year's *tshuva* cycle with a celebration of our renewed bond with our Creator. Shavuot concludes the national passage from bondage to freedom, marking the day on which God's relationship with His chosen people begins in earnest.

— **C** —————————————————————————————

Another distinct message is conveyed through the Torah's identification of Shavuot as the culmination of the Omer period: *the value of a goal reached is directly dependent upon the quality of the journey that takes you there.*

Every life milestone derives its significance, in large measure, from what comes before: the days of study leading to the bar/bat mitzvah; the

---

7. Mishna Shevi'it 1:1 and countless other sources in the Mishna and Gemara.
8. Midrash Rabba Shir Hashirim 7:2.

personal maturation that sets the stage for courtship and marriage; the years of shared love that give rise to an anniversary…

Life's special occasions would be much emptier without the struggle, growth and rich experience leading to them.

Each year, therefore, we do not return to Sinai without first passing through the Omer. To arrive at the anniversary of Matan Torah without a prior journey would have little meaning. Each year, forty-nine days of preparation, replicating the original forty-nine days of anticipation that led from the Exodus to Revelation precede our arrival. By defining the festival of Shavuot specifically in relationship to those preceding days, the Torah informs us that the most significant moment of Jewish history, like all milestones, draws its significance from the prior journey.

— **D** —

While the approaches outlined above address some of the mysteries surrounding the festival of Shavuot, the Torah's obfuscation concerning the date of Revelation itself remains a puzzle. Why does the text deliberately avoid pinpointing the most significant moment of Jewish history, to the extent that its date remains the subject of dispute to this day? Why, as well, does the Torah fail to associate this event with its apparent anniversary, the festival of Shavuot?

A fascinating, far-reaching answer is hinted at in a well-known Midrashic observation and elaborated upon by later authorities.

The Midrash focuses on the previously mentioned Torah passage, describing the arrival of the Israelites at the site of Revelation: "In the third month from the Exodus of the children of Israel from the Land of Egypt, *on this day*, they came to the Wilderness of Sinai."[9]

This text, maintain the rabbis, is even more puzzling than it first seems to be. Not only is the Torah ambiguous concerning the nation's arrival at Sinai, but the terminology actually used by the text is inherently problematic. The Torah does not say, as we would expect: "*on that day (bayom hahu)*, they came to the Wilderness of Sinai." Instead, the text reads: "*on this day (bayom hazeh)*, they came to the Wilderness of Sinai."

Why does the Torah refer to a millennia-old moment as "*this day*"?

---

9. Shmot 19:1.

Because, suggest the rabbis, the text means to convey an overarching message: "As you study Torah, [its words] should not be ancient in your eyes, but as if they were given to you 'this day.'"[10]

Or as Rashi puts it: "At all times the Torah's words should seem as new to you [variant: as dear to you] as if they were given to you today."[11]

— E

There is, I believe, much more to these rabbinic observations than meets the eye. In essence, the rabbis are emphasizing that *Revelation is not a historic event.*

The Patriarchal Era, the Exodus, the wandering in the wilderness, the entry into the land of Canaan and so much more, are periods and incidents rooted in the past. They are meant to be learned from, reexamined, re-experienced, even seen as prototypes for the present; but they are all past events.

Revelation is different. *Matan Torah* is a process that continues to this day and beyond. Every time we study a text, ask a halachic question or share a Torah thought, we stand again at Sinai receiving the Torah. Every time the rabbis apply the law to changing circumstance, suggest new insight into an age-old text or enact new legislation to protect the community, we participate in Revelation. When concerns ranging from in vitro fertilization to stem cell research to the definition of death and its impact on organ donation are actively addressed and debated within Jewish law, *Matan Torah* unfolds.

— F

We can now understand the Torah's reluctance to pinpoint both the date and the holiday marking Revelation. Either of these two acts would root *Matan Torah* in the past. Like so many other historical events, Revelation would become an event to celebrate and commemorate, rather than a process in which to participate.

The Torah, therefore, leaves it to the rabbis to determine the date on which the Israelites actually stood at Sinai and to draw the inevitable conclusion that the Shavuot festival marks that date.

---

10. Midrash Tanchuma Yitro 13.
11. Rashi, Shmot 19:1.

The text itself remains silent concerning these issues in order to remind us that we stand at Sinai today.

Points to Ponder

To the uninitiated, the allure of Torah study is often difficult to comprehend. What is this fascination with age-old, seemingly archaic text? What satisfaction can be found in poring over rabbinic observations authored centuries ago?

The following story begins to answer these questions.

Many years ago I made the acquaintance of a young man who came to Talmud study late in his educational development. One day, he turned to me and said: "You know why I love the Talmud? Because when I begin to study Talmud, *the boundaries of time disappear.* Suddenly I am sitting at a table, present at a discussion between Rabbi Akiva and Rabbi Yishmael, dating back to the beginning of the Common Era.

"As the conversation continues, Rav Huna [third century] offers a thought; Abbaye [fourth century] makes a comment, only to be countered by Rava [fourth century], as Rav Ashi [fifth century] joins in.

"Then Rashi [1040–1105] makes an observation and is immediately challenged by his descendents, the Tosafists [twelfth–thirteenth centuries]. Others soon join the discussion, including the Rambam [1135–1204] and Rabbi Yosef Karo [1488–1575], all making their positions known…

"And I, I am there too, at the table, asking my questions and adding my thoughts to a dialogue that will continue long after I am gone, as well."

To be part of an eternal conversation; to connect both with God's will and with generations long gone; *to stand at Sinai in our day*: that, in essence, is the adventure that Torah provides.

5 A Glimpse into a Hero's Heart

Context

Among the many holiday regulations found in Parshat Emor is the commandment concerning the taking of the *arba minim*, four species (*lulav*, palm branch; *etrog*, citron; *hadassim*, myrtle branches and *aravot*, willow branches), on the holiday of Succot: "And you shall take for yourselves on the first day fruit of a goodly tree, branches of palm trees, twigs of a plaited tree and willows of the brook; and you shall rejoice before the Lord, your God, for seven days."[1]

Questions

The commandment concerning the mitzva of *arba minim* appears to be internally contradictory. The passage opens by stating that the *arba minim* should be taken on the first day of the festival. This directive seems to limit the mitzva only to that day (otherwise, why mention the first day at all?). The passage, however, closes with the decree that we should "rejoice before the Lord, our God" (apparently, with the *arba minim*) for seven days.

What, exactly, are the parameters of this precept? Is it a one-day or seven-day mitzva?

Approaches

—A

Faced with the apparent contradiction in the text, the Talmudic sages derive a two-tiered approach to the mitzva of *arba minim*. Universally, they maintain, the mitzva is only a one-day precept, limited to the first day of the festival of Succot. The text thus reads: "And you shall take for yourselves on the first day..."

---

1. Vayikra 23:40.

There is, however, one critical exception. Within the confines of the Holy Temple in Jerusalem, when we are "rejoicing before the Lord, our God," the Torah mandates that the *arba minim* be taken for the full seven days of the festival.[2]

B

While this two-tiered structure reflects the biblical obligation of *arba minim*, a towering Mishnaic sage who lived at the time of the destruction of the Second Temple changes the rules.

The Mishna relates that, upon the Temple's destruction, Rabbi Yochanan ben Zakkai enacts a *takana*, a rabbinic edict (see *Shmot*: Yitro 5, *Approaches* C), mandating that the universal mitzva of *arba minim* be expanded to a full seven-day observance even outside the city of Jerusalem. Motivating Rabbi Yochanan's decision, the Mishna explains, is his desire to create a *zecher l'Mikdash*, a lasting remembrance of the newly destroyed Temple. Let the mitzva be performed universally for seven days, he reasons, so that the Temple and the observances within will never be forgotten.[3]

C

The story could end there, with Rabbi Yochanan's *takana*, and we would have gained new, valuable insight into the origins and development of the mitzva of *arba minim*.

There is, however, a greater tale to be told…

For while the Talmud does not provide formal biographies of the scholars who populate its pages, hints of their personalities and experiences do emerge. In this vein, Rabbi Yochanan's *takana* concerning the *arba minim* is one of a series of Talmudic clues which, when taken together, provide a glimpse into the heart of one of the greatest, albeit underappreciated, heroes of Jewish history. From these legal rulings and personal vignettes, Rabbi Yochanan ben Zakkai emerges not only as the man most responsible for the survival of the Jewish people during the years following the destruction of the Second Temple, but also as the architect of a plan for national continuity that has endured to this day.

---

2. Mishna Succa 3:12.
3. Ibid.

— D

As noted above, Rabbi Yochanan ben Zakkai's life spans the years before, during and after the destruction of the Second Temple in 70 CE. He reportedly lives one hundred twenty years: forty years practicing a trade, forty years in Torah study and forty years in teaching.[4] Although considered the "least" among the students of the great sage Hillel, Rabbi Yochanan distinguishes himself greatly in Torah study and in piety[5] and is eventually referred to by his teacher as "a father of wisdom, a father for generations."[6]

A complex picture emerges concerning Rabbi Yochanan's approach to conflict during the years prior to the Temple's destruction. On the one hand, this great sage is unyielding in his defense of normative halachic process and wages relentless battles against those who would subvert its course.[7] At the same time, Rabbi Yochanan is deeply concerned over the looming catastrophe that he believes will result from continued conflict with the Romans[8] and he therefore preaches restraint (albeit unsuccessfully) in that arena.[9]

Through it all, Rabbi Yochanan remains particularly devoted to the Temple, teaching in the shadow of its walls.[10]

— E

The turning point in Rabbi Yochanan's career finds this great sage in Jerusalem, a city sorely besieged from without by the Roman legions under the command of Vespasian and fractured from within by the often violent clashes between the Jewish zealots and pacifists. Desperate to act on behalf of his people, Rabbi Yochanan fakes his own death and is smuggled out of the city in a coffin by his students. As the mournful entourage approaches the city gates, the zealots standing guard against any contact with the Romans threaten to run the coffin through with a sword to verify Rabbi

---

4. Talmud Bavli Rosh Hashana 31b.
5. Ibid., Succa 28a.
6. Talmud Yerushalmi Nedarim 5:6.
7. Mishna Yadim 4:6; Tosefta Para 3:8; Talmud Bavli Bava Batra 115b; Menachot 65a.
8. Talmud Bavli Yoma 39b.
9. Ibid., Gittin 56a; Avot D'Rabi Natan 4:5.
10. Talmud Bavli Pesachim 26a.

Yochanan's death. The guards, however, are convinced to relent and Rabbi Yochanan safely exits Jerusalem.

The sage immediately makes his way to the Roman camp where he greets the general, Vespasian, with the words "Peace be upon you, O King! Peace be upon you, O King."

Vespasian responds: "You are liable to death on two accounts. First, because I am not a king – yet you call me a king. And furthermore, if I am the king, why have you not come until today?"

Rabbi Yochanan informs Vespasian that the Roman general is shortly destined to become the king and that he, Rabbi Yochanan, would indeed have appeared before Vespasian earlier had the zealots allowed him exit from Jerusalem.

Suddenly a messenger arrives from Rome with the startling news that Rabbi Yochanan's prophetic words have come true: Caesar has died and Vespasian has been appointed to ascend the throne. The newly appointed king-elect turns to Rabbi Yochanan and, in acknowledgment of the sage's wisdom, offers to fulfill his wishes.

We would expect that Rabbi Yochanan, faced with this extraordinary opportunity, would ask the Roman general to end the war with Judea or, at the very least, to lift the siege of Jerusalem, sparing the holy city and the Temple within. Amazingly, however, Rabbi Yochanan does not do so. Instead, this very scholar who had spent his days in the Temple's shadow turns his back on it, effectively consigning it to inevitable destruction. Given the opportunity to ask for anything, Rabbi Yochanan presents Vespasian with a strange request that reverberates across the ages: *Ten li Yavne v'chachameha*, "Grant me the city of Yavne and its wise men."

What is going through Rabbi Yochanan's mind? Why choose Yavne, a small city in central Israel, which is of no strategic value? Why not beseech Vespasian to spare the holy city of Jerusalem?

The Talmud explains that Rabbi Yochanan is acutely aware of the limits of Vespasian's self-proclaimed beneficence. A request as great as the sparing of Jerusalem would have been completely turned down by the Roman general. Rabbi Yochanan would have lost the opportunity to make any difference at all.[11]

Perhaps, however, Rabbi Yochanan's request is not simply a fallback

---

11. Talmud Bavli Gittin 56a–56b.

position. This great sage recognizes the full implications of the tragic journey upon which his people are about to embark. Exiled in large measure from their land, spread through the Roman Empire, they will need a powerful unifying force to hold them together. The Temple, which until now has centralized the nation's worship within their homeland, will no longer suffice. An exiled people will require a new "center," one that knows no geographical boundaries.

In short, Rabbi Yochanan recognizes that he must orchestrate his people's transition from a Temple-based society to one that will be held together solely by the "four cubits of halacha."[12] He therefore sets about the creation of a halachic center in Yavne, a center where the Sanhedrin (High Court) will sit and from which their wisdom and guidance will spread to all corners of the global Jewish community. Yavne will allow for the perpetuation of the halachic process and the survival of the Jewish nation through the dark days ahead and beyond.

Granted his wish by Vespasian, Rabbi Yochanan sees his dream begin to take root as the study of Jewish thought and law flourishes in Yavne.

— **F** —————————————————————————————————

Rabbi Yochanan's recognition of the inevitability of the Temple's destruction and his assiduous preparations for that eventuality do not in any way lessen his sorrow when the tragedy occurs: "When Rabbi Yochanan ben Zakkai heard that Jerusalem was destroyed and the Temple consumed in flames, he and his students rent their garments, and they wept, cried out and mourned."[13]

Above all, Rabbi Yochanan desperately desires to secure the memory of the Temple in the hearts and minds of the people. He therefore brilliantly counterbalances the physical loss of the Temple with the establishment of a series of *takanot*, rabbinical edicts (including the aforementioned mandate regarding the *arba minim* with which we opened our discussion). Specifically designed to be *zecher l'Mikdash*, in remembrance of the Temple, each of these *takanot*, Rabbi Yochanan hopes, will keep the glory of the Temple alive in the hearts of a people dreaming of and praying for its rebuilding.

---

12. Talmud Bavli Brachot 8a.
13. Avot D'Rabi Natan 4:5.

G

The full story behind one of these *takanot* affords us an even fuller, rare glimpse into the heart of this Talmudic sage.

The Mishna relates that originally, whenever Rosh Hashana coincided with Shabbat, the shofar was sounded only within the Temple confines (some say throughout the city of Jerusalem[14]). Upon the Temple's destruction, however, Rabbi Yochanan decrees that the shofar be sounded wherever a *beit din*, a Jewish court, convenes (one opinion limits this decree only to Yavne).[15] Clearly, this decision is designed to further concretize the transition from the Temple to the Sanhedrin at this critical juncture of Jewish history.

It remains for the Gemara, however, to tell the rest of the story…

One year, some time after the destruction of the Temple, Rosh Hashana and Shabbat coincide. Of their own volition, the people begin to converge on Yavne, reasoning that the shofar will be sounded there.

Upon witnessing this phenomenon, Rabbi Yochanan turns to his rabbinic colleagues and demands: "*Nitka*, let us sound the shofar!"

The rabbis respond (in typical rabbinic fashion), "*Nadun*, let us deliberate!" *This is not the way the law is decided, Rabbi Yochanan. We need to carefully consider the situation and weigh our options in light of the applicable regulations.*

Rabbi Yochanan answers: "*Nitka v'achar kach nadun*, let us sound the shofar and afterwards we shall deliberate!" *The people are here; the moment is urgent; they are waiting for us to respond. Let us act and then we will spend the time necessary to determine whether or not what we did was correct.*

The rabbis agree; the shofar is sounded; Rabbi Yochanan's colleagues approach him and demand: "*Nadun*, [now] let us deliberate!"

Rabbi Yochanan responds (with, I believe, a twinkle in his eye) *Kvar nishma keren b'Yavne v'ein moshivin achar ma'aseh*, "The horn has already been sounded in Yavne and one does not deliberate after the fact!" *Too late! The deed has been done and, consequently, the law has been decided.*

Under normal circumstances, Rabbi Yochanan ben Zakkai would have been the first to argue for deliberate due process in the application of the law. What sets him apart from his colleagues, however, is his ability to rec-

---

14. Rambam, *Mishneh Torah*, Hilchot Shofar 2:8.
15. Mishna Rosh Hashana 4:1.

ognize the exigency of the unusual moment and to respond, with courage and strength, to the immediate need.

— **H** —

Rabbi Yochanan could not have known in his day of the eventual success or failure of his efforts. The judgment of history is, after all, always rendered in retrospect. This great sage is, therefore, plagued by doubts concerning his own painful decisions – to the point that, weeping on his deathbed, he declares to his gathered students: "I see two paths before me, one leading to the Garden of Eden and one leading to Gehinnom, and I do not know by which I shall be taken."[16]

In the turbulent decades ahead, however, the verdict of history becomes abundantly clear. The Sanhedrin established in Yavne moves from city to city: from Yavne to Usha, back to Yavne, back to Usha, to Shefarim, to Beit Shearim, to Tsipori and finally to Teveria. Towards the end of these journeys, roughly in the year 200 CE, Rabbi Yehuda Hanasi edits the Mishna, and the Oral Law enters a new phase of development, further solidifying its place at the center of Jewish life.

The people endure and dream, past defeat, into exile, across the globe; traveling the path forged by Rabbi Yochanan ben Zakkai. With wisdom, extraordinary courage and a critical sense of balance, this great sage charts a course for his nation that guides them through their immediate crisis and throughout history.

Points to Ponder

I have often wondered what it would have been like to have been the proverbial fly on the wall, witnessing the meeting between Rabbi Yochanan ben Zakkai and Vespasian.

Two giants facing off…

On one side of the room (or tent, as the case may be), stands the Roman general, soon to be king, representing the extraordinary might of the Roman Empire. Facing him, an elderly Judean sage, representing a soon to be conquered people, on the brink of apparent exile and destruction.

And now, given the opportunity to ask for anything at all, this sage asks for an insignificant city and a group of sages like him: scholars who spend

---

16. Talmud Bavli Brachot 28b.

their time studying seemingly obscure theological concepts and applying a seemingly arcane legal code.

One can only begin to imagine Vespasian's reaction to Rabbi Yochanan's request: *Of all things to ask for… Doesn't this rabbi know what's about to happen, the overwhelming danger in which his people find themselves? Shouldn't he try to save something worthwhile, something that would at least buy his people more time, a measure of salvation? Of course I will grant him this request! It will make no difference at all.*

Were we to lay odds during this encounter, on which of the protagonists would we be willing to wager? Who, in our minds, would emerge victorious in the long run: the powerful Roman general or the frail Judean sage?

And yet…

In the Arch of Titus in Rome sits a stone block, carved with the well-known image of Judean exiles carrying the Temple Menora into captivity. Celebrating the completed Roman victory over Judea, under the command of Vespasian's son, Titus, this block also bears the words "The Jews are captive." To the Romans, however, these words meant much more. They meant: *The Jews are destroyed.* History had shown that any people exiled from their land, dispersed among other cultures, soon assimilated and disappeared.

Centuries after the Roman conquest of Judea, at the close of World War II and the greatest holocaust that any people have known, the victorious Allied armies marched through Rome and passed through the Arch of Titus. Among their number were members of the Jewish Brigade, composed solely of Jewish soldiers. An apocryphal story (elements of which are doubtless true) is told that as that brigade marched under the arch, someone took a can of blue paint and, over the words "The Jews are captive," he painted *Am Yisrael chai,* "The people of Israel live!"

Long after the Romans and, for that matter, the Egyptians, the Assyrians, Babylonians, the Greeks and so many more saw their empires crumble into dust, the Jewish nation remains, battered and persecuted, yet vibrant, alive, contributing, participating and innovating.

We have survived because of the one force that has held us together while dispersed across the globe: the force of Jewish law, emerging from Sinai, shaped and enriched by Jewish heroes across the ages – heroes like Rabbi Yochanan ben Zakkai.

Behar-Bechukotai בהר-בחוקתי

Parsha Summary

Extraordinary years, striking social legislation, promises and warnings, back to korbanot...

Parshat Behar opens as God, building on the festival cycle described in Parshat Emor, instructs the nation to count continuing cycles of forty-nine years, with each seventh year designated as Shmita *(a Sabbatical year) and each fiftieth year as* Yovel *(a Jubilee year). During* Shmita, *all agricultural activity is prohibited and the land is to be allowed to lie fallow. All produce naturally grown during this year is designated as hefker, ownerless, and therefore available to all, man and beast alike. During* Yovel, *the agricultural restrictions of* Shmita *apply and, further, far-reaching edicts are added. All Hebrew indentured servants, including those who have chosen to remain in servitude beyond the usual six-year term, must be set free and with specific exceptions, all sold land must be returned to its original owners.*[1]

Interspersed among the laws of Shmita *and* Yovel, *a series of other edicts are recorded in Parshat Behar, including:*

1. The prohibitions of financial and verbal oppression

2. The regulations concerning the redemption of land before Yovel *by the original owner or a close family member*

3. The prohibition of usury

4. The laws of eved Ivri *(a Hebrew indentured servant) and* eved Cana'ani *(a Canaanite slave)*

---

1. The laws of *Shmita* remain in effect to this day, with most halachic authorities maintaining that at least a rabbinic obligation exists in the Land of Israel in our time. The various methods through which the modern State of Israel deals with these regulations are fascinating examples of the continued application of Torah law to our time. The laws of *Yovel*, on the other hand, were suspended with the advent of the nation's first exile from the Land of Israel, to be reinstated only with the nation's return to the Land.

Parshat Behar closes with general admonitions to refrain from idolatry and to revere God's Sabbaths and the Holy Temple.

Parshat Bechukotai opens with a description of the blessings to be granted to the nation upon observance of God's statutes and commandments. The promise of these blessings is immediately followed in the text by the first of two Tochachot, *sections of rebuke, found in the Torah (the second and larger of these sections is found in the book of Devarim). Each of these* Tochachot *features stern, prophetic warnings of the terrible disasters to befall the people should they fail to follow God's will.*

Finally, the book of Vayikra concludes with a return to the theme with which it opened: korbanot. *The Torah enumerates specific rules concerning:*

1. Arachin (valuations), voluntary offerings brought to the Sanctuary based on the specific value of individuals, livestock or real estate as determined by formulas set forward in the text

2. Sanctification and redemption of animals

3. Sanctification and redemption of houses and fields

4. Redemption of ma'aser sheini, *the second tithe reserved for consumption by the owners in Jerusalem*

5. Ma'aser beheima, the tithe of animals that is brought as an offering to the Temple. While portions of the animals tithed are offered on the altar, the meat is consumed by the owners and their guests

1 Yearning to Be Free

Context

Two specific commandments to count seven cycles of seven units each, leading to a fiftieth culminating unit, appear in the Torah within the span of two contiguous parshiot.

In Parshat Emor, the Torah commanded the counting of the forty-nine days of the Omer (seven weeks, each of seven days) leading to the festival of Shavuot on the fiftieth day (see Emor 3 and 4).[1]

Now, in Parshat Behar, the Torah commands the counting of forty-nine years (seven Sabbatical cycles, each of seven years) leading to *Yovel*, the Jubilee, or fiftieth year.

A cursory review of the respective texts does, however, reveal a subtle distinction between these two precepts.

Concerning the Omer count towards the Festival of Shavuot, the Torah states: *U'sfartem lachem*, "And you shall count for yourselves"[2] (in the plural); while concerning the count towards *Yovel*, the Torah states: *V'safarta lecha*, "And you shall count for yourself"[3] (in the singular).

Questions

Is there a connection between the two disparate yet similar mitzvot of Sfirat Ha'omer and the counting towards *Yovel*, found in such close proximity within the text?

Does the seemingly minor move from plural terminology (associated with Sfirat Ha'omer) to singular terminology (associated with the counting

---

1. Ibid., 23:15–16.
2. Ibid., 23:15.
3. Ibid., 25:8.

towards *Yovel*) shed any light on the connection and/or contrast between these two mitzvot?

Approaches

—A—

The key to understanding the connection and contrast between the Omer and the *Yovel* counts may well emerge from an unexpected source, the distinction between two different dimensions of freedom in Jewish thought, *dror* and *cheirut* (see *Shmot: Bo* 3, *Approaches* B).

1. *Dror* (liberty): The removal of external constraints, physical or otherwise, that impede an individual's personal choice and independent action. *Dror* is either conferred upon an individual by an outside force or attained through severance from that force.

2. *Cheirut* (freedom): The injection of positive purpose and value into one's life. The individual who enjoys *cheirut*, by choosing to pursue a higher goal, actively frees himself from servitude to the surrounding world and its potentially enslaving forces. *Cheirut* cannot be granted by another but must be attained by an individual himself.

—B—

At the beginning of Parshat Behar, as the Torah outlines the *Yovel* laws concerning the freeing of Jewish indentured servants and the return of land to its original holders, the operant principle is *dror*: "*U'keratem dror ba'aretz l'chol yoshveha*, and you shall proclaim liberty throughout the land unto all the inhabitants thereof."[4]

This well-known passage, which enters the annals of American history with its partial inscription on the Liberty Bell in Philadelphia, has very specific meaning in its original Torah context. At the onset of the *Yovel* year, Jewish society is mandated to "proclaim liberty," by removing external constraints from certain individuals within its borders. Indentured servants are freed and land is returned to its original owners, as these individuals are liberated from bondage and poverty and afforded new possibilities for personal freedom. The full actualization of these possibilities, however, remains in the hands of the individuals themselves.

---

4. Ibid., 25:10.

The numbering of years towards *Yovel* is thus a societal count, performed through the aegis of the *beit din* (the court)[5] as it anticipates the time when Jewish society will act to "proclaim liberty" within its borders. The Torah therefore speaks of this count in singular terms: "*V'safarta lecha*, and you (*beit din*, as a single unit representing the society as a whole) shall count for yourself."

— C —

The counting of the Omer leads, on the other hand, towards a different dimension of freedom.

As noted previously (see Emor 3, *Approaches* A), many authorities view the mitzva of Sfirat Ha'omer as an act of linkage connecting the physical freedom of the Exodus with the spiritual freedom of Sinai. The nature of this spiritual freedom granted during Revelation is revealed in a fascinating Midrashic interpretation of a critical Torah passage: "And the tablets [received at Sinai] were the work of God, and the writing was the writing of God, engraved [*charut*] upon the tablets."[6]

"Read not *charut* [engraved]," the rabbis explain, "but *cheirut* [freedom]; for no man is free but he who occupies himself in the study of Torah."[7]

To the rabbinic mind, *cheirut*, full personal freedom, can only be attained through attachment to a higher goal and a higher good. Such an act of affiliation frees an individual from the limiting forces that abound in his world, enabling him to invest his life with meaning and achieve his full spiritual potential. It is this gift of *cheirut* which is offered to the Jewish nation through the laws given at Sinai.

The search for *cheirut* is therefore intensely personal and can only be performed by each individual for him- or herself. There can be no shortcuts nor can this journey towards true personal freedom be performed through a representative. When it comes to Sfirat Ha'omer, the mitzva that marks the passage towards *cheirut*, therefore, the Torah proclaims, *U'sfartem lachem*, "And you shall count for yourselves" (in the plural). Each individual is obligated to count for himself,[8] to find his own road towards personal meaning.

---

5. Torat Kohanim, Vayikra 25:8.
6. Shmot 32:16.
7. Pirkei Avot 6:2.
8. Talmud Bavli Menachot 65b.

— **D** —

Two mitzvot thus emerge within the span of two parshiot, each the mirror image of the other.

Both of these mitzvot speak of counting seven cycles of seven towards the goal of a fiftieth, culminating unit. Both represent a journey towards a specific dimension of freedom.

There, however, the parallel ends.

The counting of years towards *Yovel*, found in Parshat Behar, serves as a reminder to societies across the ages of their obligation to grant *dror*, liberty, to those under their sway; to break the chains of tyranny and prejudice that limit personal opportunity for any individual within their boundaries.

The counting of days towards the festival of Shavuot, found in Parshat Emor, on the other hand, speaks directly to the individuals themselves: *No one can grant you personal freedom. Cheirut is a God-given right which you must discover for yourselves.*

Points to Ponder

The inscription on the Liberty Bell is incomplete…

Searching for a passage to properly mark the fiftieth anniversary of Pennsylvania's original Constitution (William Penn's forward-thinking 1701 Charter of Rights), the Pennsylvania Assembly, in 1751, chose a phrase from Parshat Behar: "Proclaim liberty throughout all the land unto all the inhabitants thereof."[9]

They ignored, however, the end of the sentence: "…a Jubilee year shall it be for you, and you shall return every man unto his heritage and every man unto his family you shall return."[10]

The omission seems reasonable. This second section of text, speaking of the steps to be followed after the proclamation of liberty, is, after all, difficult to understand. What does the mandate to return to one's family and heritage have to do with the acquisition of liberty?

On a technical level, Jewish law learns important additional precepts from the second half of this sentence. The phrase "You shall return every man to his heritage" conveys, according to the rabbis, the requirement that

---

9. Vayikra 25:10
10. Ibid.

property revert to its original owners on the Jubilee year.[11] From the words "Every man unto his family you shall return," the scholars derive that all indentured servants, including those who had previously indicated a desire to stay in servitude, must be freed. Even an individual who has clearly renounced his claim to freedom is released on *Yovel*.[12]

Another fundamental idea, however, may also be rooted in the passage "…a Jubilee year shall it be for you, and you shall return every man unto his heritage and every man unto his family you shall return."[13]

With the laws of the Jubilee year, the Torah informs us that *true freedom cannot be gained through a complete severance with the past*. In order to chart a new course towards the future, the past, with all its complexities, must be reckoned with: lessons must be learned, successes valued, failures confronted.

The law turns to the Jew who has sold himself into servitude because of poverty or thievery, and forces him to go free. *You cannot run away from your past*, the Torah insists, *you must return to your roots and confront your failure*. Likewise, the Torah instructs the property owner who has sold his cherished heritage, again because of poverty: *Learn from any errors that you may have made, so that you will succeed tomorrow*.

In short, the Torah informs us that the *dror*, liberty, granted by society on *Yovel* should serve as a prelude to the personal search for *cheirut*, freedom – a search that best begins with a journey into the past.

How ironic that a passage that has come to symbolize the American struggle to break free from past allegiances actually conveys the opposite message. There are no "brave new worlds" in Jewish thought. As we strike off towards a new dawn, we simultaneously step back, into our own complex past. Therein lies a wealth of experience that will guide us in our emerging endeavors. A healthy respect for that past is the best insurance for the future.

The words engraved on the Liberty Bell tell only part of the story. Any proclamation of liberty must be accompanied by a sense of responsibility emerging from the past. Only then do we stand a chance of succeeding as individuals and as a people.

---

11. Rashi, Vayikra 25:10, based on Talmud Bavli Rosh Hashana 8b, 9b.
12. Talmud Bavli Kiddushin 15a.
13. Ibid.

2 Oppression

Context

In the midst of the detailed laws regarding the *Yovel* year, the following general mandate concerning commerce is found: "And if you make a sale to your fellow, or make a purchase from the hand of your fellow, *al tonu ish et achiv*, do not oppress one another."[1]

The prohibition emerging from this passage is identified in rabbinic literature as the prohibition of *ona'at mamon*, financial oppression.

Two sentences later the text emphasizes: *V'lo tonu ish et amito…*, "And you shall not oppress one another, and you shall fear your God; I am the Lord your God."[2]

Rather than interpreting this passage as a reiteration of the warning against financial oppression, the rabbis explain that here, the Torah references the additional proscription of *ona'at devarim*, verbal oppression.[3]

The specific term *ona'a* (oppression) also appears in conjunction with two other prohibitions in the text:

1. *Ona'at hager*: oppression of the stranger[4]
2. *Ona'at eved*: oppression of a slave[5]

Questions

What is the meaning of the term *ona'a* and to what type of "oppression" does it refer?

What feature or features unite the seemingly disparate contexts within which this term is used?

---

1. Vayikra 25:14.
2. Ibid., 25:17.
3. Talmud Bavli Bava Metzia 58b.
4. Shmot 22:20; Vayikra 19:33.
5. Devarim 23:16–17.

What are the parameters of the prohibitions of *ona'at mamon*, *ona'at devarim*, *ona'at hager* and *ona'at eved*?

Approaches

─A─

A review of the four areas of law within which the term *ona'a* appears reveals one salient uniting feature: in each case the perpetrator exploits his superior position by attacking his victim's preexisting areas of weakness.

As we review the laws of *ona'a* in their various permutations, we will encounter, once again, the remarkable sense of interpersonal responsibility that permeates Torah law.

─B─

The most obvious application of the principle of *ona'a* is found in the arena of *ona'at hager*. The rabbis understand this prohibition to include any verbal or material advantage taken of someone who occupies a vulnerable position within Jewish society, specifically a *ger tzedek*, a righteous convert.

The Hebrew term for convert is *ger*, which literally means "stranger." Far from derogatory,[6] this label is used by Jewish tradition to underscore the convert's natural emotional exposure within the community. Coming to Judaism from the "outside," the convert may yet feel himself "a stranger," not fully connected to all aspects of his chosen people and tradition. He remains particularly susceptible to taunts, insults and potential embarrassment. The Torah therefore reminds us of our own national origins as "strangers" in the land of Egypt and cautions us against oppressing the *ger* in any way.[7]

In this as in other arenas, Jewish law thus vigorously protects those who are most "at risk." Individuals guilty of oppressing the convert transgress two sets of laws: the general laws prohibiting the oppression of all others (see below) and the specific proscriptions of *ona'at hager*, designed to protect the "stranger."[8]

An additional, supplementary prohibition forbidding oppression of

---

6. We have noted, in fact, the high esteem in which converts are held in Jewish thought (see *Shmot*: Yitro 1, *Points to Ponder*).
7. Shmot 22:20; Vayikra 19:33.
8. Rambam, *Mishneh Torah*, Hilchot Mechira 14:15.

a slave is found in the book of Devarim: "You shall not turn over to his master a slave who has escaped from his master to you. With you shall he dwell in your midst in whatever place he will choose in one of your gates, which is beneficial to him; you shall not oppress him."[9]

Many authorities view this later edict as expanding the prohibition of ona'at hager to include the oppression of all gerei toshav, resident aliens (non-Jews living within our borders who have accepted upon themselves basic moral laws), as well as full converts.[10]

— C —

The Torah's concern over oppression, however, is not limited only to attacks upon society's weakest members, but extends to any unfair advantage taken of another individual during the course of the many interpersonal dealings that mark life's daily routine. Behavior that causes needless mental anguish by highlighting any individual's weak point falls into the prohibited category of ona'at devarim, verbal oppression, recorded in Parshat Behar.

Practical examples of this prohibition, mentioned in the Talmud, include:

1. Disparaging the background of a penitent
2. Misleading a prospective customer about the nature of a specific merchant's business (in order to embarrass the merchant or the buyer)
3. Inquiring about the price of a specific object without any intention to buy
4. Soliciting technical advice from someone who you know lacks the necessary knowledge or expertise
5. Suggesting to someone that his suffering is due to his own evil deeds[11]

— D —

Finally, the prohibition of ona'at mamon, financial oppression, recorded in Parshat Behar, forbids taking advantage of another individual's vulnerability in the marketplace. The halachot of ona'at mamon are highly detailed and specific, to ensure the equitable treatment of all parties in the complex arenas of finance and commerce.

---

9. Devarim 23:16–17.
10. Sifrei, Devarim 23:16.
11. Talmud Bavli Bava Metzia 58b.

As understood by the rabbis, *the biblical prohibition of onaʾat mamon fundamentally forbids deceptive pricing.*[12] Both the buyer and seller are enjoined against capitalizing on the lack of knowledge of the other concerning the market value of a specific commodity. The seller is forbidden to deceptively overcharge and the buyer is forbidden to deceptively underpay.[13] Dependent on the extent of the deceit, different paths of recourse are offered to the victim by Jewish law.

While the Tannaim, Amoraim and later authorities debate the exact parameters of *onaʾat mamon*, the majority of halachists codify the basic laws as follows:

1. If the difference between the price paid and the actual market value of the item is less than one-sixth, the sale is final and no recourse exists.[14]

2. If the difference between the price paid and the actual market value of the item is exactly one-sixth, the discrepancy is returned to the victim.[15]

3. If the difference between the price paid and the actual market value of the item exceeds one-sixth, the sale can be invalidated.[16]

4. Dependent on the case, the computation of the *onaʾa* amount is based either on one-sixth of the actual value of the item or one-sixth of the money paid.[17]

5. The time period during which the buyer can reclaim his overpayment or invalidate the sale is not open-ended, but lasts until the time necessary to show the item to an expert merchant or a family member.[18] The time period during which a seller can reclaim underpayment, however, depends on the item. If the item is common and its actual price can be easily determined, the time period during which the seller can demand payment lasts until the time necessary to make such determination. If, however, the object is unique and comparisons with similar items cannot be easily made, the seller's time period remains open-ended.[19]

---

12. Ibid., 51b; Rambam, *Mishneh Torah*, Hilchot Mechira 12:1.
13. Talmud Bavli Bava Metzia 51a.
14. Ibid., 50b.
15. Ibid., 49b, 50b.
16. Ibid., 50b.
17. Ibid., 49b, Rambam, *Mishneh Torah*, Hilchot Mechira 12:2.
18. Talmud Bavli Bava Metzia 49b.
19. Ibid., 50b, Rambam, *Mishneh Torah*, Hilchot Mechira 12:6.

6. The laws of *ona'a* are not dependent on intent. Even if the deceit is inadvertent the rules of repayment apply.[20]

7. The laws of *ona'a* only apply to cases where the injured party is consciously or inadvertently misled by the other due to his own lack of knowledge. If, however, both parties enter into the deal with a full awareness of the facts and are willing to accept either the overcharge or underpayment involved, there is no *ona'a* in the transaction and the deal is final.[21]

8. Certain transactions, including the purchase of real estate, are exempt from the laws of *ona'at mamon*.[22]

9. The market value of commodities is determined through the factoring of a wide array of variables including overhead, geographic location, personal service offered, etc.[23]

— E —

The laws of *ona'at mamon* and other similar areas of halacha are a clear indication that the Torah's belief in a system of free enterprise is tempered by the need to guard members of the community from potential abuse of that very system. While the biblical law of *ona'at mamon* is limited to the arena of deceptive pricing, numerous later *takanot* are enacted by the rabbis to further protect the consumer. Widely debated and constantly refined, these edicts address areas of commerce including: excessive profit-taking (even when no deceit is involved), hoarding and market manipulation.

— F —

Across a wide breadth of life experience, the uniform laws of *ona'a* remind us that oppression can take many forms. From the halls of commerce to the treatment of converts, from the commodity trading floors to the marketplace of ideas, the Torah uses the same terminology to consistently communicate God's demand for ethical behavior in every arena of life and to make one point abundantly clear: the weak will always be protected with the full force of Jewish law.

---

20. Rambam, *Mishneh Torah*, Hilchot Mechira 12:1.
21. Talmud Bavli Bava Metzia 51b.
22. Ibid., 56a.
23. Shulchan Aruch, Choshen Mishpat 231:20, as elaborated upon by later *poskim*.

Points to Ponder

Oppression. The very term conjures up dramatic images of slaves and taskmasters, tyrants and victims. As our study has shown, however, the strength of Torah law lies in its ability to demystify seemingly esoteric concepts, to bring them down to earth and make them concretely relevant to our lives.

Oppression can be evidenced not only in extraordinary settings but even in our own everyday, ordinary lives. Every time we take advantage of someone else's vulnerability, through word or deed; every time we misuse a position of power (however transient that position may be), we fall prey to the sin of *ona'a* and to all of its damaging consequences.

As with all interpersonal sins, the cost of such behavior is ultimately measured not only in the anguish that we cause to others, but in the ultimate price that we ourselves pay. Any temporary pleasure or gain that we may accrue through the performance of such acts ultimately pales in comparison to the irretrievable harm caused to our own sacred souls.

3 A Puzzling Exception

Context

In a sweeping set of edicts at the beginning of Parshat Behar, the Torah regulates the sale of land within Jewish society.

1. Land should be sold only in the case of dire necessity.[1]

2. Land that has been sold may be redeemed after two years by the original owner or by his relatives. The price of redemption is computed on the basis of the purchase price minus the value of the years that have passed since the sale.[2]

3. Land that has not been redeemed automatically reverts back to the original owner with the onset of the Jubilee year.[3]

The implications of these laws are nothing less than staggering. *From a Torah perspective, land cannot be sold in perpetuity, only leased for a period of time.* Properly observed, the laws regulating the sale of land ensure, in the words of Rabbi Shimshon Raphael Hirsch, "the prevention of complete permanent poverty of some families by the side of overpowering accumulation of property in the hands of the few."[4]

Once again, the Torah strikes at the critical area of land ownership, the fault line between the haves and the have-nots throughout history (see Kedoshim 3, *Approaches* C). Even an individual who becomes so destitute that he is forced to sell his family's holdings can be assured that those holdings will be returned to him or to his heirs with the arrival of the *Yovel* year, if not before.

Framing the message of these majestic laws, the text proclaims: "And the land will not be sold in perpetuity, for the land is Mine; for sojourners and residents are you with Me."[5]

---

1. Rambam, *Mishneh Torah*, Hilchot Shemita V'yovel 11:3, based on Vayikra 25:25.
2. Vayikra 25:24–28, Talmud Bavli Arachin 29b.
3. Vayikra 25:10, 13, 28.
4. Rabbi Shimshon Raphael Hirsch, Vayikra 25:34.
5. Ibid., 25:23.

There is, however, one glaring exception to the Torah's rules of land-lease. If an individual sells a residence house within a walled city, the regulations that apply are almost the opposite of those listed above. In such cases:

1. The original owner, or, upon his death, his heirs, may redeem his property only during the first year after the sale. Other relatives of the seller are prohibited from redeeming this property.

2. After the first year has passed, any opportunity for redemption has been lost. The residence is considered sold in perpetuity, with the sale unaffected even by the arrival of the Jubilee year.[6]

Questions

Why is any exception made to the general rules that govern land sales in Jewish law?

In light of the overwhelmingly significant social lessons conveyed by the general laws of land redemption and the return of land in the *Yovel* year, shouldn't these laws be applied to all transactions, including the sales of residential dwellings in walled cities?

Approaches

Confronted with the puzzling legal distinction made in the text between city dwellings and agricultural property, the scholars offer a variety of explanations.

——— **A** ———

The Ramban maintains that the Torah's laws of property purchase reflect the needs and mindset of the seller. Recognizing that the sale of a personal dwelling, such as a residence in a walled city, is emotionally wrenching and embarrassing, the Torah allows for immediate redemption within the first year of the sale. If, however, no redemption occurs within that period, it is safe to assume that the seller has given up hope of ever returning to his original home and has established himself in a new domicile. Since the seller's inability to return to his original home, therefore, causes him no

---

6. Ibid., 25:29–30.

continued real harm, the Torah allows the property to conclusively remain in the hands of the buyer.

In the case of agricultural properties and dwellings attached to them, however, the situation is vastly different. An individual's potential livelihood continues to be connected to the property that he was forced by circumstance to sell. The longer this property remains outside of his possession, the greater the ongoing damage. The Torah therefore allows for an extended period of redemption and, barring such redemption, for the full return of the property at the beginning of the Jubilee year.[7]

— B —

The Chizkuni offers two rationales for the distinction between city dwellings and rural property.

In an approach similar to that of the Ramban, this scholar first explains that God is only concerned for the return of property upon which the owner's livelihood depends. Fields and the dwellings attached to them are therefore open to an extended redemption period and, barring such redemption, must be returned to the original owner upon the commencement of the *Yovel* year.

In his second explanation, however, the Chizkuni makes a one-hundred-eighty-degree turn by suggesting that these laws may actually reflect the needs and mindset of the purchaser, rather than those of the seller. An individual who purchases a city dwelling, the Chizkuni explains, generally intends to do so in perpetuity. After all, individuals are rarely comfortable living in the homes of others. The Torah, therefore, grants the purchaser full ownership of the dwelling after the first year has passed.

By their very nature, however, agricultural properties and the dwellings attached to them are more transient in terms of habitation, as evidenced by the fact that sharecroppers and workers often live in others' fields. The purchaser of such property acquires no personal connection to the land and consequently develops no need for continued ownership. These properties, therefore, remain open for redemption and are returned to the original owner with the arrival of the *Yovel* year.[8]

---

7.   Ramban, Vayikra 25:29.
8.   Chizkuni, Vayikra 25:29.

C

For his part, Rabbi Shimshon Raphael Hirsch sees in the complex and divergent laws of land sale and redemption a divine societal "grand plan" designed to create "an urban population occupied with agriculture."[9] Rural dwelling places attached to agricultural property are protected, like the properties themselves, from permanent sale. The return of these properties to their original owners at the *Yovel* year would ensure that, as a rule, "every field and vineyard would have as its proprietor a householder in the neighboring town."[10] Jewish society would thus be characterized in the main by a blend of "town-bred intelligence"[11] and the natural, uncomplicated outlook on life fostered by connection with nature and the land.[12]

Only in walled cities would a population become experientially divorced from the land, focused on trade and industry, as opposed to agricultural work. In such cities, land itself becomes less significant as an educational, stabilizing force and may, therefore, be sold in perpetuity. Population centers of this nature, however, were clearly regulated in both size and number, limited to locations that were walled at the time of Yehoshua, before they were inhabited by the Israelites.[13]

D

Finally, a wonderfully creative, practical approach to the laws of dwellings in walled cities is offered by the nineteenth–twentieth-century Lithuanian scholar Rabbi Meir Simcha Hacohen of Dvinsk, in his classic work the *Meshech Chochma*. Through the eyes of this scholar, the issue before us translates into a clash between communal and personal need, with communal concerns emerging triumphant.

The Meshech Chochma notes that walled cities played a crucial military role in the defense of the Land of Israel, as a major line of resistance against invading armies. The laws of land redemption and return could not be applied to these population centers without severely weakening the residential stability essential to their role.

---

9. Rabbi Shimshon Raphael Hirsch, Vayikra 25:34.
10. Ibid.
11. Ibid.
12. Ibid.
13. Ibid.

If every fifty years dwellings within walled cities returned to their original owners, the resultant population upheaval would sorely undermine each city's infrastructure. Vast numbers of newcomers would arrive, unfamiliar with the ways of the area; neighbors would be strangers to each other; personal relationships, years in the making, would suddenly be destroyed; the community's ability to act together in any concerted fashion would be sorely compromised.

Such a phenomenon would place the entire country in grave danger.

Therefore, although the laws of redemption and return should really apply to all property, including residences in walled cities, the Torah creates an exception. The personal rights of the owners are overruled by communal need; and the overarching social laws of land redemption and return are set aside in favor of national security.[14]

Points to Ponder

At face value, the Meshech Chochma's observations concerning the military role of walled cities hardly seem relevant to our lives. Modes of warfare have obviously changed since the time of the Torah. Even in Israel where, unfortunately, our readiness for conflict must be constant, we have more effective weapons at our disposal than walled population centers.

And yet, with a little imagination, I believe that we can hear the Meshech Chochma speaking directly to us. After all, our Jewish communities do lie on the frontlines of an ongoing struggle for continued Jewish existence in a challenging world. In Israel, issues of physical survival are clearly played out on a daily basis across the country. In the diaspora it is the battle for spiritual survival that is more keenly felt. Everywhere in the world, in equally significant yet varying ways, strong Jewish communal structure protects us against serious threats to our Jewish way of life.

How unfortunate, then, that in the diaspora, where strong involvement in the community is our best hope of maintaining our Jewish identity, we often take our synagogue communities for granted, failing to appreciate their pivotal place in our personal and national lives. So accustomed are we to being part of such settings, we rarely stop to think about how different things would be without them.

Synagogues at their best fulfill the role implicit in their Hebrew title

---

14. Meshech Chochma, Vayikra 25:29.

beit knesset, "house of gathering." More than simply a house of prayer, the synagogue has become the central locus of our religious lives, providing both a safe communal harbor and an environment encouraging spiritual growth. Within such shuls, participants develop into an extended family, celebrating each other's occasions of joy, sharing each other's sorrow. Generations gather, enabling congregants to learn life lessons from each other's worlds and experiences. Through involvement with the *beit knesset*, children learn that they belong to something bigger. Within its walls, they form lifelong friendships and acquire much of their world outlook.

How lonely and isolating it must be, particularly in an increasingly turbulent world, for those who find themselves without the support provided by such communities. How critical these congregations are – particularly for us, a people within a people throughout the diaspora – striving to maintain our unique faith and traditions.

In the battle to maintain Jewish identity, particularly in the diaspora, synagogue communities are today's "walled cities," our first line of defense in the struggle for spiritual survival. Like those walled cities of yore, therefore, our own communities must be carefully protected against challenges that threaten to undermine their stability and effectiveness.

The battle must be waged, for example, against the growing phenomenon of "shtieblization," the fragmentation of large congregations into small scattered prayer settings with little or no connection. Such venues make no real demands upon their participants and provide little sense of collective responsibility beyond the shared Shabbat prayer. In many neighborhoods, the proliferation of *shtieblach* has created an environment where neighbors no longer know each other and where people often define themselves by the shuls to which they do *not* go.

Even within large, vibrant synagogue settings, potential dangers lurk. A growing sense of triumphant insularity, particularly in the Orthodox community, prevents any meaningful sharing with those "outside." Unaffiliated Jews feel less and less connected to thriving Jewish communities in their own backyards, while the communities themselves do little to change that. I have often wondered how "successful" Modern Orthodox congregations, such as my own, will one day be judged. Will the credit we receive for our own internal accomplishments be offset by our lack of involvement with the disappearing American Jewish community beyond our walls?

Finally, internally, our synagogues could certainly use some fine tuning. How many congregations today can boast of prayer services that are spiritually uplifting? Do participants in the service spend more time talking or praying? Do they feel connected at all to the experience of prayer? What percentage of the congregation participates in ongoing Torah study and daily prayer with a minyan? Are the children of the community involved in synagogue youth programming and activities, or have they become too over-programmed and jaded to care? Are the different groupings within the synagogues engaged with and learning from each other or are their relationships colored by misunderstanding and mistrust? Has the community mastered the art of welcoming and integrating new members without causing the long-standing congregants to feel that they are being "pushed out"?

Centuries ago, the cities that represented the first line of defense against the enemy had to be, according to the Meshech Chochma, finely tuned and functioning. If not, God forbid, disaster could result.

Our own synagogue communities need constant attention as well. They stand on the frontlines of the battle for our future.

4 A Casual Curse

Context

As Parshat Bechukotai and the book of Vayikra draw to a close, God delivers a stinging rebuke and warning to the Israelites. Known as the *Tochacha Haketana*, the small rebuke (in contrast to a second, larger rebuke found in the book of Devarim), this section contains a series of frighteningly prophetic descriptions of the tragedies that will befall the nation should they fail to follow God's ways.

At the core of this *tochacha*, a word is found that, in this conjugation, appears nowhere else in the Torah text. Here, however, this term, *keri*, is repeated no less than seven times within the span of twenty sentences. According to most authorities (see below), this term apparently connotes "casualness" or "happenstance" and is derived from the root *kara*, to happen.

The passages of the *Tochacha* within which the term *keri* appears are:

1. "And if you will walk with me *keri*…"[1]
2. "And if in spite of these things you will not be chastised towards me, and you will walk with me *keri*…"[2]
3. "And then I [God], too, will walk with you with *keri*…"[3]
4. "And if with all this you will not hearken unto Me, and you will walk with Me with *keri*…"[4]
5. "And I will walk with you with a fury of *keri*…"[5]

---

1. Vayikra 26:21.
2. Ibid., 26:23.
3. Ibid., 26:24.
4. Ibid., 26:27.
5. Ibid., 26:28.

6. "And they will confess their sin and the sin of their fathers, for the treachery with which they have betrayed Me, and also for having walked with Me with *keri*."[6]

7. "And I, too, shall walk with them with *keri*…"[7]

Questions

By using the term *keri* so prominently at both ends of the *Tochacha's* equation, in both the description of the nation's possible transgression and in the description of God's possible response, the Torah apparently emphasizes a critical idea, central to the very nature of sin and punishment. *If we could only understand this concept*, the text seems to say, *we could finally recognize where we go wrong. We could strike to the core of our failures and their consequences, finding a way to break the recurring, tragic cycle that plagues our relationship with the Divine.*

And yet, the text remains frustratingly unclear.

Why, at this point, does the Torah suddenly introduce, for the first and only time, the word *keri*?

Once introduced, why is this term repeated so often in such a short span of text?

Above all, within the context of the *Tochacha*, in the realm of both sin and punishment, what does the word *keri* actually mean?

Approaches

— **A** —

Confronted with this puzzling term and its use in the *Tochacha*, numerous commentaries propose a wide variety of interpretations.

Both Rashi and his grandson, the Rashbam, for example, introduce a basic translation upon which most commentaries build. These scholars translate the word *keri* to mean "casual" or "inconsistent" (derived, as stated above, from the root *kara*, to happen). If the nation sins by worshiping God in an erratic, inconsistent manner, Rashi and the Rashbam explain, God

---

6. Ibid., 26:40.
7. Ibid., 26:41.

will respond in kind and will relate to the nation haphazardly and unpre-
dictably, as well.[8]

A number of other commentaries, including Rabbeinu Bachya and
the Ohr Hachaim, choose a related but different path. The term *keri*, these
scholars maintain, describes a flawed world outlook that can lead to immeasurable sin. An individual who sees the world in a fashion of *keri* perceives no pattern to the events unfolding around him. In place of Divine
Providence, this individual observes only random coincidence; and in
place of punishment for sin, accidental misfortune. For such an individual,
tshuva (return to the proper path) becomes increasingly unattainable. In
a haphazard world governed by arbitrary forces, after all, there exists little
incentive for change.[9]

Going a step further, the Ohr Hachaim perceives in God's reaction –
"And then I [God], too, will walk with you with *keri*…"[10] – a carefully calibrated "measure for measure" response to the nation's failing. If the people
refuse to see a divinely ordained pattern in the world around them, God
will withdraw, making it even more difficult for them to perceive His presence. The punishments to follow will seem even more random, bearing no
obvious connection to the nation's sins. The people's failure to recognize
God's imminence will thus prove frighteningly prophetic, for God will respond with "distance."[11]

For his part, Rabbi Shimshon Raphael Hirsch interprets the sin associated with the word *keri* as "indifference" to God's will. Those guilty of this
transgression find considerations other than God's will central to their lives
and their sporadic obedience to Torah law is thus purely coincidental. God
responds to this sin in kind, says Hirsch, by removing His Divine protection from the nation and allowing the natural course of world history to
determine their fate. The welfare of the Jewish people will be advanced only
coincidentally, when that welfare happens to correspond to the interests
and needs of the powerful nations around them.[12]

Finally a group of other scholars, Onkelos chiefly among them, diverge
from the above explanations entirely and explain the term *keri* to mean

---

8. Rashi, Vayikra 26:21.
9. Rabbeinu Bachya, ibid.; Ohr Hachaim, ibid.
10. Vayikra 26:24.
11. Ohr Hachaim, ibid.
12. Rabbi Shimshon Raphael Hirsch, Vayikra 26:21, 23–24.

"stubbornness" or "harshness." If the nation stubbornly refuses to obey based upon God's law, God's response will be harsh and unforgiving.[13]

—— B ——

A clearer understanding of the puzzling term *keri* and its repeated use in the *Tochacha* can be gained if we consider the basic approach of Rashi and the Rashbam (who interpret the term to mean a casual approach to God's will) in light of the "rules" that govern our own life experiences.

Many years ago, I asked the participants in one of my synagogue classes to name the one most important component in any successful interpersonal relationship. Expecting a plethora of suggestions, I was surprised when they unanimously responded with the one word which I had earlier defined for myself as my own answer: *trust.*

Our associations with each other, from partnerships to friendships to marriages, can endure many blows and setbacks. One wound, however, invariably proves fatal: *the total loss of trust.* When mutual trust is gone and cannot be regained; when the relationship no longer feels safe and secure; when each participant no longer believes that the other consistently has his partner's best interests at heart, the relationship is doomed.

God thus turns to the Israelites and proclaims: "And if you will walk with me *keri*…"

If I find that you are deliberately inconsistent in your commitment to Me; if I find that you are only at My door when you choose to be; if I find that I cannot trust you to seek My presence and relate to Me continually; then I will respond in kind…

"And then I [God], too, will walk with you with *keri*"

You will no longer be able to count on My continuing presence in your lives. I will distance Myself and not be there when you expect Me to be. Our relationship will become casual and inconsistent; all trust will be lost…

God will forgive many failings and sins, but when we lose His trust, the punishments of the *Tochacha* are the result.

Points to Ponder

The text's prominent use of the puzzling word *keri* in the *Tochacha* brings our study of Vayikra full circle…

---

13. Targum Onkelos, Vayikra 26: 21, 23.

This complex central book of the Torah, with its disparate laws ranging from minute, mysterious rituals to towering ethical edicts, makes one real demand upon the reader.

We are challenged to earn God's trust.

Judaism is not a smorgasbord. The Torah emphasizes that we cannot pick and choose the elements of observance that suit our fancy. Each law, from a seemingly minor sacrificial detail to a powerful edict such as "Love your fellow as yourself," has its place and its purpose. Each halachic element is an essential component in the tapestry of trust meant to be woven between God and his people.

In structure and content, the book of Vayikra reminds us that when we earn God's trust through faithful adherence to His multifaceted law, we will be able to trust in God's continued presence within our lives.

Sources

Abravanel – Rabbi Don Yitzchak Abravanel; biblical commentator, philosopher, statesman, diplomat (Portugal, Spain, Italy, 1437–1508).

The last great figure of Spanish Jewry, the Abravanel served during his lifetime as finance minister to the kings of Portugal, Spain and Italy. The Abravanel used his high position and great wealth to benefit his brethren and spared no effort in petitioning the Spanish king and queen, at the time of the Spanish Inquisition, to reverse the edict banishing the Jews from Spain. Failing in that effort, the Abravanel himself suffered expulsion in 1492 with the rest of the exiles.

The Abravanel authored many works including major commentaries on the Torah, other books of Tanach, *Pirkei Avot*, the Haggada and the Rambam's *Guide to the Perplexed*. His commentaries are divided into chapters, each of which is introduced by the list of questions and problems which he intends to address in the chapter. The Abravanel often applied the lessons learned from Scripture to issues confronting the Jewish society of his day.

Abudarham, David ben Yosef – Liturgical commentator (Spain, fourteenth century).

A member of a distinguished family, the Abudarham authored *Sefer Abudarham*, an important guide to the laws, customs and texts of the Jewish prayer service. His work was designed to address a declining understanding of the meaning of the prayers and of the rituals associated with them.

The Abudarham drew upon sources in the Talmud Bavli, the Talmud Yerushalmi, Geonic literature and earlier and later commentaries. He makes extensive use of the Siddur of Rav Saadia Gaon and may well have been the last to see an original of this book.

The *Sefer Abudarham* remains a critical source for Spanish, Provencal, French and Ashkenazi practices and customs surrounding the prayer service.

Alshich, Moshe – Rabbi, scholar, halachist, commentator (Turkey, Israel, Syria, 1508–1593).

Born in Adrianople, Turkey, the Alshich emigrated at a young age to Tzfat, Israel, where he studied under and was ordained by Rabbi Yosef Caro. The Alshich gained such prominence as a teacher, orator, halachic authority and communal leader that he was granted the title *Hakadosh* (the holy one), a title reserved for a few select rabbinic figures across Jewish history. The Alshich's last years were spent in Damascus, Syria.

Among other works, the Alshich published volumes of his popular lectures and sermons relating to various sections of Tanach (Torah, Prophets and Writings). Particularly noteworthy is his commentary on the Torah, *Torat Moshe*, which follows a homiletic approach and is filled with practical lessons on ethics and morals.

Auerbach, Shlomo Zalman – Talmudic scholar, rosh yeshiva, halachic authority, one of the major halachic decisors of the twentieth century (Palestine/Israel, 1910–1995).

Born in the Shaarei Chesed neighborhood of Jerusalem founded by his grandfather, Rabbi Shlomo Zalman Porush, Auerbach's early years were already marked by advanced scholarship. He mastered the entire Talmudic tractate of Kiddushin by the age of eleven and distinguished himself during his period of study at the Etz Chaim Yeshiva in Jerusalem. His first major published work, *Meorei Eish,* dealt with the issue of electricity and Shabbat.

Auerbach studied under the renowned sage Rabbi Tzvi Pesach Frank and enjoyed close relationships with major sages including Rabbi Chaim Ozer Grodzinski and the two major leaders of the Charedi (fervently observant) community through the early and middle years of the twentieth century: the Chazon Ish (Rabbi Avraham Yeshaya Karelitz) and Rabbi Elazar Menachem Shach.

Auerbach reflected scholarly brilliance, an incisive and analytic mind and a warm and enveloping love for all Jews as he rose to become the preeminent halachic authority of his time in Israel. His classes as rosh yeshiva of the Kol Torah Yeshiva in Jerusalem were renowned and his countless students continue to shape the course of Orthodox Judaism.

Aviner, Shlomo Chaim Hacohen – Rabbi, rosh yeshiva, author, Religious Zionist leader (France, Israel, 1943–).

Born in Lyon, France, Aviner played a major role in the Bnei Akiva

Zionist youth movement, eventually becoming its national director. In 1996, Aviner immigrated to Israel, settling in Kibbutz Sdei Eliyahu in the northern Jordan Valley. After serving as rabbi of Kibbutz Lavi in the Galilee and as rabbi of Moshav Keshet in the Golan Heights, Aviner assumed the rabbinic position in Beit El, the position that he currently occupies. Aviner is also rosh yeshiva of the Ateret Kohanim Yeshiva in the Old City of Jerusalem, an institution that has played a major role in establishing and preserving a Jewish presence throughout the Old City.

One of the leading rabbis of the National Religious movement, Aviner has carefully staked out nuanced yet often controversial positions on the difficult issues facing Religious Zionism today. He has published numerous volumes including: commentary on the Torah and Tanach, a Haggada and analyses of the thought of renowned Religious Zionist scholars.

Avnei Nezer – Rabbi Avraham ben Ze'ev Nachum Bornstein of Sochaczew; Chassidic Rebbe (grand rabbi), Talmudic scholar, halachist (Poland, 1839–1910).

The first Rebbe of the Sochatchover dynasty, Bornstein earned early fame as a child prodigy and, at the age of fourteen, married the daughter of the renowned Chassidic leader Rabbi Menachem Mendel of Kotsk.

Bornstein occupied a number of rabbinical posts before assuming, in 1883, the position of rabbi in the city of Sochaczew, where he remained until his death.

Emerging as one of the greatest halachic scholars of his generation, Bornstein founded a yeshiva and trained numerous disciples who became scholarly Chassidic leaders in their own right.

Bornstein's two major works were *Avnei Nezer*, his collection of responsa on the four sections of the *Shulchan Aruch* (which earned him the personal title the Avnei Nezer), and *Eglei Tal*, a study of the laws of Shabbat.

Avot D'Rabi Natan – An interpretive expansion on the Mishnaic tractate of *Pirkei Avot* (see below).

Apparently dating from the Mishnaic period, *Avot D'Rabi Natan* is essentially a companion piece to *Pirkei Avot*.

In many cases, *Avot D'Rabi Natan* acts as a commentary to the existing text of *Pirkei Avot*, elaborating on and enriching the Mishna through anecdotes and exegetical interpretation. On other occasions, each of these texts presents material not found in the other.

Babad, Yosef – Rabbi, Talmudic scholar, halachic authority (Poland, 1800–1874).

Few life details are known concerning Babad, who served as a rabbi in several cities in Galicia before being appointed chief of the rabbinic court in Tarnopol in 1857.

His primary work was the renowned *Minchat Chinuch*, a major commentary and expansion on the *Sefer Hachinuch*.

Bass, Shabbetai ben Yosef – Biblical and Talmudic scholar, bibliographer, printer (Poland, Czechoslovakia, Germany, Holland, 1641–1718).

Following the murder of his parents in a pogrom in Kalisz, Poland, Bass and his elder brother fled to Prague. There he received both a thorough Talmudic and general education and was appointed bass singer (hence his name) in the renowned Altneu Shul of Prague.

Bass's love of books drew him to publishing and printing. Between 1674 and 1679, he visited libraries in Poland, Germany and Holland, stopping in various centers of Jewish scholarship. In Amsterdam he studied the art of printing and proofreading and published a series of works, including his renowned supercommentary on Rashi, the *Siftei Chachamim*, as well as a Hebrew bibliography of twenty-two hundred Judaic works, citing books, authors, contents, format and place and year of printing. Subsequently, Bass established a successful printing press in Dyhernfurth, Germany, but was plagued by a series of misfortunes including anti-Semitic accusations that led to his brief arrest. The last years of his life were devoted to the second edition of his bibliographical material, which he never completed.

Bechor Shor – Biblical commentator, Talmudic scholar, poet (France, twelfth century).

A member of the group of medieval scholars known as the Tosafists, Bechor Shor was a student of the renowned Talmudic scholar and commentator Rabbeinu Yaakov Tam. Little is known of the details of Bechor Shor's life, and controversy swirls around his possible identification as the Tosafist Rabbi Yaakov ben Yitzchak of Orleans.

In addition to his annotations on the Talmud, Bechor Shor authored a biblical commentary noteworthy for its concentration on *pshat* combined with a general respect for earlier Midrashic literature.

Beit Halevi – Rabbi Yosef Ber Soloveitchik; rabbi, Talmudic scholar, rosh yeshiva, halachist (Belarus, Poland, Russia, 1820–1892).

The Beit Halevi was the great-grandson of Rabbi Chaim Volozhiner and the great-grandfather of Rabbi Yosef Dov Soloveitchik.

Incisive, brilliant and determined in his approach to Talmud study, the Beit Halevi also distinguished himself through extraordinary acts of kindness towards the poor and needy.

The Beit Halevi's life was marked by numerous personal and professional transitions. In 1854, after years of study in the cities of Brody, Lemberg and Minsk, he assumed the position of co-rosh yeshiva of the Yeshiva of Volozhin, partnering with Rabbi Naftali Tzvi Yehuda Berlin (the Netziv). Over time, however, it became apparent that differences in approach and temperament precluded the ability of these great leaders to work together. After ten years of service to the yeshiva, therefore, the Beit Halevi left Volozhin to become the rabbi of Slutsk. In 1875 he relinquished that position and in 1878 he became the rabbi in Brisk, where he remained until his death. His son Chaim (Reb Chaim Brisker) succeeded him.

His numerous published works, including commentary on the Talmud, responsa, sermons and halachic novella, were all printed under the title *Beit Halevi*.

Bleich, J. David – Rabbi, Talmudic scholar, halachic authority (United States, 1936–).

Professor of Talmud (rosh yeshiva) at the Rabbi Isaac Elchanan Theological Seminary (RIETS) of Yeshiva University, head of that seminary's postgraduate institute for the study of Talmudic jurisprudence and family law, professor of law at the Benjamin Cardozo School of Law, rabbi of Congregation Bnei Jehuda in New York, Bleich has achieved a well-earned reputation as a contemporary authority on Jewish law and ethics.

Among the volumes authored or edited by Bleich are *Contemporary Halachic Problems*, *Judaism and Healing*, *Providence in the Philosophy of Gersonides*, *Time of Death in Jewish Law*, *With Perfect Faith: Foundations of Jewish Belief* and *Jewish Bioethics*. His countless articles cover a myriad of topics in Jewish thought and law.

Caro, Yosef – *Hamechaber* (the author); scholar, halachist, author of the *Shulchan Aruch* (Set table), the universally accepted, authoritative code of Jewish law (Spain and/or Portugal, Turkey, Israel, 1488–1575).

Born either in Spain or Portugal, Caro fled to Turkey with his family upon the expulsion of Jews from Portugal, in 1497. Living successively in the cities of Istanbul, Adrianople, Nikopol and Salonika, Caro studied with numerous scholars, many of whom shaped his mystical life perspective.

In 1522, at the age of thirty-four, Caro began to write his monumental *Beit Yosef*, a project which would occupy him for twenty years and which he concluded only after moving to Tzfat, Israel. With this work, Caro strove to create order out of the multiplicity of codes and halachic rulings that had developed in Jewish law over the centuries. Caro traced each law to its origins, discussed the law's development through an analysis of divergent opinions and rendered authoritative practical rulings. In order to avoid unnecessary duplication, Caro fashioned the *Beit Yosef* as a commentary to the *Arba Turim* of Rabbi Yaakov ben Asher.

While the *Beit Yosef* was considered by Caro to be his most important scholarly writing, it is the more succinct digest of that work, the *Shulchan Aruch*, for which this scholar is eventually immortalized. The *Shulchan Aruch*, with its ordered, succinct presentation of practical Jewish law, quickly became the authoritative legal code for world Jewry and the point of departure for halachic works that followed.

Among Caro's other contributions was the *Kesef Mishneh*, an extensive commentary on the Rambam's *Mishneh Torah*.

Charlop, Zevulun – Contemporary rabbi, scholar, educator (United States, 1929–).

A renowned scholar, educator and preacher, Charlop graduated from Yeshiva College in 1951 and received *smicha* from the Rabbi Isaac Elchanan Theological Seminary (RIETS) of Yeshiva University in 1954. That same year he assumed the position of rabbi of the Young Israel of Mosholu Parkway in the Bronx, New York, a position that he holds to this day.

From 1971 to 2007, Charlop served as dean of RIETS. He currently holds the positions of dean emeritus of RIETS and special advisor to the president of Yeshiva University on yeshiva affairs.

The author of numerous articles, essays and studies, Charlop comes from a long line of rabbinic leadership. His father, Rabbi Jechiel Charlop, was ordained at RIETS in 1921 and served as the rabbi of the Bronx Jewish Center for forty-six years. His grandfather, Rabbi Yaakov Moshe Charlop, was an associate of Chief Rabbi Avraham Yitzchak Kook and served as rosh yeshiva of Merkaz HaRav Yeshiva in Jerusalem from its inception.

Chatam Sofer – Rabbi Moshe ben Shmuel Sofer; rabbinic leader, Talmudic scholar, halachist, biblical commentator (Germany, Hungary, 1762–1839). A child prodigy, the Chatam Sofer entered yeshiva at the age of nine and was delivering public lectures by the age of thirteen. After years of intensive study, he assumed rabbinic and teaching positions in several communities before accepting, in 1807, his primary position in Pressburg, Hungary. There he established a major yeshiva which housed, at its height, five hundred students, many of whom went on to become influential leaders in their own right.

Reacting to the newly developing Reform movement, the Chatam Sofer vehemently opposed any changes or innovations in Jewish practice. He is considered by many to be one of the most influential figures in the development of Chareidi Judaism (the most theologically conservative form of Orthodox Judaism today). The Chatam Sofer authored numerous important responsa (answers to halachic questions) as well as oft-studied commentaries on the Torah and Talmud.

Chizkuni – Rabbi Chizkiya ben Manoach Chizkuni; biblical commentator (France, thirteenth century).

Almost nothing is known about the personal life of the Chizkuni, a classical biblical commentator who lived in Provence around the year 1250. The Chizkuni's commentary, which focuses on the *pshat* (simple meaning) of the text, is based, according to the author, upon a number of earlier sources. In particular, the Chizkuni often elaborates upon the observations of Rashi.

The commentary of the Chizkuni first appeared in print in Venice in 1524.

Da'at Zekeinim Miba'alei Hatosafot – A compilation of Torah commentary authored by the Tosafists (a large group of twelfth- to thirteenth-century medieval rabbis whose critical and explanatory glosses are basic to the study of Talmud).

The period of the Tosafists began after the completion of Rashi's commentaries; the first Tosafists were actually Rashi's sons-in-law and grandsons. The Talmudic commentaries of the Tosafists are characterized by lengthy analyses of difficult passages and by a willingness to critically review the positions of their predecessors, particularly Rashi.

Preserved in manuscript for centuries, the *Da'at Zekeinim Miba'alei Hatosafot* was first formally published in 1783.

Eiger, Akiva – Rabbi, Talmudic scholar, halachic authority (Germany, 1761–1873).

A figure of exemplary kindness and humanity, Eiger earned a place of major leadership within the German Jewish community based on his extraordinary scholarship. His early years were spent in study first in his hometown of Eisenstadt, then in Breslau and Lissa. In 1791, Eiger accepted a position in Märkisch-Friedland where he established a yeshiva. In 1814 he became the rabbi in Posen, establishing yet another, larger, yeshiva.

Eiger was a strong opponent of the Reform and Haskala movements yet was sensitive to, and made adjustments for, the changing educational needs of his day. He was extremely modest, eschewing honorific titles, and remained uncomfortable reaping any material benefit from his rabbinical services. He interfaced with the secular authorities, leading an 1807 delegation of Jewish leaders in negotiations with the French government over Jewish rights in the newly established duchy of Warsaw. Eiger received a message of thanks from Frederick William III for service rendered during the cholera epidemic of 1831.

Eiger's numerous works include critical glosses and notes to the Mishna, Talmud and *Shulchan Aruch*.

Epstein, Baruch Halevi – Commentator, scholar, author (Russia, 1860–1942).

The son of Yechiel Michel Epstein, Baruch Halevi studied under the tutelage of both his father and his uncle, the Netziv.

Although he was offered numerous rabbinic positions in such major centers as Pinsk, Moscow and Petrograd, Epstein opted to earn his livelihood as a bookkeeper and to devote his free time to Torah study. The author of numerous volumes, he is best known for his monumental *Torah Temima*. In this work, he connects passages of the Talmud and Midrash to their sources in the written text and comments extensively on the topics they raise.

Epstein, Kalonymus Kalman Halevi – Chassidic rabbi, preacher and commentator (Poland, circa 1753–1823).

A disciple of the famed Chassidic sages, Rabbi Elimelech of Lizhensk and Yaakov Yitzchak ("the Seer") of Lublin, Epstein established a Chassidic presence in Krakow, to the strong opposition of the established Jewish community. Epstein, however, persevered and succeeded in promulgating Chassidic tradition throughout western Galicia.

Epstein's primary work was the *Ma'or Va'shemesh*, a commentary on the Torah, replete with information on the lives and accomplishments of the Chassidic masters.

Ettlinger, Jacob – Rabbi, scholar, halachist (Germany, 1798–1871).

Ettlinger received his early education from his father, a rabbi in Karlsruhe, and continued his studies in Würzburg, where he also attended university until an anti-Semitic outbreak forced him to leave. In 1826 he was appointed district rabbi for the districts of Ladenburg and Ingolstadt and settled in Mannheim, where he founded a yeshiva. Ten years later, he was appointed chief rabbi of Altona, where he established another yeshiva and where he remained until his death.

Ettlinger was a deep, unswerving traditionalist and a strong opponent of the developing Reform movement. In that vein, he led a major rabbinic protest against the conference of the Reform rabbis in Brunswick in 1844.

A prolific author, Ettlinger's powerful influence was felt in his lifetime and beyond, particularly through the continued work of his renowned students, Rabbis Shimshon Raphael Hirsch and Azriel Hildesheimer.

Feinstein, Moshe – Reb Moshe; rabbi, preeminent Torah sage and halachic authority of the twentieth century (Russia, America, 1895–1986).

After serving as rabbi of Luban (near Minsk) for sixteen years, Reb Moshe immigrated to the United States in 1937. Settling in the Lower East Side, where he remained for the rest of his life, he assumed the position of rosh yeshiva at Mesivta Tiferes Yerushalayim. Under his guidance, this institution became a leading American yeshiva.

Reb Moshe was regarded by most leading rabbinic contemporaries as the *Gadol Hador*, the greatest Torah stage of his generation, and his decisions on Jewish law were accepted as authoritative by Orthodox Jews throughout the world. He played a major role in defining the continuing interface between halacha and issues of modernity, rendering decisions on a wide range of issues including artificial insemination, transplantation surgery, end-of-life medical care, abortion, financial ethics, business and labor disputes, etc.

Close to two thousand of Reb Moshe's responsa are contained in *Igrot Moshe*, a multivolume work arranged according to the sections of the *Shulchan Aruch*. His commentary on the Torah was published posthumously under the title *Darash Moshe*.

Gombiner, Avraham Abele ben Chaim Halevi – *Dayan*, Talmudic scholar, halachic authority and commentator (Poland, Lithuania, circa 1637–1683).

Fleeing his hometown, Gombin, after the murder of his parents during the Chmielnicki massacres of 1648, Gombiner eventually made his way to Lithuania where he studied with his relative Yitzchak Yaakov Gombiner. He later moved back to Poland where he was appointed head of the yeshiva in Kalicz and *dayan* (rabbinic judge).

Gombiner is best known for his classic work the *Magen Avraham*, a commentary on the *Orach Chaim* section of the *Shulchan Aruch*. This authoritative commentary, which incorporates the customs and practices of Gombiner's contemporary Poland, is written in concise, terse style and demonstrates the author's scholarship, broad knowledge of halachic literature and deep respect for communal custom.

Hacohen, Meir Simcha of Dvinsk – Rabbi, talmudic scholar, biblical commentator (Latvia, Lithuania, 1843–1926).

Renowned as a brilliant Talmudic scholar and beloved as a compassionate leader, Rabbi Meir Simcha served as rabbi of the city of Dvinsk for forty years. In 1906 he turned down a rabbinic position in Jerusalem as a result of the entreaties of the Dvinsk community who argued that his departure would "destroy" not only their community but the entire diaspora. During World War I when most of the Jewish community fled Dvinsk, leaving behind only the poorest inhabitants, Rabbi Meir Simcha remained, declaring that as long as there were nine Jews in the city he would be the tenth.

Among his most important works were the *Meshech Chochma* and *Ohr Sameach*, commentaries on the Torah and on the Rambam's *Mishneh Torah*, respectively.

Hirsch, Shimshon Raphael – Rabbi, biblical commentator, rabbinic leader, philosopher (Germany, 1808–1888).

In the wake of the emancipation, traditional Judaism was desperately in need of a powerful leader to guide the transition of Orthodoxy into a new world marked by greater freedom. Rabbi Shimshon Raphael Hirsch successfully filled that role.

In 1851, Hirsch relinquished a prominent rabbinic post to become the rabbi of eleven individuals who had separated from the general community of Frankfurt am Main in response to that community's shift towards

Reform Judaism. From those humble beginnings, Hirsch built a model Orthodox community of five hundred members.

Hirsch developed a philosophy of *Torah im Derech Eretz* (lit.: Torah and the way of the land) which envisioned a relationship between traditional observant Judaism and the modern world. Much controversy exists today as to the exact dimensions of the relationship envisioned by Hirsch. There is no question, however, that Hirsch's contributions were instrumental in the development of German Orthodox Jewry and paved the way for the development of today's Modern Orthodox community throughout the Jewish world. Hirsch published many works including *Nineteen Letters*, in which he brilliantly responds to the major philosophical questions of his day; *Horeb*, a text outlining his approach to Jewish belief and practice; and an extensive, thought provoking, commentary on the Torah.

Hoffman, David Tzvi – Biblical and Talmudic scholar and commentator, halachic authority (Germany, Hungary, Austria, 1843–1921).

Educated in Hungarian yeshivot, as well as the Hildesheimer Seminary in Eisenstadt, Hoffman later studied in the universities of Vienna, Berlin and Tübingen.

Hoffman lectured at the Hildesheimer Rabbinical Seminary in Berlin and assumed the position of the seminary's rector upon Hildesheimer's death in 1899. By the end of his life, Hoffman was recognized as the preeminent halachic scholar of the German Orthodox Jewish community and regularly fielded questions on a wide array of subjects from rabbis throughout Germany.

While Hoffman was a violent opponent of the Reform Jewish movement, his responsa show great awareness of contemporary concerns and evidence a willingness to show leniency, where possible, in areas of halacha. His commentaries on the books of Vayikra and Devarim demonstrate deep knowledge of rabbinic sources as well as a facility with the archaeological data of his time.

Horowitz, Yeshaya ben Avraham Halevi – The *Shla Hakadosh*; rabbi, *dayan*, halachic authority, kabbalist, community leader (Bohemia, Poland, Germany, Palestine, circa 1565–1630).

Born in Prague, Horowitz moved with his father as a youth to Poland, where he studied under a number of prominent teachers and quickly earned an exceptional scholarly reputation. After rising to the position of *av beit din* (head of the rabbinical court) in a number of locations, in

1606 he was appointed to that position in the *beit din* in Frankfurt am Main, Germany, one of the most important rabbinical courts of his time. He returned to Prague after the expulsion of the Jews from Frankfurt, assuming the prestigious rabbinical position there. After the death of his wife in 1621, he immigrated to Israel, settling in Jerusalem and assuming the position of rabbi of the Ashkenazic community. After being kidnapped by a local pasha and ransomed for an exorbitant sum, Horowitz moved to Tzfat. He died in Teveria where his grave is still visited to this day.

Among his many works, Horowitz's *Shnei Luchot Habrit* is his most well known, and he became recognized as the "Holy *Shla*" (abbreviated from the first letters of this work's title). Interweaving halachah, homilies and kabbalistic teachings, this work is designed to give direction to the reader as to how to lead an ethical life. The *Shnei Luchot Habrit* and Horowitz's other works reflect the vast breadth of his teachings, which combine outstanding halachic acumen, deep mystical search and strong ethical mandate.

Ibn Chaim, Aharon ben Avraham – *Dayan,* commentator (Morocco, Italy, Palestine, 1545–1632).

Born in Fez, Morocco, where he studied under his father and other teachers, Ibn Chaim served for a period on the rabbinic court in Fez. He left for Egypt in 1606 and then traveled to Venice, Italy, in 1609, where he published the work for which he is best known, the *Korban Aharon.* This work features an extensive commentary on the *Sifra* (the halachic Midrash on Vayikra), as well as an introduction detailing the development and application of the principles that guide the process of Oral Law.

After traveling to a number of countries in the Far East, Ibn Chaim finally settled in Jerusalem, where he remained until his death.

Ibn Ezra – Rabbi Avraham ben Meir Ibn Ezra; biblical commentator, philosopher, poet, grammarian, physician, astronomer/astrologer (Spain, Egypt, North Africa, Italy, France, England, Israel, 1092–1167).

Over the course of an impoverished and itinerant life, the Ibn Ezra made a profound contribution to Jewish scholarship. A prolific poet, the Ibn Ezra produced treatises on Hebrew grammar, mathematics, astronomy/astrology and philosophy.

The Ibn Ezra's greatest contribution, however, was made through his renowned commentary on the Torah and other books of Tanach (an acronym for the biblical canon – Torah, Nevi'im, Ketuvim: the five books of Moses, the Prophets and the Writings). This work, which inspired numerous supercommentaries, is singular for its strong use of grammatical principles to uncover the *pshat* of the text. While the Ibn Ezra's commentary included a great deal of exegetical material authored by his predecessors, he did not shy away from offering his own original observations.

Kleiman, Yaakov Hacohen – Contemporary scholar and genealogist (Israel).

A resident of the Jewish Quarter in the Old City of Jerusalem, Kleiman is heavily involved in the study of Jewish genealogy, specifically the lineage of the *kehuna*. Rabbi Kleiman lectures on Temple studies at Aish HaTorah, Jerusalem. He is co-director with Rabbi Nachman Kahana of the Center for Kohanim, an organization dedicated to fostering readiness and knowledge of Temple traditions among Kohanim. He is also the author of the book DNA *and Tradition* (Jerusalem: Devora, 2004), exploring the chromosomal link between all Kohanim.

Kli Yakar – Rabbi Ephraim Shlomo ben Chaim of Luntshitz; *dayan*, biblical commentator, orator (Poland, Bohemia, 1550–1619).

At an early age, the Kli Yakar earned a reputation as a spellbinding speaker and traveled in that capacity through numerous cities and towns. Subsequently, he served as rosh yeshiva and *av beit din* (head of the Jewish court) in Prague.

His renowned commentary on the Torah, the *Kli Yakar*, is largely homiletic in style.

Kook, Avraham Yitzchak Hacohen – Leading rabbinic authority, scholar and halachist; first chief rabbi of the newly established Jewish presence in the land of Palestine (Lithuania, Palestine, 1865–1935).

Born in Griva, Latvia, Kook quickly earned a reputation as a child prodigy and, early on, showed great independence of mind and thought. He studied briefly at the famed Yeshiva of Volozhin under the tutelage of the Netziv and in 1887, at the age of twenty-three, assumed his first rabbinic position in Zaumel. This was followed by a rabbinic position in Baumel in 1895.

In 1904, Kook moved to Palestine (then under Ottoman rule), where he assumed the rabbinic position in Jaffa. There he became heavily involved in outreach to Jews of all walks of life and religious backgrounds. He identified with the Zionist movement, seeking a greater role for Torah and halacha in the Jewish settlement in Palestine.

World War I found Kook in Europe (having traveled there to foster Zionist ideology within the religious community), unable to return to Palestine. He accepted a temporary position in London during the war years and returned to Palestine after the conclusion of hostilities. Upon his return, Kook was appointed to the chief rabbinate in Jerusalem and, with the formation of the position in 1921, was elected first Ashkenazic chief rabbi of Palestine.

Kook's influence upon twentieth-century Jewish thought was profound, as he mapped out a unique path in support of religious Zionism. He was able to blend mystical speculation with practical activity and managed to see good in all participants in the Zionist enterprise, across the religious spectrum. At the same time, he did not shy away from encouraging secular Jews towards greater piety and the Orthodox community towards greater involvement in national and world affairs.

Kook's deep love for the whole of the Jewish people and his vision of the newly established Jewish presence in Palestine as the beginning of divine redemption laid the groundwork for the developing character of the Religious Zionist movement in the decades that followed.

Ktav Sofer – Rabbi Shmuel Binyamin Sofer; rabbi, rosh yeshiva, commentator (Hungary, 1815–1871).

Oldest son of the famed Chatam Sofer and grandson, on his mother's side, of the renowned Rabbi Akiva Eiger; the Ktav Sofer succeeded his father in 1839, at the age of 24, as the rabbi of Pressburg, Hungary, and as the rosh yeshiva of the famed Pressburg Yeshiva.

Serving as rabbi of Pressburg for thirty-three years, the exact number of years that his father had served before him, the Ktav Sofer followed his father's legacy of opposition to radical change as he preached strict adherence to the tenets and practices of traditional Judaism. In 1868, the long nascent conflict between the Hungarian Orthodox and Reform Jews finally erupted at a Jewish congress convened in Budapest. As a result, largely under the leadership of the Ktav Sofer, a separate Orthodox community was established.

The Ktav Sofer authored a commentary on the Torah as well as volumes of responsa and Talmudic commentary all under the title *Ktav Sofer* (by which the author himself became known).

Landau, Yechezkel ben Yehuda – The Noda b'Yehuda; *dayan*, rabbi, Talmudic scholar, halachic authority (Poland, Austria, Russia, Bohemia, 1713–1793).

A member of a wealthy and distinguished family tracing its roots to Rashi, Landau was born in Opatow, Poland, and was educated in Vladimir-Volinski and Brody. Endowed with extraordinary intellectual ability, a commanding personal presence and a unique ability to communicate with others, Landau was appointed to a position as *dayan* (halachic judge) in Brody at the age of twenty-one and to the position of rabbi of Yampol at the age of thirty. In 1754, he rose to the rabbinate of Prague and of the whole of Bohemia.

With these latter positions as his platform, Landau exerted tremendous influence over the broad Jewish community of his time as a rabbi, mentor, judge, halachic arbiter and representative of the community to the governmental authorities. Deeply traditional, he was nonetheless cautiously open to positive elements of secular culture, encouraging a proper relationship with non-Jews and fostering a feeling of patriotism for the country. He was a bold, innovative halachic arbiter and his volumes of responsa, the *Noda b'Yehuda* (the title by which Landau, himself, became known), are considered classics to this day. Among Landau's other works was the *Dagul Mei'rivava*, a commentary on the *Shulchan Aruch*.

Leibowitz, Dr. Nehama – Biblical scholar and commentator, teacher (Israel, 1905–1997).

Born in Riga, Latvia, Nehama Leibowitz was awarded a doctorate from the University of Berlin in 1930 and emigrated that same year to the British Mandate of Palestine. Over the course of her career, Leibowitz taught for decades at a Religious Zionist teachers seminary, lectured at Tel Aviv University, where she was appointed full professor, delivered regular radio addresses on Voice of Israel radio and lectured in a multitude of settings throughout the country.

Leibowitz is best known for her *gilyonot* (lit.: pages), stencils on the weekly Torah reading which she distributed to all interested. Her incisive analytical approach to text made these *gilyonot* immensely popular and through their distribution she rekindled intense interest in the study of biblical text and commentary throughout the Jewish world. Later Leibowitz produced formal studies, which were eventually collected into books on the Torah. Leibowitz was awarded the Israel Prize for education in 1957.

Maharal – Rabbi Yehuda Loew; rabbi, Talmudic scholar, philosopher, commentator (Poland, Bohemia, 1525–1609).

Born to a noble family that traces its lineage to King David, the Maharal was one of the most influential Jewish thinkers of the postmedieval period. So expansive was his influence that Rav Avraham Yitzchak Hacohen Kook (the first chief rabbi of Israel) once proclaimed that the Maharal was "the father of the approach of the Vilna Gaon on the one hand and the father of the Chassidic movement on the other."

After serving as rabbi of Nikolsburg in the province of Moravia for twenty years, the Maharal moved to Prague in 1573, there opening a yeshiva and mentoring numerous outstanding disciples. After leaving for a brief period to serve as rabbi in the city of Posen, the Maharal returned to Prague in 1598 to assume the position of chief rabbi.

A renowned educator, the Maharal criticized his contemporaries for not heeding the advice of the Mishna which counsels that children should be taught subjects that are age appropriate. "The fools nowadays," he proclaimed, "teach boys Torah with the commentary of Rashi, which they do not understand and also Talmud which they cannot yet grasp." While clearly rooted in the world of Torah the Maharal embraced the study of secular subjects, particularly mathematics.

A prolific writer, the Maharal was held in high esteem by Jews and non-Jews alike. His statue was erected in 1917 at the entrance to the province town hall by the municipal authority, and his synagogue, the Altneu Shul, stands to this day.

Midrash Hagadol – Collection of Midrashim compiled in the late thirteenth century by the Yemenite scholar Rabbi David ben Avraham Adani.

This work, culled from ancient Tannaitic (Mishnaic) sources, was preserved in manuscript for centuries and studied primarily within the Yemenite community. European scholars, within the last 150 years, have printed carefully edited versions of the text. The Midrash Hagadol serves as a significant record of many teachings from the Mishnaic and Talmudic period which are found in no other source.

Midrash Rabba – A collection of Midrashic anthologies on various books of Tanach.

Although the title "Rabba" is shared by all of these anthologies, they are not a cohesive work but a series of Midrashic texts edited in different centuries and in various locales. Bereishit Rabba (Midrash Rabba Bereishit) was compiled in the sixth century and consists of wide-ranging ethical teachings, homilies, maxims, parables and metaphors all connected (albeit sometimes loosely) to the text of Bereishit.

Midrash Tanchuma – A compilation of Midrashim, many of which are ascribed to the Talmudic sage Tanchuma bar Abba.

Rav Tanchuma bar Abba, who lived in Israel during the second half of the fourth century CE, was a student of the renowned sage Rav Huna and a major author of *aggadot* (Midrashic tales). The text ascribed to his name has appeared over the centuries in various versions.

Midreshei Halacha – A group of Tannaitic expositions on the Torah designed to identify the sources of the 613 mitzvot within the Torah text.

In contrast to *Midreshei Aggada* (homiletical Midrashim such as the Midrash Rabba, Midrash Tanchuma, etc.), *Midreshei Halacha* are primarily halachic in purpose. Nonetheless, they contain much aggadic material, as well. While the contents of the *Midreshei Halacha* date to the Mishnaic period, the redaction of the extant texts apparently occurred much later. Numerous theories, in fact, concerning the categorization and dating of these Midrashim have been offered by scholars and historians.

Because practically no halachic legislation derives from the book of Bereishit, *Midreshei Halacha* are only found in connection with the books of Shmot, Vayikra, Bamidbar and Devarim. These Midrashim are referred to by various titles such as *Mechilta, Sifra, Sifrei* and *Torat Kohanim*.

Mishna – First official written summary of the Oral Law.

The editing of the Mishna by Rabbi Yehuda Hanasi at the end of the second century CE marked a major transformation in the mode of transmission of Jewish tradition. Until this time, the distinction between Written Law (*Torah She'bi'chtav*) and Oral Law (*Torah She'b'al Peh*) had been studiously maintained, the latter memorized and transmitted verbally across the centuries. Driven by the fear, however, that the Oral Law would be lost if not recorded in writing, Rabbi Yehuda developed the six "orders" of the Mishna. This pioneering sage, however, preserved the character of the Oral Law by recording the Mishnaic edicts in short, cryptic style which requires immediate further oral explication.

The sages of the Mishna are known as the Tannaim.

Mizrachi, Eliyahu – Talmudic scholar, biblical commentator, rabbi, rosh yeshiva, halachic authority (Turkey, 1450–1526).

Born and educated in Constantinople, Mizrachi rose to become the foremost rabbinic authority in the Ottoman Empire of his day. Mizrachi was firm and unbending in his legal positions and responded to halachic queries addressed to him from far and wide. His grueling daily schedule encompassed communal leadership, the stewardship of a yeshiva, extensive teaching, the rendering of legal decisions and scholarly writing.

In addition to his major achievements in the area of Jewish scholarship and communal leadership, Mizrachi also studied and wrote on secular subjects, particularly mathematics and astronomy.

Mizrachi's crowning achievement – and the project which he personally considered his most important – was his monumental supercommentary on Rashi. This extensive work became the basis for continued study and analysis by later commentaries.

Nachshoni, Yehuda – Contemporary biblical scholar and commentator (Israel).

Nachshoni is the author of one of the most comprehensive works on the weekly parsha, *Hagot B'parshiot HaTorah* (available in an English translation by Shmuel Himelstein: *Studies in the Weekly Parashah: The Classical Interpretations of Major Topics and Themes in the Torah*, ArtScroll Judaica Classics [New York: Mesorah, 1989]). In this work he presents a series of essays on each parsha, raising critical questions and offering a wide array of approaches from the classical to the contemporary.

Netziv – Rabbi Naftali Tzvi Yehuda Berlin; Talmudic scholar, rosh yeshiva, biblical commentator (Poland, Russia, 1817–1893).

For forty years beginning in 1854, the Netziv served as the rosh yeshiva of the Yeshiva of Volozhin. The Netziv's scholarship, coupled with a deep personal love for all of his students, transformed the yeshiva into the largest such institution of its time and a major spiritual center for the Russian Jewish community. His opposition to the secularization of the yeshiva eventually brought him into conflict with government authorities and, according to some versions, led to the yeshiva's closing in 1892 (others suggest that the closure was due to internal upheaval). The Netziv was one of the early supporters of Jewish settlement in the Land of Israel.

Among the Netziv's publications was his popular biblical commentary, the *Ha'ameik Davar*, in which he emphasized the consonance between Talmudic interpretation and the *pshat* of the Torah text.

A son of the Netziv's first marriage was Rabbi Chaim Berlin, who became chief rabbi of Moscow and subsequently chief rabbi of the Ashkenazic community in Yerushalayim; a son of his second marriage was Rabbi Meir Berlin (later Bar-Ilan), a leader of the religious Zionist Mizrachi movement who inspired the creation of Bar-Ilan University (named in his memory).

Ohr Hachaim – Rabbi Chaim Ibn Attar; rabbi, biblical commentator, Talmudic scholar, kabbalist (Morocco, Israel, 1696–1743).

One of the most prominent rabbis in his native land of Morocco, the Ohr Hachaim decided in 1733 to resettle in the Land of Israel. He was, however, detained along the way in Livorno, Italy, by leading members of the Jewish community who established a Talmudic academy for him. Finally arriving in Jerusalem in 1742, the Ohr Hachaim served as the head of the Beit Midrash Knesset Yisrael until his death.

The Ohr Hachaim's commentary on the Torah combines textual analysis with Talmudic and kabbalistic insights. Over the years, this commentary has become particularly popular within the Sephardic and Chassidic communities.

Onkelos – Convert to Judaism, scholar and author of the seminal Aramaic translation of the Torah, *Targum Onkelos* (Rome, Israel, 35–120 CE).

According to tradition, Onkelos was the nephew of the Roman emperor Titus (who, as a general, was responsible for the destruction of the Second Temple).

After his conversion, Onkelos authored *Targum Onkelos*, a monumental interpretive translation of the Torah into Aramaic. This translation, which received the approbation of Onkelos' teachers, the Mishnaic scholars Rabbi Eliezer and Rabbi Yehoshua, offers striking insights into the text. So authoritative did this work become that the rabbis of the Talmud decreed that the weekly reading of the Torah portion should include the reading of the *Targum*, as well. *Targum Onkelos* is included in almost all published editions of the Torah today.

Peli, Pinchas – Scholar, author, poet (Palestine/Israel, 1930–1989).

Born in Jerusalem to a Chassidic family by the name of Hacohen, Peli adopted his pen name, which means "wonder." Peli combined a traditional yeshiva education with advanced academic degrees from Hebrew University in Jerusalem and a doctorate received under the tutelage of Rabbi Abraham Joshua Heschel in America.

Peli served as professor of Jewish thought and literature at the Ben-Gurion University in the Negev and as visiting professor in numerous universities in the United States, Argentina and Japan. During his tenure as visiting professor at Yeshiva University from 1968 to 1970, Peli developed a close relationship with Rabbi Joseph Dov Soloveitchik and eventually published a volume based on the Rav's oral discourses entitled *Al Hatshuva*, (*On Repentance*).

Peli authored numerous other volumes, poems and short stories.

Pirkei Avot – Mishnaic tractate containing the ethical pronouncements of the Tannaitic sages.

Pirkei Avot is singular within the Talmud in its focus upon ethical maxims as opposed to legal stricture. Many of Judaism's best-known proverbs and moral observations are contained within this tractate.

Elsewhere, the Talmud proclaims, "He who desires to be pious, let him practice the teachings of [*Pirkei*] *Avot*."

Rabbeinu Bachya – Rabbi Bachya ben Asher; biblical commentator, *dayan*, preacher (Spain, 1263–1340).

A disciple of the renowned Talmudist Rabbi Shlomo ben Aderet (the Rashba), Rabbeinu Bachya served as a preacher and a *dayan* (rabbinical judge) in Saragossa, Spain. Rabbeinu Bachya is best known for his commentary on the Torah, which combines *pshat*, Midrash, philosophy and Kabbala. Each weekly parsha is introduced by an ethical discussion citing a verse from Proverbs.

Rabbeinu Chananel – Chananel ben Chushiel; Talmudic scholar, halachic authority, commentator (Tunisia, 990–1055).

Rabbeinu Chananel lived in the city of Kairouan, Tunisia, where he studied under the tutelage of his father, Chushiel ben Elchanan, head of the Kairouan yeshiva. Following in his father's footsteps, Rabbeinu Chananel eventually earned the title *Reish Bei Rabbanan* (chief among the rabbis), accorded by the Babylonian academies of his day.

Rabbeinu Chananel wrote the first authoritative commentary on the Talmud, great sections of which are preserved and recorded on the actual pages of specific Talmudic tractates. In contrast to the later commentary of Rashi, Rabbeinu Chananel's work is not a running interpretation of the entire text. Instead, he summarizes and explains the main arguments of the Gemara and issues halachic decisions on the matters in question. He relies greatly on the positions of the Babylonian Geonim, and thus serves as an important bridge between the teachings of the Geonim and the scholars of North Africa and those of the scholars of Europe and Israel. Many later commentaries rely heavily on his work.

Rabbeinu Chananel also wrote a commentary on the Torah, only portions of which have been preserved.

Ralbag – Rabbi Levi ben Gershon; Talmudic scholar, commentator, philosopher, mathematician, astronomer/astrologer (France, 1288–1344).

Little is known about the life of this revolutionary Jewish philosopher who authored works ranging from biblical commentary to acclaimed philosophical and mathematical treatises. His major philosophical text, *Sefer Milchamot Hashem* (The Wars of the Lord), was composed over a twelve-year period and earned the Ralbag renown well beyond the Jewish community.

In opposition to the generally accepted position of classical Judaism, the Ralbag maintained that God deliberately limits his own omniscience with regard to his foreknowledge of human acts. By stating that God knows the choices available to us but consciously chooses not to know the specific decisions that we will make, the Ralbag addressed the age-old dilemma of how man's free will can exist in the face of God's omniscience.

Rambam – Rabbi Moshe ben Maimon, also known as Maimonides; widely recognized as the greatest post-Talmudic authority on Jewish law and thought (Spain, Morocco, Egypt, 1135–1204).

The Rambam's works include *The Guide to the Perplexed*, a philosophical work on Jewish theology; *Sefer Hamitzvot*, a compendium of the 613 commandments of the Torah; a commentary on the Mishna; and his magnum opus, the *Mishneh Torah*, a masterful, comprehensive code of Jewish law. In his commentary on the Mishna, the Rambam delineated thirteen principles still considered to be the cornerstones of Jewish belief. His *Mishneh Torah* launched the course for halachic codification across the ages and served as the forerunner of other essential texts such as the *Arba Turim* and the *Shulchan Aruch*.

A royal physician and world-class philosopher, the Rambam made a monumental impact upon the development of Jewish tradition and law, reflected in the well-known dictum inscribed on his tomb: "From Moshe (Moses) to Moshe (Rambam) no one arose like Moshe."

Ramban – Rabbi Moshe ben Nachman, also known as Nachmanides; biblical and Talmudic commentator, scholar, physician (Spain, Israel, 1194–1270).

The Ramban's commentary on the Torah combines *pshat*, Midrash and kabbalistic insights. A towering figure in the history of Jewish scholarship, the Ramban authored numerous works on the Talmud as well as Jewish law and thought. His vigorous defense of Judaism in the face of Christian attack culminated in a public disputation with the Jewish apostate Pablo Christiano, in the presence of King James of Spain in 1263.

The Ramban's deep love for the Land of Israel is manifest in his writings and in his philosophy of Jewish law. In 1267, at the age of seventy-two, the Ramban settled in the Land of Israel and worked vigorously to rebuild Jerusalem's Jewish community.

Ran – Rabbi Nissim ben Reuven; Talmudic scholar, rabbi, halachist, philosopher, physician (Spain, 1290–1380).

Widely recognized as the greatest rabbinic authority of his time, the Ran served as rabbi of Barcelona and responded to thousands of halachic inquiries from across the Jewish diaspora. The Ran is best known for his practical commentary on the halachic work of Rabbi Yitzchak ben Yaakov Alfasi (the Rif). Through this commentary, the Ran achieved a revered position in the world of Talmudic scholarship. The Ran's compendium of sermons, *Drashot HaRan,* provides insight into many of the basic tenets of Jewish faith.

Rashbam – Rabbi Shmuel ben Meir; biblical commentator, Talmudic scholar (France, 1080–1158).

The Rashbam, Rashi's grandson, was a leading member of the Tosafists (a large group of medieval rabbis whose critical and explanatory glosses are basic to the study of the Talmud). The Rashbam's commentary on the Torah is remarkable for its bold adherence to *pashut pshat* even when the *pshat* leads to controversial conclusions. The Rashbam took issue with his renowned grandfather's periodic Midrashic interpretation of the text and, in fact, claimed, "I debated with him [Rashi] and he admitted to me that, if he had the time, he would be obligated to author other commentaries based upon the straightforward explanations of the text…."

So great was the storm concerning some of the Rashbam's views that his commentary on the first chapters of Bereishit was omitted in many earlier editions of the Bible.

Rashi – Rabbi Shlomo Yitzchaki; arguably the greatest of all biblical and Talmudic commentators (France, 1040–1105).

Rashi's commentary on the Torah, considered an essential companion to the study of the text, combines *pshat* with the periodic referencing of Midrash (when he feels such referencing is necessary for textual comprehension).

In addition to commentaries on the Prophets and Writings, Rashi also authored an indispensable running commentary on the Talmud, known for its brevity and clarity.

No course of study in the Torah or Talmud is considered complete without the accompanying study of Rashi's commentary.

Rema – Rabbi Moshe Isserles; Talmudic scholar, *dayan*, rosh yeshiva, preeminent halachic authority for Ashkenazic Jewry (Poland, 1520–1572).

Born in Cracow, Poland, the Rema studied in Lublin where he married the daughter of Rabbi Shalom Shachna, the rosh yeshiva. Upon his wife's untimely death at the age of twenty, the Rema honored her memory with the building of a synagogue which stands in Cracow to this day. The Rema's second wife also came from a scholarly family.

The Rema distinguished himself as an outstanding scholar at an early age and by 1550 was a member of the Cracow Beit Din (religious court). He established a yeshiva in Cracow, supported its students through his own resources and earned a worldwide reputation as a brilliant and effective *posek* (halachic arbiter). Humble and self-effacing, the Rema was, nonetheless, so confident and incisive in his halachic positions that he became known to his contemporaries as the "Maimonides of Polish Jewry." Like Maimonides, the Rema also pursued secular knowledge through the study of history, astronomy and philosophy.

While the Rema authored many works, he is best known for his *Mapa* (Tablecloth), a series of annotations inserted into the body of Rabbi Yosef Caro's halachic compendium, the *Shulchan Aruch* (Set table). These glosses append the legal positions and customs of Ashkenazic Jewry to Caro's Sephardic-oriented work, thus transforming the *Shulchan Aruch* into the primary universal code of law for the entire Jewish nation.

Ritva – Rabbi Yom Tov ben Avraham Asbili; Talmudic scholar and commentator (Spain 1250–1330).

Born in Seville, the Ritva studied in Barcelona and is mentioned in an official document of 1280 of the Kingdom of Aragon as a leading rabbinic figure of the community of Saragossa. Rising to prominence at a young age, he eventually became the acknowledged spiritual leader of Spanish Jewry.

Firmly convinced of the truth of the maxim "There are many ways in which the Torah can be interpreted, all of them the words of the living God," the Ritva argued for an understanding of the widely conflicting positions of earlier scholars, such as the Rambam and the Ramban.

The Ritva is best known for his masterful commentary on the Talmud, which combines a wealth of earlier source material with incisive original thought.

Rosanes, Yehuda ben Shmuel – Rabbi, halachic authority (Turkey 1657– 1727).

Born in Constantinople, Rosanes spent his early years engaged in Torah study and working in the business of his uncle and father-in-law, Abraham Rosanes. Due to his scholarship and talent, he rose to great prominence within the Turkish Jewish community and was appointed to the chief rabbinate of Constantinople.

Rosanes took an active role in condemning and denouncing the Sabbateans (followers of Shabbetai Tzvi, a rabbi and kabbalist who claimed to be the messiah and eventually converted to Islam).

Rosanes is best known for his *Mishneh LaMelech*, a scholarly and incisive commentary on the *Mishneh Torah* of the Rambam. This work was edited and published by his student, Jacob Culi, after Rosanes' death.

Saadia Gaon – Talmudic scholar, philosopher, halachist (Egypt, Babylonia, 882–942).

Arguably the greatest scholar of the Geonic period (late sixth–eleventh centuries), Saadia Gaon is also considered by many to be the "father of Jewish philosophy." Sensing the twin dangers posed to rabbinic Judaism by Karaism (a movement that accepted the written but not the oral law) and rationalistic thought, Saadia developed a systematic philosophy of Judaism which examined its truths and teachings in the light of reason.

Saadia played a major role in a calendar controversy between the Jerusalem and the Babylonian scholarly communities which threatened to create a dangerous schism concerning the fixing of festival dates. At the request of the Babylonian scholars, Saadia effectively refuted the position of Aharon ben Meir, the head of the Jerusalem Academy, and solidified the supremacy of the Babylonian scholars. Both as a result of this effort and in the merit of his extraordinary abilities, Saadia was appointed head of the famed Babylonian Academy of Sura in 928, at the age of forty-six.

So important were Saadia's contributions to Jewish thought that, centuries later, the Rambam proclaimed in his *Iggeret Teiman*: "Were it not for Saadia, the Torah would almost have disappeared from among Israel."

Sefer Hachinuch – Systematic analysis of the six hundred thirteen commandments of the Torah, published anonymously in thirteenth-century Spain.

Following the order of the Torah text, the Ba'al Hachinuch (as the anonymous author of the *Sefer Hachinuch* is called) links each mitzva to the parsha in which it is found and discusses both the philosophical underpinnings and halachic parameters of that mitzva.

Sforno – Rabbi Ovadia Sforno; biblical commentator, Talmudic scholar, philosopher, physician (Italy, 1470–1550).

The Sforno's broad-based education earned him recognition in many fields including law, philosophy, mathematics, medicine, Hebrew language and Hebrew literature. When the famous German humanist Johan Reuchlin desired to perfect his knowledge of Hebrew literature, Cardinal Domenico Grimani advised him to approach the Sforno. A prolific writer, the Sforno is best known for his clear commentary on the Torah and many books of Tanach. These works reflect great respect for the *pshat* of the text and are written in a beautiful, almost lyrical style.

Shabbetai ben Meir Hacohen – The Shach; Talmudic scholar, *dayan*, halachic authority and commentator (Poland, Lithuania, 1621–1662).

Born in Amstivov, Lithuania, Shabbetai moved to Poland, studying in Tykocin, Krakow and Lublin. While still young, he returned to Vilna, where he married a woman from a wealthy family, descended from the Rema (Rabbi Moshe Isserles). Financially supported by his father-in-law, the Shach was able to devote his time solely to study.

After serving for a period of time in the *beit din* (rabbinical court) in Vilna, Shabbetai returned to Krakow where, in 1646, he published his classic work, the *Siftei Kohen*, a commentary on the Yoreh Deah section of the *Shulchan Aruch* (thus he became known by the title the *Shach*, comprised of the initials of the title of this work). Towards the end of his life, Shabbetai expanded his commentary to include the Choshen Mishpat section of the *Shulchan Aruch*, as well. The *Siftei Kohen* revealed Shabbetai's towering intellect, incisive mind and mastery of Jewish law and is widely accepted as an authoritative source for halachic decisions.

Shabbetai was forced to flee repeatedly in order to escape the religious persecution and slaughter of Polish Jewry during his lifetime. In 1651, he published *Megilat Eifa*, which portrays the suffering of the Jewish community at the hands of Chmielnicki and his followers.

Siddur – The Jewish prayer book.

The Siddur mirrors the historical journey of the Jewish people. While the earliest prayers were primarily spontaneous, prayer services became codified over time, stemming from various sources.

Biblically mandated prayers include the Shma Yisrael, the Birkat Kohanim (priestly blessing) and the Birkat Hamazon (grace after meals). The central prayer of the Jewish liturgy, known as the Amida (the standing [prayer]), was edited by Rabbi Gamliel and his colleagues in Yavne, after the destruction of the Second Temple.

The earliest true Siddur was drawn up in the ninth century by Rav Amram Gaon, at the request of the Jewish community of Spain. One hundred years later, Rav Saadia Gaon compiled a Siddur, as well. Critical to the development of the Jewish prayer book was the Machzor Vitri, edited in the eleventh century by Simcha ben Shmuel, a student of Rashi. The Machzor Vitri contained all the regular prayers according to the custom of northern France.

The Siddur continues to evolve to this day, as evidenced by prayers included in many contemporary prayer books relating to the welfare of the State of Israel and its armed forces.

Soloveitchik, Yosef Dov – The Rav; rabbi, pioneering spiritual leader of the Modern Orthodox movement in America and throughout the Jewish world (Lithuania, America, 1903–1993).

Scion of a two-hundred-year-old rabbinic dynasty, the Rav arrived in America in 1932 armed with an education that combined traditional Lithuanian Talmudic studies and a Ph.D. in philosophy from the University of Berlin. He assumed a rabbinic position in Boston where he established the Maimonides School and played a major role in many facets of the community's development. In 1941, he succeeded his father, Rabbi Moshe Soloveitchik, as the head of the Rabbi Isaac Elchanan Theological Seminary rabbinic school of Yeshiva University. For decades thereafter he commuted weekly between Boston and New York.

The Rav combined vast Torah and secular knowledge, a deeply analytical mind, powerful teaching ability and majestic oratorical skill with a magnetic leadership personality. Through his classes, widely attended public lectures, writings and policy decisions he furthered the philosophy of encounter between the highest form of Torah knowledge and the best secular scholarship of Western civilization. Advisor and teacher to tens of thousands, the Rav shaped the course of Modern Orthodox philosophy through the twentieth century and beyond.

Sternbuch, Moshe – Rabbi, *dayan*, halachic authority (London, South Africa, Israel).

Head of the rabbinical court of the *Eida Hachareidit* (a prominent communal organization based in Jerusalem representing a substantial community of fervently observant Ashkenazic Jews), Sternbuch was born in London, England. Orphaned at an early age, he studied in numerous settings before assuming a rabbinic position in Johannesburg, South Africa. While in Johannesburg, Sternbuch earned wide recognition for the quality of his rabbinic leadership.

Upon immigrating to Israel, Sternbuch assumed the position as rabbi of the Gra synagogue in Har Nof, Jerusalem (a synagogue named after the Vilna Gaon). A widely renowned halachic arbiter, Sternbuch is the author of numerous works, including *Moadim U'zmanim*, a series of volumes containing in-depth expositions on halachic topics associated with the festival cycle.

Sternbuch's philosophical views are reflective of the fervently observant Eida Hachareidit of which he is a major leader and include strong opposition to Zionism and to the secular government of the State of Israel, which the Eida considers to be heretical.

Talmud Bavli – Babylonian Talmud; foundational compilation of the halachic (legal) and aggadic (ethical-homiletical) discussions of the sages of the Babylonian academies from the second through the fifth centuries CE.

The scholars of the Talmud, known as the Amoraim, expound at great length upon the concise teachings of the Mishna, often digressing to discuss loosely related issues and ideas. Structurally, the style of the Talmud Bavli can best be described as "conversation in suspended animation," reflecting the origin of its subject matter, which was memorized and transmitted orally for centuries before its eventual written recordation.

Together with the Mishna, the Talmud Bavli serves as the basic source for the continually developing Oral Law.

Talmud Yerushalmi – Jerusalem Talmud; collection of the teachings of the sages of the Israeli academies from 200 to 350 CE.

Like the Talmud Bavli, the Talmud Yerushalmi centers on the discussions of the Amoraim (Talmudic scholars) concerning the Mishna. The Talmud Yerushalmi, however, is smaller in scope, more fragmented, and more difficult to study than its Babylonian counterpart; consequently, over the centuries, the Yerushalmi has exerted less influence upon the development of Jewish law. The return to the land of Israel in recent years has given birth to a renewed interest in the Talmud Yerushalmi and the laws it contains pertaining to the land.

Targum Yonatan – Interpretive Aramaic translation of the Torah commonly attributed to Yonatan ben Uziel. The correct name of this translation, according to most biblical scholars, is Targum Yerushalmi (Jerusalem Targum [translation]). Probably due to a printer's error (in Hebrew, as in English, the first letters of Targum Yerushalmi and Targum Yonatan are the same), the work was mistakenly labeled Targum Yonatan and attributed erroneously to Yonatan ben Uziel, an outstanding pupil of the renowned Mishnaic sage Hillel. Yonatan ben Uziel did produce a famous translation of the Books of the Prophets which, according to the Talmud, reflects the interpretation of the prophets Chagai, Zacharia and Malachi. The Talmud makes no mention, however, of a Targum on the Torah produced by this sage. The erroneous attribution is perpetuated in many current Chumashim. To address the issue, scholars refer to this biblical translation as the Targum Pseudo-Yonatan.

The Targum Pseudo-Yonatan contains much aggadic material from various sources and is both translation and commentary. The actual date of its composition remains a matter of dispute.

Vilna Gaon – Rabbi Eliyahu ben Shlomo Zalman (Lithuania, 1720–1797).

Also known by the acronym the *Gra* (Gaon Rabbi Eliyahu), the Vilna Gaon is considered one of the greatest Talmudic scholars of the past two centuries and is recognized as the "founding father" of the Lithuanian (non-Chassidic) yeshiva movement.

The Gaon demonstrated extraordinary ability as a youngster, delivering a learned discourse in the Great Synagogue of Vilna at the age of six and a half.

A man of iron will, the Gaon devoted every waking moment of his life to all facets of Torah study. He reportedly never slept for more than two hours in a twenty-four-hour period and studied in an unheated room in the winter, placing his feet in cold water to prevent himself from falling asleep.

The Gaon's Talmudic methodology was sharp and incisive, standing in stark contrast to the lengthy *pilpul* (discussion) approach of the Polish yeshivot. He was a harsh opponent of the Chassidic movement, believing that the Chassidim replaced serious intellectual search with a superficial emotional approach.

The Gaon's influence upon the trajectory of modern Jewish scholarship cannot be overstated. He reframed the approach to Talmud study, authored over seventy works on wide-ranging aspects of Torah thought and mentored select students who became foremost Torah scholars in their own right.

Wessely, Naphtali Herz – Haskala linguist, poet and scholar (Germany, Denmark, Holland, 1725–1805).

Rooted in the traditional education of his youth, Wessely was nonetheless greatly influenced by the teachings of the Haskala movement (which preached openness to secular culture). Wessely's educational theory, in which he proposed the study of secular subjects "common to the human race" as a prerequisite foundation to the study of Torah, placed him at odds with Orthodox luminaries of the day, including the Vilna Gaon.

On the other hand, Wessely's linguistically based scriptural commentary shows wide knowledge of traditional sources and was well received within the scholarly Orthodox community. Among his works is a commentary on the book of Vayikra, written at the request of Moses Mendelssohn (father of the Haskala movement) for inclusion in the *Biur* (Mendelssohn's Hebrew commentary on the Torah written in collaboration with Solomon Dubno, Aaron Yaroslov and Wessely).

Yalkut Shimoni – An important, comprehensive Midrashic anthology compiled in the twelfth or thirteenth century.

The *Yalkut Shimoni* contains over ten thousand aggadic and halachic observations on the entire Torah text. Both the authorship and the exact date of the *Yalkut*'s publication are the subject of dispute.

Yosef, Ovadia – Rabbi, Talmudic scholar, *dayan*, preeminent halachic authority, former Sephardic chief rabbi of Israel, spiritual leader of the Shas Party in the Israeli Knesset (Israel, 1920–).

Born in Baghdad, Yosef moved with his family to Palestine when he was four years old. He received his rabbinic ordination at the age of twenty, and in 1945 was appointed to the Sephardic *beit din* (rabbinical court) of Jerusalem. In 1947, he accepted two positions; as head of the *beit din* in Cairo and as deputy chief rabbi of Egypt. After returning to Israel in 1950, Yosef served on the rabbinical courts of Petach Tikva and Jerusalem. During this period he published a number of critically acclaimed texts including the first two volumes of his major work, *Yabia Omer*. In 1968 he assumed the position of chief Sephardic rabbi of Tel Aviv and in 1973 he was elected chief Sephardic rabbi of Israel.

Yosef's immeasurable contributions in many spheres have transformed the Jewish world. He is considered the leading living Jewish halachic authority by the Sephardic and Eastern Jewish communities and is one of the most important halachists in several generations. His responsa are highly regarded by scholars throughout the world.

Yosef has worked assiduously to improve the status of the Sephardic and Eastern Jews in Israel and has exerted major political influence through his leadership of the Shas Party. He has taken courageous and, at times, controversial positions on numerous issues and continues to wield extraordinary influence in many arenas.

Zohar – Central work in the literature of Kabbala (Jewish mysticism).

The Zohar is essentially a collection of several sections containing Midrashim and discussions on a wide array of topics.

The Zohar's main section is arranged according to the parshiot of the Torah text, although the latter part of the book of Bamidbar and the book of Devarim are not completely covered. Other portions of the work include the teachings and experiences of the second-century Tanna Rabbi Shimon bar Yochai; mystical studies on specific sections of the Torah and other books of Tanach; and discourses on a variety of topics including the nature of God, the origin and structure of the universe, good and evil, man's relationship to God, etc.

While the authorship of the Zohar is subject to dispute, many traditionalists have, for centuries, traced its origins to Rabbi Shimon bar Yochai.

Index

והאמרי והפרזי והחוי והיבוסי אל ארץ זבת
חלב ודבש ושמעו לקלך ובאת אתה וזקני
ישראל אל מלך מצרים ואמרתם אליו יהוה
אלהי העבריים נקרה עלינו ועתה נלכה נא
דרך שלשת ימים במדבר ונזבחה ליהוה
והיה הוא יהיה לך לפה ואתה
ואת המטה הזה תקח בידך אשר
את האתת
וילך משה וישב אל יתר חתנו